BEST

SHORT STORIES

Introductory Level

10 Stories for Young People

with Lessons for Teaching the Basic Elements of Literature

JAMESTOWN PUBLISHERS

a division of NTC/CONTEMPORARY PUBLISHING GROUP
Lincolnwood, Illinois USA

Editorial Development: Patricia Opaskar, Mary Ann Trost
Cover Design: Steve Straus
Cover Illustration: Michael Steirnagle
Interior Design: Steve Straus
Interior Illustrations: Units 1, 7: Antonio Castro; Units 2, 8: Lynne Colorio;
Units 3, 4: Jim Abel: Units 5, 6: Holly Jones

ISBN: 0-89061-889-5 (hardbound)
ISBN: 0-89061-844-5 (softbound)

Published by Jamestown Publishers,
a division of NTC/Contemporary Publishing Group, Inc.,
4255 West Touhy Avenue,
Lincolnwood (Chicago), Illinois, 60712-1975, U.S.A.
© 1998 NTC/Contemporary Publishing Group, Inc.

00 01 02 03 04 MV 10 9 8 7 6 5 4 3

Acknowledgments

Acknowledgment is gratefully made to the following publishers, authors, and agents for permission to reprint these works. Every effort has been made to determine copyright owners. In the case of any omissions, the Publisher will be pleased to make suitable acknowledgments in future editions.

"The Professor of Smells" by Laurence Yep. Text copyright © 1989 by Laurence Yep. Used by permission of HarperCollins Publishers.

"Tuesday of the Other June" by Norma Fox Mazer. Reprinted by permission of Norma Fox Mazer. Copyright 1986 by Norma Fox Mazer. All rights reserved. Originally appeared in *Short Takes: A Short Story Collection for Young Readers,* Lothrop, Lee & Shepard Books, 1986.

"Almost a Whole Trickster," by Gerald Vizenor. Reprinted by permission of the author.

"President Cleveland, Where Are You?" from *Eight Plus One* by Robert Cormier. Copyright © 1965 and renewed 1993 by Robert Cormier. Reprinted by permission of Pantheon Books, a division of Random House, Inc.

Many Moons by James Thurber. Copyright © 1943 by James Thurber. Copyright © renewed 1971 by Helen Thurber and Rosemary A. Thurber. Reprinted by arrangement with Rosemary A. Thurber and the Barbara Hogenson Agency.

"Catch the Moon" from *An Island Like You: Stories from the Barrio* by Judith Ortiz Cofer. Copyright © 1995 by Judith Ortiz Cofer. Reprinted by permission of Orchard Books, New York.

"The Richer, the Poorer" by Dorothy West. Permission granted by Bertha Klausner International Literary Agency, Inc.

"The Long Rain" by Ray Bradbury. Reprinted by permission of Don Congdon Associates, Inc. Copyright © 1950 by Love Romances, Inc., renewed 1977 by Ray Bradbury.

"Lob's Girl" from *A Whisper in the Night* by Joan Aiken. Copyright © 1984 by Joan Aiken. Used by permission of Bantam Doubleday Dell Books for Young Readers.

Contents

To the Student

A short story is a work of fiction that can usually be read in a single sitting. You are about to read short stories by some of the finest writers in the world. Some of these stories will make you laugh and some will touch your heart. Some stories will give you chills and some will make you think about life in a new way. All of them will make you admire the skill of the storytellers who set them down on paper.

Storytelling is an ancient art. Before people had writing materials and the ability to turn language into writing, they told stories. For thousands of years, stories have been told wherever people gather—around campfires, in villages, in people's homes, and in theaters. Fables, folktales, and fairy tales are examples of short stories told long ago. These stories were passed down from generation to generation. Over the years, they were changed and added to by storytellers. Finally, they were written down for people to read.

The plot of a short story usually revolves around a single important event in a character's life and involves one main conflict. Authors of short stories must build interest in characters and events without wasting words. Such efficient storytelling takes a great deal of skill.

As you read the ten short stories in this book, you will be able to see how the authors constructed them. You will learn about the elements of a short story and study the techniques that writers use to make their stories come alive. You will also have a chance to try these techniques in your own writing.

Unit Format and Activities

- Each unit begins with an illustration of a scene from a story in the unit. The picture will help you make some predictions about the story.

- The Introduction begins with a summary of the story and information about the author. It introduces an important literary concept and gives you an opportunity to explore what you know about developing this concept in your own writing. Finally, there are questions for you to consider as you read and a list of vocabulary words and their definitions.

- The full text of the story makes up the next section.

- Following each story are questions that test your comprehension of story events and your critical thinking skills. Your answers to these questions and to other exercises in the unit should be recorded in a personal literature notebook. Check your answers with your teacher.

- Your teacher may provide you with charts to record your progress in developing your comprehension skills: The Comprehension Skills Graph *records* your scores and the Comprehension Skills Profile *analyzes* your scores—providing you with information about the skills on which you need to focus. You can talk with your teacher about ways to work on those comprehension skills.

- The next section contains three lessons, which begin with a discussion of the literary concept that is the unit's focus. Each lesson illustrates a technique the author uses to develop that concept. For example, you will see how an author uses dialogue, action, and change to create characters.

- Short-answer exercises test your understanding of the author's techniques as illustrated by short excerpts from the story. You can check your answers to the exercises with your teacher and determine what you need to review.

- Each lesson also includes a writing exercise that guides you in creating your own original work using the techniques you have just studied.

- Discussion guides and a final writing activity round out each unit in the book. These activities will help sharpen your reading, thinking, speaking, and writing skills.

Reading the short stories in this book will enable you to recognize and appreciate the skills it takes to write an interesting story. When you understand what makes a story good, you become a better reader. The writing exercises and assignments will help you become a better writer by giving you practice in using the authors' techniques to make your own stories interesting.

Unit 1   Plot

The Professor of Smells
by Laurence Yep

About the Illustration

Describe what you think might be happening here. Use details from the illustration as clues. Give reasons for your answers.

These questions will help you begin to think about the story:

- Where do you think this scene takes place?

- Who do you think the main character is?

- What unusual thing is the man wearing on his face? Why do you suppose he is wearing it?

- What is in the bird's nest? How do you suppose those things got there? What might the man do when he finds them?

Unit 1

Introduction

About the Story

"The Professor of Smells" is based on a traditional Chinese folktale. Its main character is an unlucky gambler named Chung. After he loses all of his money, Chung tricks his wife into giving him all of her money for gambling. When he loses even that money, he is determined to reform. However, to distract his wife from the lost money, Chung makes up a story. He says that he has gained a fantastic sense of smell. He has the ability to find anything just by smelling. His wife tells all the neighbors that Chung can smell out lost objects, and he discovers that his silly story has gotten out of hand. When the emperor calls on Chung to use his great smelling ability, the gambler realizes his trickery may cost him his life.

The gambling game in this story begins with a random number of beans under an overturned bowl. Bettors guess a number from 0 to 3. Then the person running the game picks up the bowl and removes beans in groups of four. When all groups of four are gone, there are between 0 and 3 beans left. Whoever guessed the right number wins.

Gamblers in old China thought they might get good luck from the patron of gamblers, called the Pure White Lord. They would pray to this supernatural being or burn incense sticks before his picture to honor him.

About the Author

Laurence Yep is an award-winning author who has also taught creative writing and Asian American studies at the University of California in Berkeley and in Santa Barbara. He writes realistic fiction, science fiction, and fantasy for children, young adults, and adults. Many of his works deal with characters who, because of race or personal characteristics, do not fit into the culture surrounding them. His concern for the outsider grew out of his own experience.

Yep was born in San Francisco in 1948. Although his parents were Chinese, his family lived in an African American neighborhood where his father owned a store. Yep attended a bilingual school in Chinatown, where he was ridiculed for speaking only English. He first came into contact with white culture when he entered high school. It was in high school that he started writing.

Yep's writing frequently reflects his Chinese American heritage, as in his Newbery Honor novel, *Dragonwings;* in books about Chinese American young people of today, such as *Child of the Owl* and *Sea Glass;* and in the collection of Chinese folktales that is the source of this story, *The Rainbow People.*

About the Lessons

The lessons that follow "The Professor of Smells" focus on plot, an important part of every short story. The *plot* is the sequence of events in a story. First, the author introduces readers to the characters and setting of the story. Next, he or she presents a problem that the characters must face. Events build up to the *climax*—the turning point of the story. Finally, the plot winds down and comes to an ending, or *resolution*.

Writing: Developing a Plot

As you read "The Professor of Smells," you will be able to observe some of the elements that make a good plot. Completing the writing exercises in this unit will help you develop a plot outline of your own. The following activities will help you begin to think about what your plot might include.

- List the titles of at least three stories, books, or movies that you have enjoyed. Include thrillers, adventures, comedies, and so on.

- Start planning a plot of your own. Write one or more ideas for each of these story elements:

  Type of story (adventure, mystery, comedy, etc.)

  Setting (where and when the story takes place)

  Characters (who is in the story)

  Major problem the main character faces

- Think about how the plots develop in the stories you like. For each pair of characteristics below, decide which you prefer for your own plot.

  1) getting to know the characters before the action starts *or* starting with the action

  2) the action happening in other lands and times *or* happening in your world

  3) emphasis on danger and thrills *or* stress on characters and ideas

Before Reading

The questions below will help you see how the author has developed the plot of "The Professor of Smells." As you read the story, try to answer these questions concerning its plot:

- Who is the main character in the story? What problem does he face? How does his problem change throughout the story?

- What is the most exciting part of the story?
- Is the problem solved by the end of the story? How?

Vocabulary Tips

This story includes some words that may be unfamiliar to you but are useful for understanding the story. Below you will find some of these words, their definitions, and sentences that show how the words are used. Look over the words before you begin to read.

reprimand   to scold sharply. After the runner was called out at second, his manager <u>reprimanded</u> him for missing a sign.

skeptically   doubtfully; requiring proof. The unfriendly audience watched the magician <u>skeptically</u>.

irritably   in an impatient, easily annoyed manner. If the phone rings after 10 P.M., Mom always answers <u>irritably</u>.

haughtily   in a way that shows pride in oneself and scorn for others. During his visit to our school, the singer turned away <u>haughtily</u> when a girl asked him for an autograph.

kowtow   the act of kneeling and touching the ground with the forehead to show great respect. We agreed that whoever lost the game had to make a <u>kowtow</u> to the winner.

diligently   in a careful, hard-working manner. Cherie studied <u>diligently</u> for the science test.

dais   a raised platform. The queen's throne was on a <u>dais</u> in the great hall.

The Professor of Smells

Laurence Yep

Once there was a gambler named Chung. He would bet on anything. He would bet on the weather. He would bet on how many cockroaches were in a cupboard. He once even bet that the sun would set in the east.

His poor wife used to pull at her hair because of his gambling. She worried so much that she yanked her hair into spikes.

One day, he came home without any money. He found his wife in their small vegetable patch. Her ducks waddled around her feet, quacking and eating the insects that her hoe turned up. "I was winning," he said to his wife. "But I made just one bad bet. Give me some of your egg money and I'll double it for you."

She shook her head. "As they say, 'Don't fill the jar when it's cracked.'"

Chung promised desperately, "If I don't win this time, I'll give up gambling for good."

His wife believed him because she wanted to, and went and got her money. Each cash was a round coin with a square hole through which a string had been run. Although she had saved a year to get two strings of a hundred cash each, she gave them both to him.

He went straight back to the wine shop where his friends were gambling. By the door was a picture of the

Pure White Lord. He stood in rich robes and held a pair of dice in his hand.

In front of the picture was a small, narrow table on which sat a cup of dirt. He lit an incense stick and thrust it into the dirt beside all the other burning sticks.

The owner was standing in front of a large table. His hands rested on a big bowl that was turned over. He moved the bowl around in quick circles so that the beans inside rattled against the sides. "Who'll bet? Who'll bet? Better to be wealthy than healthy. Better to be rich than digging a ditch. Who'll bet? Who'll bet?"

Chung found a spot on a bench and slapped his two strings of cash down. He stared hard at the bowl. He felt magical and powerful all at the same time. He felt like he could see the beans inside. He knew just how many were there. "One," he declared.

The owner nodded and finished taking all the bets. Then he lifted the bowl and with a single chopstick drew the beans away, four at a time.

When only half the beans were gone, Chung's experienced eyes saw that there would be three beans left. He had lost all of his wife's egg money. "Chung," he reprimanded himself, "you were so sure. Where did you go wrong?"

One of Chung's friends was a big man with messy hair. Although the big man never seemed to work, he always had money and he always had good luck. He had doubled his money. "Chung, why don't you just give your money away?" He laughed as he jingled his winnings in the air.

It was a magical, musical sound to Chung. He didn't care about his promise to his wife. "Chung," he said to himself, "you just have to squeeze some more money out of your wife."

On his way home, he thought and thought about different plans when he happened to pass by the coffin maker's. As he heard the sound of the saw, he had an idea.

When the coffin maker saw Chung, he grunted. "I don't have any money. And even if I did, I wouldn't loan it to you."

But Chung scooped up a handful of shavings. "May I?"

Puzzled, the coffin maker shrugged. "Be my guest."

Chung sprinkled the wood shavings all over himself and then ran into his house. "If you give me money, you'll be the happiest woman in the world." He lifted his wife up and whirled her around in a circle.

"Put me down." She slapped at his shoulders until he obeyed. Then she smoothed out her blouse. "No more money for gambling."

"That's all done." Chung dusted the shavings from his hair and shoulders. "Sawing wood is so much more fun."

"It is?" the wife asked in surprise.

"I lost the money, so I left. But then I saw a new house being built. When I stopped to watch, the carpenter invited me to help." He shoved his arm forward and then drew it back as if he were sawing. "I had so much fun that the carpenter said I could become his apprentice. I just have to pay him one string of cash."

The wife looked around their barren house. They slept on mats under a moth-eaten quilt. They now had only one pot to their name and two cracked dishes. "But we don't have any money."

"It's a shame," Chung sighed. "The fee is usually higher, but the carpenter liked me."

"We mustn't waste this chance." The wife looked

sadly at her ducks. "My ducks are almost like pets. And we sell the eggs for money."

"It's just temporary. I'll sell them. Then with my wages, I'll buy your ducks right back," the gambler promised.

As soon as he had sold the ducks, he went right back to the wine shop and plunked his money down. "I know it's one this time," he said.

But the number of beans was two.

Chung stood there in a daze. "That's impossible."

His big friend tapped him on the shoulder. "Are you going to set up house there, or are you going to let a player get into the game?"

Chung sadly stepped outside and stopped in front of the pawnshop. He finally realized the enormity of what he had done. "Chung," he said to himself, "you're rotten through and through. You've taken everything from your wife—even her pet ducks. I wouldn't blame her if she left you now. Why did you have to gamble?"

He walked through the village, desperately trying to think of some story that would fool her. As he wandered by a tinsmith, he saw something flash in the dirt. He bent hopefully, thinking that it might be money, but it was only an old piece of tin about the length of his finger.

"Chung, maybe you could disguise yourself." He playfully put the tin over his nose. To his surprise, it fit perfectly and that gave him another idea. He went back into the wine shop and borrowed a knife. With the knife he punched two holes into the piece of tin. Then he got some string from the wine shop and tied the tin over his nose.

Sneaking home, he saw his wife at the stove. Rice bubbled on the stove. Next to it was a duck's egg.

His wife was cutting up some vegetables. But she cut too fast. Giving a little cry, she lifted her knife and sucked at the cut on her finger.

Chung quietly left his house. Then he came back inside and said loudly, "Woman, what do you have for a hungry working man?"

"How is my carpenter?" The wife turned around happily. But the smile left her face. Instead, she just stared. "What happened to your nose?"

"I've found a better profession." He tapped a nail against the tin so that it rang. "I'm a professor of smells."

The wife folded her arms skeptically. "You lost all my money and all my ducks. I trusted you."

"No, no, I can smell out anything." He pointed to the dinner that lay covered up by lids. "My educated nose tells me that you have cooked rice, an omelet, and vegetables for our dinner. Am I right?"

His wife snorted. "Anyone could smell food in a kitchen."

But then he sniffed the air first to his left and then to his right. "I smell blood." He looked at her accusingly. "What an odd sort of dinner?!"

His wife held up her cut finger. "I cut my finger just now. That's what you must have smelled."

He turned in profile. "I told you this was an educated nose." He clinked a fingernail against the tin. "I can find anything by smell."

"Then you can find lost things?" the wife asked in delight.

Chung was so busy congratulating himself on his cleverness that he didn't think. "Anything," he swore.

His wife served his dinner and went outside. As Chung ate, he could hear his wife boasting about her husband's new profession to their neighbors. She added, "For a small fee, he will find anything you've lost."

Chung nearly choked on a mouthful of rice.

"Even my great-aunt's thimble?" a woman asked.

Chung knocked himself on his head. "Chung, you've gotten yourself into an even worse mess." Outside, his proud wife was taking down a list of lost objects that he was to find.

The next day, the professor of smells made a big show of sniffing the air. He walked all around their village. Then he went out the gates and sat down in the orchard. The tin hurt his nose, so he took it off and set it on a rock. It would not be long before everyone knew he was a liar. Then the whole village would make fun of him, and his wife would be angry.

Suddenly a big magpie landed and tried to pick up the tin. Chung waved his hand irritably. "Leave me *something*." The magpie took off.

As Chung watched it rise through the orchard trees, he had another thought. If the magpie liked bright things, maybe the magpie had stolen other bright things. He took out the list and looked at it. The missing items were all shiny things.

Picking up his tin nose, he raced up the slope after the magpie. Sometimes he tripped over rocks, sometimes over tree roots; but the determined gambler always stumbled to his feet and kept the magpie in sight. Finally, the magpie roosted in a tall tree.

Climbing the tree, he found the magpie's nest near a hole in the tree. Putting his hand inside, he pulled out a thimble. Eagerly he took out all the other missing items.

Once on the ground, he buried each item in the orchard and carefully memorized their locations. Then he went back into the village, again sniffing. "I'm close.

I'm close!" And when h⌐ had gathered a small crowd, he led them back to the orchard.

Sniffing the air, he ran back and forth among the fruit trees. Finally, he pointed at one neighbor. "Your thimble is here."

The woman skeptically dug into the dirt and straightened in amazement. She held the thimble up for everyone to see. "This is it! But how did it get here?"

Chung shrugged. "I'm a professor of smells, not of reasons."

One by one, he found the other items to the growing amazement of the crowd. His proud wife collected the fees; and they returned to the village and bought back her ducks.

Soon his fame spread throughout the district. Then one day a sedan chair came to their house. Out stepped a man in expensive robes. He bowed to the startled wife. "I must see the professor of smells. I've lost my prize pig."

The wife tilted back her head regally. "I'll see if he's free."

As soon as she was in the house, she rushed over to the sleeping mat and woke him. "There's a rich man outside who wants you to find his pig."

No magpie would have stolen a pig. "I'm too tired," Chung said.

His wife poked him in the chest. "Professors aren't supposed to be temperamental."

Chung hated to disappoint his wife. "I could listen to him, I suppose," Chung said, and put on his tin nose.

When he went outside, the rich man bowed. "I was going to breed new stock with this special pig. Now I've lost her. Please, Professor, won't you help me?"

Chung was going to refuse politely, but his wife

stepped in front of him. "The professor," she said haughtily, "is a busy man. His skills are in much demand."

The rich man bowed again. "I'm desperate." He took a pouch from his sleeve and held it out. "I hate to insult him with money. However, these gold coins will meet some of his expenses. Once he finds the pig, he's welcome to a second pouch."

Before Chung could stop her, his wife had taken the pouch. "And what does your pig look like?"

"She's all brown except for a white spot around her eye." The rich man drew a circle around his right eye.

When the rich man left, Chung's wife hugged him. "Everyone said you were worthless when we got married. But I knew. I had faith."

Chung did not have the heart to tell her the truth. But then he muttered to himself, "Chung, if a magpie didn't steal the pig, someone else might have." So he asked his wife for a little cash.

"You're not going to go back to gambling, are you?" his wife asked.

"No, but I need wine to sharpen my nose." He went to the wine shop. Once inside, he took off the tin nose and looked around until he saw his man.

Then he paid for a jar of warm wine. He did not drink at all. Instead, he sat down by his big friend. He kept filling the big man's cup. Soon the big man was very drunk. He looked around the wine shop and then crooked a finger at Chung. "You're a good fellow. You just have the luck of a slug. You're welcome to a barbecue next week."

"I like pork," Chung said carefully.

The big robber slapped a hand on Chung's shoulder. "Then you're in luck. I've got the pig of all pigs for you. I found her in her own little house—just like she was a person. And the floor was all tile. I never saw the like."

Chung pretended to think a moment. Then he shook his head. "You don't know how long it's been since I've had pork, but I went to a wise old woman. She said I could only eat brown pigs with white circles around their eyes. I don't think there is any such animal."

The big robber slapped Chung on the back. "It must be this pig's destiny to be your dinner. That's the exact description of the animal I . . . uhh . . . found."

Chung realized this could only be the rich man's pig. He looked over at the picture of the Pure White Lord. "Help me," he begged the picture, "not for my sake but for my wife's. And I swear I won't ask for your help again."

"What did you say?" the big robber asked.

"Nothing." Chung counted out his cash. "I don't suppose you'd like a little game?"

"That'll be the easiest money I'll ever make." The robber grinned. He held up a hand. "Let's play scissors, paper, and rock."

They began to match hands, but the Pure White Lord must have wanted to get rid of Chung. This time Chung won and kept on winning. In no time, he had the robber's money and the pig too.

Then the professor of smells led the pig back to the grateful rich man and received the second pouch of gold.

Naturally, the fame of the professor of smells spread far and wide after that. Chung enjoyed his new reputation and the respect he now received, but his wife enjoyed it even more. "I knew he was special," his wife would boast to their neighbors. "And now everyone knows."

And Chung said to himself, "Chung, there isn't a better wife than her. If you're enjoying good times, it's for her merits—not yours."

So when his old friends would come around, he would refuse to go gambling with them.

But one day a company of soldiers marched into the village and straight to Chung's door. They set a sedan chair down and an official in elegant robes climbed out.

"Professor Chung," the official announced solemnly, "word has reached His Imperial Highness of your special skills. He begs you to come to the capital right away. His jade seal has been lost. No document is official without it. The government is paralyzed. An army of soldiers and clerks has searched the palace; but they could find nothing. Your country turns to you now in its hour of need. You must find the lost seal."

Chung, the gambler thought to himself, you're in for it now. And out loud he said, "It's impossible. I have no such talents."

"This is no time to be modest," his wife hissed at him.

The official tapped him with his fan. "Your wife is right. Anyway, you have no choice. His Imperial Highness summons you."

Chung clutched at his head and bowed. "You have to believe me. I'm telling the truth. I'm a fraud."

But the official signed to some soldiers. They picked up the protesting Chung and dumped him into a second chair.

All the way to the palace, Chung imagined what would happen. "Chung," he said to himself, "it's only fair if they torture you. You've been a cheat and a liar all your life. But then they'll punish your wife and all your kin and all your neighbors, and that isn't fair."

By the time they had reached the audience hall, he had scared himself thoroughly with such thoughts. He was so frightened that he walked straight up to the dragon throne. All the officials and soldiers stared in disbelief. Even the emperor was amazed.

One of his advisors pointed a finger at Chung. "Don't you know you're supposed to make three kowtows and nine bows? You should lose your head for such an insult."

But the emperor was intrigued. "He's either a fool or an extraordinary man."

Chung thought that this was his way out. "Well, if you don't want my help, I'll just leave." He turned on his heel and started to walk out.

The emperor quickly made up his mind. "Wait!" he called.

Chung faced the emperor again. "What is it now?"

The emperor flushed an angry red, but he swallowed his pride. "Professor Chung, you have forty days to prove your skills as an extraordinary man. In that time, you will either help me find my jade seal or I will help you find some manners." He smiled unpleasantly. "And you won't like your lessons."

Chung began that very hour to look all over the palace. It wasn't just one big building but dozens. Some were rooms where the emperor and his family stayed. Others were government offices and soldiers' barracks and quarters for the servants. There were even gardens and parks.

Chung went diligently through the rooms and over the grounds. Whenever anyone saw him, he would pretend to sniff the air vigorously. But by the thirty-ninth day, he had covered only half of the palace.

He slumped miserably against the wall and moaned. He knew he could not succeed where an army had failed. "Chung," he said out loud to himself, "you're done for. You can't fool the emperor anymore."

Now it so happened that one of the king's advisors happened to be in the hallway outside of the office. He stopped dead in his tracks and stared at Chung. It was the same advisor who had wanted Chung's head. "You can't prove a thing!" the advisor said.

"I was just talking to myself," Chung said.

"It's a bad habit." The advisor walked away hastily.

The gambler suddenly had a hunch, and this hunch was stronger than anything he had felt when he was gambling. "Chung, maybe the White Lord is taking pity on you still." He followed the advisor and found out his name was Chung just like his.

"Aha!" Chung said to himself.

The professor of smells nosed around the capital and found that the advisor lived as royally as a prince. He had a fancy palace of his own and an army of servants. "Aha and double aha! My namesake likes to live high on the hog," the professor of smells said.

Next the professor of smells went to some of the fancy gambling places and the expensive restaurants and antique dealers. The advisor owed everyone.

"Chung," he said to himself, "you're having a streak of luck. You might as well follow it out to its end."

He returned to the palace and started sniffing down one hallway and up another. When he found the advisor, he circled him, sniffing, snorting, and sneezing. "There's a smell of jade to you."

The advisor held up the jade ornaments that decorated his sash. "Of course, you idiot."

But the professor of smells went on smelling the advisor. "No, this has an inkish smell to it. Sort of a sealish scent."

The advisor gathered himself up stiffly. "You're imagining things."

Chung tapped the side of his nose with a loud clink.

"You doubted me, but this is no ordinary nose. It can

smell out seals. It can smell out debts and even where they're from," and Chung named a half dozen places. "If I were the thief and I owed that much money, then I might be desperate enough to come up with a scheme. I might hold the imperial seal for ransom. Or I might sell it to some rival of the emperor's. Then they could get their decrees made official."

The advisor sank to his knees and bowed his head. "You truly are a professor of smells. Despite my debts, I still have a considerable fortune. You can have half of it if you can keep me from disgrace."

Chung felt like singing and dancing for joy. However, he managed to keep a stern face. "Well, since we have the same name, we must have the same ancestor some time back in the past. For his sake, bring the seal to me and then resign."

The advisor gratefully obeyed Chung's orders, and Chung buried the seal in one of the gardens under a magnolia tree.

The next day he marched straight into the audience hall. The emperor glared down at Chung. "I see you haven't learned any manners."

But Chung put up a hand for silence and began to sniff.

"What is it?" the emperor demanded.

"Quiet," Chung snapped. "All that talk distracted me last time." He walked right up the dais to the dragon throne and sniffed the emperor's fingers. Then he began to sniff the air. "Yes, Chung," he mumbled to himself, "that's it." Still sniffing the air, he ran out of the audience hall.

The emperor sat on his throne in astonishment. Then he suddenly jumped to his feet. Raising the hem of his long gown, he looked around at his equally amazed court. "Let's see what this extraordinary man is up to." And he scampered after the professor of smells with the rest of the court close at his heels.

Mumbling to himself all the time, Chung led them on a merry chase through one building after another. He scuttled up stairs, leaped through windows, and climbed walls. The emperor and his court had quite forgotten their dignity now. Finally, when their elegant silk robes were all torn and dirty and they were panting like a blacksmith's bellows, Chung led them to the magnolia tree.

"It's the scent of the flowers that threw me off." He circled all around the tree and suddenly began digging in the spot where he had buried the jade seal. "And here the little devil is!"

Wiping it off, he presented it to the emperor. As the emperor took it, he stared down at the hole. "But how did it ever get there?"

Chung simply smiled. "Your Highness, I am a humble professor of smells—not of reasons."

"You must teach this talent to others," the emperor said.

"Alas, Your Majesty. I've strained my nose night and day in your service. I'm afraid it's quite used up." Chung removed his tin nose. "The professor of smells is no more."

Between the grateful emperor and his ex-advisor, Chung went home loaded down with wealth and fame. And he and his wife lived quite comfortably for the rest of their lives.

But he never gambled again. He knew that he had used up enough luck for a dozen professors of smells.

Reviewing and Interpreting the Story

Record your answers to these comprehension questions in your personal literature notebook. Follow the directions for each part.

Reviewing Try to complete each of these sentences without looking back at the story.

Identifying
Cause and Effect

1. Chung puts the piece of tin over his nose because

    a. it will protect his nose from getting sunburned.

    b. he thinks wearing something made of tin is lucky.

    c. he is afraid his wife will slap him for losing her duck money.

    d. he is hoping he can disguise himself.

Identifying
Sequence

2. Chung follows the magpie to its nest after

    a. the magpie tries to pick up his piece of tin.

    b. Chung buries the thimble and other things.

    c. Chung's wife collects money from her neighbors.

    d. a rich man asks Chung to find his pig.

3. Chung talks his wife into selling her ducks by telling her he wants to

    a. become a wine merchant.

    b. become a professor of smells.

    c. become a carpenter.

    d. make one last bet.

4. Chung decides to stop gambling when he realizes that

    a. it would be more fun to be a professor of smells.

    b. his wife wants him to stop.

    c. his gambling hurts his faithful wife.

    d. he has always been unlucky.

5. Which of the following is the most accurate list of scenes in this story?

    a. a small Chinese village, a busy highway, and a palace

    b. a small Chinese village and a palace

    c. a small Chinese village, an orchard, and a palace

    d. a small Chinese village, an orchard, a busy highway, and a palace

Interpreting To answer these questions, you may look back at the story if you like.

Analyzing

6. Which of these events does not indicate that Chung thinks quickly and logically?

    a. He tells the emperor's messenger that he is a fraud.
    b. After a short talk with the advisor named Chung, he investigates him.
    c. When the magpie tries to pick up his piece of tin, he decides that the bird might be a thief.
    d. He uses whatever he happens upon— wood shavings, a piece of tin— to trick his wife.

Predicting Outcomes

7. In the years following Chung's visit to the palace, which of these situations is most likely to occur?

    a. The pig thief will stop robbing and gambling and become a solid citizen.
    b. The emperor will rule wisely, sniffing out and solving problems on his own.
    c. The advisor will confess his crime and be pardoned.
    d. Chung's wife will keep some ducks as pets, without bothering to sell their eggs.

8. Chung suspects that a man he knows stole the pig because the man

    a. is big and has messy hair.

    b. never seems to work, but always has money.

    c. is so lucky at gambling.

    d. always laughs at Chung and his bad luck.

Making
Generalizations

9. The most important lesson of this folktale is that

    a. it's better to depend on your mind than on your luck.

    b. you should think for yourself, not imitate others.

    c. honesty is always the best policy.

    d. gambling is a disease.

Understanding
Story Elements
(Character)

10. The two most important characters in this story are Chung and

    a. his wife.

    b. the emperor.

    c. the pig thief.

    d. the emperor's advisor named Chung.

Now check your answers with your teacher. Study the questions you answered incorrectly. What types of questions were they? Talk with your teacher about ways to work on those skills.

Plot

Every story has a beginning, a middle, and an end. In planning a story, an author decides on a main character, presents a problem, and then tells how the problem is resolved. All of the events, or things that happen in a story, make up its plot. To create a good story, an author chooses the events of a plot carefully. One event leads to another and captures readers' interest by making them wonder what happens next.

A condition or action at the beginning of the plot sets up the problem. For example, the author might choose to have a main character—a hiker—threatened by a wild animal. The rest of the plot revolves around the hiker's struggle to resolve or end the problem. The author might have the hiker outrun the animal, make friends with it, kill it, or be killed by it. The order in which the author presents the events is important. He or she must show readers how one event causes or leads to the next.

If a story has a strong plot, readers are impatient to find out what event will happen next. After finishing the story, they can look back and see how all the events fit together like the links of a chain.

Generally, a plot has five separate stages: introduction or exposition, rising action, climax, falling action, and resolution.

In this unit we will look at the following ways in which author Laurence Yep develops the plot of "The Professor of Smells":

1. In the beginning of the story, Yep uses *exposition* to introduce the main character and to present the conditions that will create the problem the character faces.

2. In the middle of the story, the *rising action* shows how efforts to meet the problem lead to further events. All of these events build to the *climax*.

3. The climax is the point in the story when the struggle against the problem reaches a turning point. The events that happen at the climax signal that there are changes to come.

4. At the end, the *falling action* and *resolution* bring the story to a satisfactory conclusion. Yep reports how the struggle comes to an end and what happens to the characters afterward.

1 • Exposition and Rising Action

Exposition. The first section of a story is called the *introduction,* or *exposition*. In this part the author introduces the characters, the setting, and the problem. Notice how much we learn about the main character of "The Professor of Smells" in its first paragraph:

> Once there was a gambler named Chung. He would bet on anything. He would bet on the weather. He would bet on how many cockroaches were in a cupboard. He once even bet that the sun would set in the east.

These details tell us how thoughtless Chung was in his eagerness to gamble. Many people might bet on the weather, because in most parts of the world there is no way to be certain what tomorrow will be like. But everyone knows that the sun will always set in the west. Chung had to ignore facts and common sense to make a bet about that.

The author never states, "This story is set in a small village in China long ago." However, the details about the vegetables and animals that Chung's wife raises indicate that the setting is a small village. The descriptions of the money and the wine shop indicate that the time is long ago.

> He found his wife in their small vegetable patch. Her ducks waddled around her feet, quacking and eating the insects that her hoe turned up.
>
> His wife believed him because she wanted to, and went and got her money. Each cash was a round coin with a square hole through which a string had been run. Although she had saved a year to get two strings of a hundred cash each, she gave them both to him.

He went straight back to the wine shop where his friends were gambling. By the door was a picture of the Pure White Lord. He stood in rich robes and held a pair of dice in his hand.

The exposition also introduces us to the problem facing the main character. Clearly, Chung's problem is his gambling.

Rising Action.   In this section of a story, the problem grows more and more complicated. Even when it looks as if the character has solved the difficulty, we discover that it was merely replaced by a bigger worry or threat. Each event makes it more difficult for the main character to resolve the problem.

At the beginning of "The Professor of Smells," Chung has a simple problem: He likes to gamble but has no money to gamble with.

> . . . "I was winning," he said to his wife. "But I made just one bad bet. Give me some of your egg money and I'll double it for you."

Although he gets the money, Chung's problem doesn't end. He simply loses the money and needs more.

> . . . "Chung," he said to himself, "you just have to squeeze some more money out of your wife."

Again, getting the last of his wife's money doesn't help Chung because he loses that too. His problem has grown more serious.

> Chung sadly stepped outside and stopped in front of the pawnshop. He finally realized the enormity of what he had done. "Chung," he said to himself, "you're rotten through and through. You've taken everything from your wife—even her pet ducks. I wouldn't blame her if she left you now. Why did you have to gamble?"

Now Chung is anxious to keep his wife from learning about his stupidity. He comes up with the tin nose and the story about his great ability to smell things.

"Then you can find lost things?" his wife asked in delight.

Chung was so busy congratulating himself on his cleverness that he didn't think. "Anything," he swore.

His wife served his dinner and went outside. As Chung ate, he could hear his wife boasting about her husband's new profession to their neighbors. She added, "For a small fee, he will find anything you've lost."

Chung nearly choked on a mouthful of rice.

As surprised as Chung is at this point, he has even more surprises in store as his pretended smelling ability leads to bigger challenges and almost costs him his life. Throughout the rising action, each event leads to new difficulties. Rising action is the longest stage in any plot.

Exercise 1

Read this passage, which follows Chung's discovery that his large friend has the stolen pig. Use what you have learned in this lesson to answer the questions.

"Nothing." Chung counted out his cash. "I don't suppose you'd like a little game?"

"That'll be the easiest money I'll ever make." The robber grinned. He held up a hand. "Let's play scissors, paper, and rock."

They began to match hands, but the Pure White Lord must have wanted to get rid of Chung. This time Chung won and kept on winning. In no time, he had the robber's money and the pig too.

Then the professor of smells led the pig back to the grateful rich man and received the second pouch of gold.

Naturally, the fame of the professor of smells spread far and wide after that. . . .

But one day a company of soldiers marched into the

village and straight to Chung's door. They set a sedan chair down and an official in elegant robes climbed out.

"Professor Chung," the official announced solemnly, "word has reached His Imperial Highness of your special skills. He begs you to come to the capital right away. His jade seal has been lost. No document is official without it. The government is paralyzed. An army of soldiers and clerks has searched the palace; but they could find nothing. Your country turns to you now in its hour of need. You must find the lost seal."

1. Why does Chung suggest that the robber play a game of chance with him? What information has the author already given about both Chung and the robber that makes this action a logical move on Chung's part?

2. What is the immediate, enjoyable result of Chung's cleverness? How does his cleverness lead to a far more serious problem? How might the story have changed if Chung had lost the game with the robber?

Check your answers with your teacher. Review this part of the lesson if you don't understand why an answer was incorrect.

Writing on Your Own 1

Review your lists and notes from Developing a Plot on page 5. Follow these steps:

- Choose a setting—a place and time for your story. Write two or more complete sentences describing where and when your story will take place.

- Decide who your main character will be and what problem he or she will face. Write a paragraph that describes the situation at the beginning of the story.

- What could your character do to try to solve the problem? What worse problem can result from that action? Plan the rising action in your story briefly, using a chart like the one that follows for "The Professor of Smells." Provide at least four events in your plot.

Event	Chung tells wife he can find things by smell.	

⬇

Event	Wife tells neighbors.

⬇

Problem	Wife and neighbors expect Chung to find lost items.

⬇

Event	He follows bird to find lost things.

⬇

Event	Chung's fame spreads.

⬇

Event	Rich man expects Chung to find lost pig.

⬇

Event	He gambles with robber to win back lost pig.

⬇

Event	Chung's fame spreads farther.

⬇

Problem	Emperor expects Chung to find his lost seal.

2 • Climax

The *climax* of any story is the point at which the problem is the most intense. Emotions of both characters and readers are at a high point. Whatever happens now will bring victory or defeat to the main character.

In a novel, the climax may require an entire chapter or more. In a short story, it may take up several paragraphs. There is not always a clear break between the rising action and the climax, or between the climax and the falling action. At a certain point, however, you feel that the struggle has come to a head. A decision on the problem cannot be postponed any longer. Often the climax is called the "turning point." The character can never go back to things as they used to be.

In the introduction and rising action of "The Professor of Smells," Chung repeatedly makes trouble for himself. When he uses trickery to get out of one situation, it gets him into a worse fix. Yet Chung never seems to learn anything from his experiences. Even when he is most anxious, he expects to find a way to avoid the consequences of what he has done.

For example, when he realizes that his gambling is harmful to his wife and must stop, Chung uses the tale about his smelling ability to escape her just anger. When he thinks that his neighbors will laugh at him, he wanders away from town to avoid their laughter. He stays outside of town until he finds a solution that makes him look good. When he wants to get the stolen pig from a fellow gambler, he relies on help from the Pure White Lord to carry him to victory.

However, when the emperor calls on him, Chung realizes he is in more serious trouble than ever before. He is so desperate that he momentarily turns to the truth to escape the emperor's call. "You have to believe me," he tells the official who was sent for him. "I'm telling the truth. I'm a fraud."

Still, when he is brought before the emperor, Chung once again gambles that he can find a way out. Because of his fear, he forgets how to behave before the emperor. Even the emperor is puzzled by his actions and says, "He's either a fool or an extraordinary man." At that, Chung decides that he can try to fool even the emperor.

Chung thought that this was his way out. "Well, if you don't want my help, I'll just leave." He turned on his heel and started to walk out.

The emperor quickly made up his mind. "Wait!" he called.

Chung faced the emperor again. "What is it now?"

The emperor flushed an angry red, but he swallowed his pride. "Professor Chung, you have forty days to prove your skills as an extraordinary man. In that time, you will either help me find my jade seal or I will help you find some manners." He smiled unpleasantly. "And you won't like your lessons."

The last paragraph above ushers in the climax. All of Chung's gambling, lies, and tricks have brought him to a critical point, where he must either succeed or pay for his actions.

Exercise 2

Read this passage and answer the questions about it using what you have learned in this lesson.

Chung began that very hour to look all over the palace. It wasn't just one building but dozens. Some were rooms where the emperor and his family stayed. Others were government offices and soldiers' barracks and quarters for the servants. There were even gardens and parks.

Chung went diligently through the rooms and over the grounds. Whenever anyone saw him, he would pretend to sniff the air vigorously. But by the thirty-ninth day, he had covered only half of the palace.

He slumped miserably against the wall and moaned. He knew he could not succeed where an army had failed. "Chung," he said out loud to himself, "you're done for. You can't fool the emperor anymore."

Now it so happened that one of the king's advisors happened to be in the hallway outside of the office. He stopped dead in his tracks and stared at Chung. It was the same advisor who had wanted Chung's head. "You can't prove a thing!" the advisor said.

1. Chung begins his task of searching the palace with optimism. At what point does his attitude change? Why? Does he have any further plans to avoid punishment for his tricks?

2. Why does the advisor stop to speak to Chung? What clue does his statement provide? Explain how the climax is at the same time both a critical downturn in Chung's hopes and an upturn in his luck.

Check your answers with your teacher. Review this part of the lesson if you don't understand why an answer was incorrect.

Writing on Your Own 2

In this exercise you will write a paragraph or two to develop a climax using your notes from Writing on Your Own 1. Follow these steps:

- Review the events you have outlined so far. Does the last event on your list bring the problem to a climax, a moment of high excitement or danger? If not, add events to the outline to take your character to a point of no return.

- Think about how your character will react to the situation. What can he or she do to resolve the problem in either a good or a bad way? Write a paragraph or two telling about the climax and your character's reaction.

- Reread the climax you just wrote. You may wish to add details to make the events more exciting or to suggest how this turning point will change the plot.

3 • Falling Action and Resolution

Falling Action. This stage of a story includes all the events following the climax. These events show how actions taken at the climax work out. In some stories, the falling action is very short. In others, there is quite a bit of action at this stage.

In "The Professor of Smells," the falling action includes everything that happens after Chung cries out to himself, "Chung, you're done for" and hears the emperor's advisor respond, "You can't prove a thing!" At that moment, Chung and the reader suspect that the advisor has the missing seal. But you don't know whether Chung can obtain the seal and save himself, or whether he must accept the emperor's punishment. You learn the results of the climax in the falling action. The author includes details about how Chung investigates the advisor, sharing the excitement of his detective work with the reader.

> The professor of smells nosed around the capital and found that the advisor lived as royally as a prince. He had a fancy palace of his own and an army of servants. "Aha and double aha! My namesake likes to live high on the hog," the professor of smells said.
>
> Next the professor of smells went to some of the fancy gambling places and the expensive restaurants and antique dealers. The advisor owed everyone.

Even after the advisor confesses to Chung, the author keeps you reading to discover how Chung will return the jade seal to the emperor without disgracing the advisor and without getting himself into a deeper mess.

Resolution. At this stage, the author shows the reader how the problem is resolved. You see how the main character grows or is destroyed by the changes he or she has experienced. You discover, too, how the events of the story affect other characters.

Usually, the excitement dies down gradually between the climax and the end of the story. As this happens, the author ties up other "loose ends." Compare, for example, the excitement in the first paragraph of this passage with the calmness in the last.

Mumbling to himself all the time, Chung led them on a merry chase through one building after another. He scuttled up stairs, leaped through windows, and climbed walls. The emperor and his court had quite forgotten their dignity now. Finally, when their elegant silk robes were all torn and dirty and they were panting like a blacksmith's bellows, Chung led them to the magnolia tree.

"It's the scent of the flowers that threw me off." He circled all around the tree and suddenly began digging in the spot where he had buried the jade seal. "And here the little devil is!"

Wiping it off, he presented it to the emperor. As the emperor took it, he stared down at the hole. "But how did it ever get there?"

Chung simply smiled. "Your Highness, I am a humble professor of smells—not of reasons."

Exercise 3

Read this passage and answer the questions about it using what you have learned in this lesson.

"You must teach this talent to others," the emperor said.

"Alas, Your Majesty, I've strained my nose night and day in your service. I'm afraid it's quite used up." Chung removed his tin nose. "The professor of smells is no more."

Between the grateful emperor and his ex-advisor, Chung went home loaded down with wealth and fame. And he and his wife lived quite comfortably for the rest of their lives.

But he never gambled again. He knew that he had used up enough luck for a dozen professors of smells.

1. How can you tell that Chung has truly learned the dangers of tricking people?

2. What do you learn about the state of characters other than Chung at the end of the story?

Check your answers with your teacher. Review this part of the lesson if you don't understand why an answer was incorrect.

Writing on Your Own 3

Use what you have learned in this lesson to plan the falling action of your plot and its resolution. Follow these steps:

- Review the climax that you developed for your story in Writing on Your Own 2. Decide whether your character will succeed or fail. Then use a plot outline chart to list the events of the falling action that will take your character from the climax to the end you have in mind.

- What more does your reader need to know about the fate of your main character? What additional facts could you include about him or her? Write a resolution of no more than two paragraphs that tells the condition of the main character at the end of the story.

Discussion Guides

1. Imagine that Chung's wife meets his large friend, the robber, at a party. To be sociable, they tell each other a little about themselves and try to identify people they both know. They try to decide whether the Chung that she is married to is the Chung

that the robber has met at the wine shop. What might come out in the conversation? Work with a partner to develop a short dialogue between these two characters. Then present your dialogue to your class or another group.

2. When the emperor calls for Chung, he expects that his story about being a "professor of smells" will be exposed as a lie. He tells himself, "It's only fair if they torture you. You've been a cheat and a liar all your life." Do you agree that he deserves punishment? Which of his actions were illegal or hurtful to others? Has he done any good deeds to make up for his misdeeds? With a group, discuss Chung's behavior throughout the story. At the end of your discussion, the group should vote to determine whether Chung deserves punishment and, if so, to recommend his sentence.

3. What clues do you get from this story about life in China long ago? Work with a partner or a small group to review the story for details about the way the village looked, how rich people traveled, what people did for fun, how the government worked, and so on. Discuss the details to discover whether everyone interprets them the same way. Discuss, too, what else you can infer about daily life and about attitudes and beliefs of the time. Conclude your discussion by listing the three aspects of this life that your group considers most interesting.

Write a Plot Outline

Throughout this unit, you have been developing the plot of an original story, working out each of the five parts in order from beginning to end. In the process, you may have found that all your parts work well together. On the other hand, by the time you worked on your resolution, you may have decided that your introduction was dull. The rising action may have had missing steps. Or perhaps the climax disagreed with what came before or after.

Now you are going to put all these parts together to revise and complete your plot outline. If you have questions about the writing process, refer to Using the Writing Process, beginning on page 306.

- Assemble the writing you did for Developing a Plot at the beginning of the unit and for each of the Writing on Your Own exercises.

- Review and compare your work on the following assignments: *a)* notes for developing a plot, *b)* descriptions of setting and character, *c)* outline of events in the rising action, *d)* the climax, *e)* the list of events in the falling action, and *f)* the resolution. Look over your outline. Decide which work you can use and which needs to be improved or replaced. You may discover, for example, that you cannot use a well-written description simply because you changed the plot since writing that part.

- Building on what you have, fill in the missing parts to complete your plot outline. Make sure that your finished outline includes the following elements:

  1) an introduction that describes the setting, the main character, and his or her problem

  2) rising action in which the problem grows more serious

  3) a climax, or turning point

  4) falling action in which the climax is worked out

  5) a resolution

- Share your finished plot outline with a partner for feedback. Ask your partner to point out areas that are unclear or that don't seem to fit the plot. Make any revisions you agree with.

- Proofread your outline for errors in spelling, grammar, and punctuation. Make a corrected copy and save it in a portfolio of your writing.

- . If you wish, write a story using your plot outline as a guide.

Unit 2 Character

Tuesday of the Other June
by Norma Fox Mazer

About the Illustration

Describe what you think is happening in this scene. Use details from the illustration as clues. Give reasons for your answers.

These questions will help you begin to think about the story:

- Where does this scene take place?

- Who do you think the main character is?

- How do you think the girl who is being pushed into the water feels?

- Do you think the laughing bystanders are her friends? Why or why not?

Unit 2

Introduction

About the Story

On Tuesday, the first day of swimming class at the Community Center, June meets another girl named June. The Other June immediately starts bullying June, pinching her, and calling her names. Each week thereafter, the Other June teases June and makes her look weak and foolish in front of her friends. June, following her peace-loving mother's advice, is powerless to fight back. Soon, every Tuesday becomes Awfulday, a day to be feared all week long. After the swim class finally ends, June and her mother move to a new apartment. She hopes it is far away from the Other June, but to her dismay, finds that now she will be in school with her enemy every single day. Read to find how June deals with the Other June.

About the Author

Norma Fox Mazer was born in 1931 in New York City and grew up in Glens Falls, New York. She attended Antioch College in Yellow Springs, Ohio, and Syracuse University in New York. She has written a number of award-winning novels for young adult readers. Most of her writing focuses on the choices that young people make as they move from childhood to adulthood. Her characters often tackle problems such as discrimination, lack of self-esteem, and the need for self-understanding. Ms. Mazer won the Newbery Honor Medal in 1988 for her novel *After the Rain* about a girl's close relationship with her ill grandfather. She often writes together with her husband Harry Mazer.

Other short stories by this author can be found in collections such as *Dear Bill, Remember Me? and Other Stories*, and *Summer Girls, Love Boys and Other Short Stories*.

About the Lessons

The lessons that follow "Tuesday of the Other June" focus on character. A *character* is a person, animal, or thing that takes part in the action of a story. You come to know the characters in a short story in a variety of ways. Often the writer helps you know the characters both inside and outside, that is, how they think and feel as well as how they look and sound. The best characters are those who seem to come alive, as if you could really know such a person in everyday life.

Writing: Creating a Character

A good character is one that you will remember long after you finish reading a story or seeing a play or movie. Creating a memorable character takes planning and thought. In the course of this unit, you will create your own interesting character and write a character sketch showing him or her in action. The suggestions below will help you get started.

- Think of an imaginary character who is familiar, much like a person you might meet in your neighborhood or your classroom. The character could be one you like or one you would try to avoid meeting. You will need to describe how this person looks, speaks, acts, and feels, so choose someone you can make interesting and believable.

- Jot down a few notes about how the character looks and sounds. First just write some phrases. Then write a few sentences to introduce your reader to the appearance of the character.

- Read your sentences to a friend or classmate and listen to his or her sentences about a character. Decide if your characters are realistic. Discuss what details you can add to make your characters more believable.

Before Reading

The questions below will help you see how the author has developed the realistic characters who appear in "Tuesday of the Other June." As you read the story, keep these questions in mind:

- What do you know about June and the Other June, based on what they say?

- What do you know about both Junes from what they do?

- How is June different at the end of the story from the way she was at the beginning of the story?

Vocabulary Tips

This story includes a few words that may be unfamiliar to you but are useful for understanding the story. Below you will find some of these words, their definitions, and sentences that show how the words are used. Look over the words before you begin to read.

heave to pull on or haul. The sailor <u>heaved</u> the thick rope onto the deck.
wheeze to make a sound like hoarse breathing. The washing machine <u>wheezed</u> and whined just before it fell silent.
frisk to move playfully. I like to watch my dog <u>frisk</u> around the park on our daily walks.

Tuesday of the Other June

Norma Fox Mazer

"Be good, be good, be good, be good, my Junie," my mother sang as she combed my hair; a song, a story, a croon, a plea. "It's just you and me, two women alone in the world, June darling of my heart, we have enough troubles getting by, we surely don't need a single one more, so you keep your sweet self out of fighting and all that bad stuff. People can be little-hearted, but turn the other cheek, smile at the world, and the world'll surely smile back."

We stood in front of the mirror as she combed my hair, combed and brushed and smoothed. Her head came just above mine; she said when I grew another inch she'd stand on a stool to brush my hair. "I'm not giving up this pleasure!" And she laughed her long honey laugh.

My mother was April, my grandmother had been May, I was June. "And someday," said my mother, "you'll have a daughter of your own. What will you name her?"

"January!" I'd yell when I was little. "February! No, November!" My mother laughed her honey laugh. She had little emerald eyes that warmed me like the sun.

Every day when I went to school, she went to work. "Sometimes I stop what I'm doing," she said, "lay down my tools, and stop everything, because all I can think about is you. Wondering what you're doing and if you need me. Now, Junie, if anyone ever bothers you—"

"—I walk away, run away, come on home as fast as my feet will take me," I recited.

"Yes. You come to me. You just bring me your trouble, because I'm here on this earth to love you and take care of you."

I was safe with her. Still, sometimes I woke up at night and heard footsteps slowly creeping up the stairs. It wasn't my mother, she was asleep in the bed across the room, so it was robbers, thieves, and murderers, creeping slowly . . . slowly . . . slowly toward my bed.

I stuffed my hand into my mouth. If I screamed and woke her, she'd be tired at work tomorrow. The robbers and thieves filled the warm darkness and slipped across the floor more quietly than cats. Rigid under the covers, I stared at the shifting dark and bit my knuckles and never knew when I fell asleep again.

In the morning we sang in the kitchen. "Bill Grogan's GOAT! Was feelin' FINE! Ate three red shirts, right off the LINE!" I made sandwiches for our lunches, she made pancakes for breakfast, but all she ate was one pancake and a cup of coffee. "Gotta fly, can't be late."

I wanted to be rich and take care of her. She worked too hard, her pretty hair had gray in it that she joked about. "Someday," I said, "I'll buy you a real house and you'll never work in a pot factory again."

"Such delicious plans," she said. She checked the windows to see if they were locked. "Do you have your key?"

I lifted it from the chain around my neck.

"And you'll come right home from school and —"

"—I won't light fires or let strangers into the house

and I won't tell anyone on the phone that I'm here alone," I finished for her.

"I know, I'm just your old worrywart mother." She kissed me twice, once on each cheek. "But you are my June, my only June, the only June."

She was wrong, there was another June. I met her when we stood next to each other at the edge of the pool the first day of swimming class in the Community Center.

"What's your name?" She had a deep growly voice.

"June. What's yours?"

She stared at me. "June."

"We have the same name."

"No we don't. June is *my* name, and I don't give you permission to use it. Your name is Fish Eyes." She pinched me hard. "Got it, Fish Eyes?"

The next Tuesday, the Other June again stood next to me at the edge of the pool. "What's your name?"

"June."

"Wrong. Your—name—is—Fish—Eyes."

"June."

"Fish Eyes, you are really stupid." She shoved me into the pool.

The swimming teacher looked up, frowning, from her chart. "No one in the water yet."

Later, in the locker room, I dressed quickly and wrapped my wet suit in the towel. The Other June pulled on her jeans. "You guys see that bathing suit Fish Eyes was wearing? Her mother found it in a trash can."

"She did not!"

The Other June grabbed my fingers and twisted. "Where'd she find your bathing suit?"

"She bought it, let me go."

"Poor little stupid Fish Eyes is crying. Oh, boo hoo hoo, poor little Fish Eyes."

After that, everyone called me Fish Eyes. And every Tuesday, wherever I was, there was also the Other June—at the edge of the pool, in the pool, in the locker room. In the water, she swam alongside me, blowing and huffing, knocking into me. In the locker room, she stepped on my feet, pinched my arms, hid my blouse, and knotted my braids together. She had large square teeth, she was shorter than I was, but heavier, with bigger bones and square hands. If I met her outside on the street, carrying her bathing suit and towel, she'd walk toward me, smiling a square, friendly smile. "Oh well, if it isn't Fish Eyes." Then she'd punch me, *blam!* her whole solid weight hitting me.

I didn't know what to do about her. She was training me like a dog. After a few weeks of this, she only had to look at me, only had to growl, "I'm going to get you, Fish Eyes," for my heart to slink like a whipped dog down into my stomach. My arms were covered with bruises. When my mother noticed, I made up a story about tripping on the sidewalk.

My weeks were no longer Tuesday, Wednesday, Thursday, and so on. Tuesday was Awfulday. Wednesday was Badday. (The Tuesday bad feelings were still there.) Thursday was Betterday and Friday was Safeday. Saturday was Goodday, but Sunday was Toosoonday, and Monday—Monday was nothing but the day before Awfulday.

I tried to slow down time. Especially on the weekends, I stayed close by my mother, doing everything with her, shopping, cooking, cleaning, going to the laundromat. "Aw, sweetie, go play with your friends."

"No, I'd rather be with you." I wouldn't look at the clock or listen to the radio (they were always telling you the date and the time). I did special magic things to keep the day from going away, rapping my knuckles six times on the bathroom door six times a day and never, ever touching the chipped place on my bureau. But always I woke up to the day before Tuesday, and always, no matter how many times I circled the worn spot in the living-room rug or counted twenty-five cracks in the ceiling, Monday disappeared and once again it was Tuesday.

The Other June got bored with calling me Fish Eyes. Buffalo Brain came next, but as soon as everyone knew that, she renamed me Turkey Nose.

Now at night it wasn't robbers creeping up the stairs, but the Other June, coming to torment me. When I finally fell asleep, I dreamed of kicking her, punching, biting, pinching. In the morning I remembered my dreams and felt brave and strong. And then I remembered all the things my mother had taught me and told me.

Be good, be good, be good, it's just us two women alone in the world . . . . Oh, but if it weren't, if my father wasn't long gone, if we'd had someone else to fall back on, if my mother's mother and daddy weren't dead all these years, if my father's daddy wanted to know us instead of being glad to forget us—oh, then I would have punched the Other June with a frisky heart, I would have grabbed her arm at poolside and bitten her like the dog she had made of me.

One night, when my mother came home from work, she said, "Junie, listen to this. We're moving!"

Alaska, I thought. Florida. Arizona. Some place far away and wonderful, some place without the Other June.

"Wait till you hear this deal. We are going to be caretakers, troubleshooters for an eight-family apartment building. Fifty-six Blue Hill Street. Not janitors, we don't do any of the heavy work. April and June, Troubleshooters, Incorporated. If a tenant has a complaint or a problem, she comes to us and we either take care of it or call the janitor for service. And for that little bit of work, we get to live rent free!" She swept me around in a dance. "Okay? You like it? I do!"

So. Not anywhere else, really. All the same, maybe too far to go to swimming class! "Can we move right away? Today?"

"Gimme a break, sweetie. We've got to pack, do a thousand things. I've got to line up someone with a truck to help us. Six weeks, Saturday the fifteenth." She circled it on the calendar. It was the Saturday after the last day of swimming class.

Soon, we had boxes lying everywhere, filled with clothes and towels and glasses wrapped in newspaper. Bit by bit, we cleared the rooms, leaving only what we needed right now. The dining-room table staggered on a bunched-up rug, our bureaus inched toward the front door like patient cows. On the calendar in the kitchen, my mother marked off the days until we moved, but the only days I thought about were Tuesdays—Awfuldays. Nothing else was real except the too fast passing of time, moving toward each Tuesday . . . away from Tuesday . . . toward Tuesday. . . .

And it seemed to me that this would go on forever, that Tuesdays would come forever and I would be forever trapped by the side of the pool, the Other June whispering *Buffalo Brain Fish Eyes Turkey Nose* into my ear, while she ground her elbow into my side and smiled her square smile at the swimming teacher.

And then it ended. It was the last day of swimming class. The last Tuesday. We had all passed our tests and, as if in celebration, the Other June only pinched me twice. "And now," our swimming teacher said, "all of you are ready for the Advanced Class, which starts in just one month. I have a sign-up slip here. Please put your name down before you leave." Everyone but me crowded around. I went to the locker room and pulled on my clothes as fast as possible. The Other June burst through the door just as I was leaving. "Good-bye," I yelled, "good riddance to bad trash!" Before she could pinch me again, I ran past her and then ran all the way home, singing, "Good-bye . . . good-bye . . . good-bye, good riddance to bad trash!"

Later, my mother carefully untied the blue ribbon around my swimming-class diploma. "Look at this! Well, isn't this wonderful! You are on your way, you might turn into an Olympic swimmer, you never know what life will bring."

"I don't want to take more lessons."

"Oh, sweetie, it's great to be a good swimmer." But then, looking into my face, she said, "No, no, no, don't worry, you don't have to."

The next morning, I woke up hungry for the first time in weeks. No more swimming class. No more Baddays and Awfuldays. No more Tuesdays of the Other June. In the kitchen, I made hot cocoa to go with my mother's corn muffins. "It's Wednesday, Mom," I said, stirring the cocoa. "My favorite day."

"Since when?"

"Since this morning." I turned on the radio so I could hear the announcer tell the time, the temperature, and the day.

Thursday for breakfast I made cinnamon toast, Friday my mother made pancakes, and on Saturday, before we moved, we ate the last slices of bread and cleaned out the peanut-butter jar.

"Some breakfast," Tilly said. "Hello, you must be June." She shook my hand. She was a friend of my mother's from work, she wore big hoop earrings, sandals, and a skirt as dazzling as a rainbow. She came in a truck with John to help us move our things.

John shouted cheerfully at me, "So you're moving." An enormous man with a face covered with little brown bumps. Was he afraid his voice wouldn't travel the distance from his mouth to my ear? "You looking at my moles?" he shouted, and he heaved our big green-flowered chair down the stairs. "Don't worry, they don't bite. Ha, ha, ha!" Behind him came my mother and Tilly balancing a bureau between them, and behind them I carried a lamp and the round, flowered Mexican tray that was my mother's favorite. She had found it at a garage sale and said it was as close to foreign travel as we would ever get.

The night before, we had loaded our car, stuffing in bags and boxes until there was barely room for the two of us. But it was only when we were in the car, when we drove past Abdo's Grocery, where they always gave us credit, when I turned for a last look at our street—it was only then that I understood we were truly going to live somewhere else, in another apartment, in another place mysteriously called Blue Hill Street.

Tilly's truck followed our car.

"Oh, I'm so excited," my mother said. She laughed. "You'd think we were going across the country."

Our old car wheezed up a long steep hill. Blue Hill Street. I looked from one side to the other, trying to see everything.

My mother drove over the crest of the hill. "And now—ta da!—our new home."

"Which house? Which one?" I looked out the window

and what I saw was the Other June. She was sprawled on the stoop of a pink house, lounging back on her elbows, legs outspread, her jaws working on a wad of gum. I slid down into the seat, but it was too late. I was sure she had seen me.

My mother turned into a driveway next to a big white building with a tiny porch. She leaned on the steering wheel. "See that window there, that's our living-room window . . . and that one over there, that's your bedroom. . . .

We went into the house, down a dim cool hall. In our new apartment, the wooden floors clicked under our shoes, and my mother showed me everything. Her voice echoed in the empty rooms. I followed her around in a daze. Had I imagined seeing the Other June? Maybe I'd seen another girl who looked like her. A double. That could happen.

"Ho yo, where do you want this chair?"

John appeared in the doorway. We brought in boxes and bags and beds and stopped only to eat pizza and drink orange juice from the carton.

"June's so quiet, do you think she'll adjust all right?" I heard Tilly say to my mother.

"Oh, definitely. She'll make a wonderful adjustment. She's just getting used to things."

But I thought that if the Other June lived on the same street as I did, I would never get used to things.

That night I slept in my own bed, with my own pillow and blanket, but with floors that creaked in strange voices and walls with cracks I didn't recognize. I didn't feel either happy or unhappy. It was as if I were waiting for something.

Monday, when the principal of Blue Hill Street School left me in Mr. Morrisey's classroom, I knew what

I'd been waiting for. In that room full of strange kids, there was one person I knew. She smiled her square smile, raised her hand, and said, "She can sit next to me, Mr. Morrisey."

"Very nice of you, June M. Okay, June T, take your seat. I'll try not to get you two Junes mixed up."

I sat down next to her. She pinched my arm. "Good riddance to bad trash," she mocked.

I was back in the Tuesday swimming class only now it was worse, because every day would be Awfulday. The pinching had already started. Soon, I knew, on the playground and in the halls, kids would pass me, grinning. "Hiya, Fish Eyes."

The Other June followed me around during recess that day, droning in my ear, "You are my slave, you must do everything I say, I am your master, say it, say, 'Yes, master, you are my master.'"

I pressed my lips together, clapped my hands over my ears, but without hope. Wasn't it only a matter of time before I said the hateful words?

"How was school?" my mother said that night.

"Okay."

She put a pile of towels in a bureau drawer. "Try not to be sad about missing your old friends, sweetie, there'll be new ones."

The next morning, the Other June was waiting for me when I left the house. "Did your mother get you that blouse in the garbage dump?" She butted me, shoving me against a tree. "Don't you speak anymore, Fish Eyes?" Grabbing my chin in her hands, she pried open my mouth. "Oh, ha, ha, I thought you lost your tongue."

We went on to school. I sank down into my seat, my head on my arms. "June T, are you all right?" Mr. Morrisey asked. I nodded. My head was almost too heavy to lift.

The Other June went to the pencil sharpener. Round and round she whirled the handle. Walking back, looking at me, she held the three sharp pencils like three little knives.

Someone knocked on the door. Mr. Morrisey went out into the hall. Paper planes burst into the air, flying from desk to desk. Someone turned on a transistor radio. And the Other June, coming closer, smiled and licked her lips like a cat sleepily preparing to gulp down a mouse.

I remembered my dream of kicking her, punching, biting her like a dog.

Then my mother spoke quickly in my ear: *Turn the other cheek, my Junie, smile at the world and the world'll surely smile back.*

But I had turned the other cheek and it was slapped. I had smiled and the world hadn't smiled back. I couldn't run home as fast as my feet would take me, I had to stay in school—and in school there was the Other June. Every morning, there would be the Other June, and every afternoon, and every day, all day, there would be the Other June.

She frisked down the aisle, stabbing the pencils in the air toward me. A boy stood up on his desk and bowed. "My fans," he said, "I greet you." My arm twitched and throbbed, as if the Other June's pencils had already poked through the skin. She came closer, smiling her Tuesday smile.

"No," I whispered, *"no."* The word took wings and flew me to my feet, in front of the Other June. *"Noooooo."* It flew out of my mouth into her surprised face.

The boy on the desk turned toward us. "You said something, my devoted fans?"

"No," I said to the Other June. "Oh, no! No. No. No. No more." I pushed away the hand that held the pencils.

The Other June's eyes opened, popped wide like the eyes of somebody in a cartoon. It made me laugh. The boy on the desk laughed, and then the other kids were laughing too.

"No," I said again, because it felt so good to say it. "No, no, no, no." I leaned toward the Other June, put my finger against her chest. Her cheeks turned red, she squawked something—it sounded like "Eeeraaghyou!"— and she stepped back. She stepped away from me.

The door banged, the airplanes disappeared, and Mr. Morrisey walked to his desk. "Okay. Okay. Let's get back to work. Kevin Clark, how about it?" Kevin jumped off the desk and Mr. Morrisey picked up a piece of chalk. "All right, class—" He stopped and looked at me and the Other June. "You two Junes, what's going on there?"

I tried it again. My finger against her chest. Then the words. "No—more." And she stepped back another step. I sat down at my desk.

"June M," Mr. Morrisey said.

She turned around, staring at him with that big-eyed cartoon look. After a moment she sat down at her desk with a loud slapping sound.

Even Mr. Morrisey laughed.

And sitting at my desk, twirling my braids, I knew this was the last Tuesday of the Other June.

Reviewing and Interpreting the Story

Record your answers to these comprehension questions in your personal literature notebook. Follow the directions for each part.

Reviewing Try to complete each of these sentences without looking back at the story.

Recalling Facts

1. June's mother is named
   a. April.
   b. May.
   c. June.
   d. Tilly.

Identifying Cause and Effect

2. The Other June chooses June to bully because
   a. June is the smallest girl in the class.
   b. she doesn't want to share her name with June.
   c. she doesn't like June's clothes.
   d. June is the class leader and the Other June wants to replace her.

Recognizing Story Elements (Setting)

3. This story is set
   a. during the American Revolution.
   b. at a time in the distant future.
   c. at the present time.
   d. in the dead of winter.

4. It is easy for the Other June to terrorize June because June

   a. is too weak to fight back.

   b. is afraid to upset her mother by not following her directions.

   c. wants the attention the Other June gives her.

   d. is not popular with her classmates.

5. The first thing June does is

   a. yell "Good-bye, good riddance to bad trash!" to the Other June.

   b. poke the Other June in the chest and say, "No—more."

   c. move to a new apartment.

   d. sign up for the Advanced Class.

Interpreting   To answer these questions, you may look back at the story if you like.

6. From what the Other June says about June's clothes, it is probably true that June and her mother are

   a. not rich enough to buy fine clothes.

   b. interested in keeping up with the latest fashions.

   c. from a foreign country and dress in unusual styles.

   d. quite wealthy.

7. The next time June faces a difficult situation, she will most likely

   a. run away from it as fast as she can.

   b. ask her mother to help her overcome
      her problems.

   c. face it with courage.

   d. smile cheerfully and forget her prob-
      lems.

8. June probably doesn't tell her mother
   about her problems with the Other June
   because she

   a. is ashamed.

   b. wants to forget the Other June while
      she is at home.

   c. doesn't think her mother would be of
      any help in solving the problem.

   d. doesn't want to worry her mother, who
      works so hard and loves her so much.

9. By the end of the story, June learns a lesson about dealing with people that can be
   stated this way:

   a. Smile at the world and the world will
      smile back.

   b. Sometimes you have to stand up for
      your own rights.

   c. Good friends are hard to find.

   d. Don't judge a person until you've
      walked a mile in his or her shoes.

10. The turning point in the story comes when

    a. June meets the Other June.

    b. June's mother says they are going to move.

    c. the rest of the class starts laughing at the Other June.

    d. June decides to stand up to the Other June.

Now check your answers with your teacher. What types of questions did you answer incorrectly? Talk with your teacher about ways to work on those skills.

Character

Think about the stories you like best and remember most clearly. If you're like most people, you will probably be able to picture the people in the stories immediately. You feel that you know some fictional characters as well as, or maybe even better than, the people you see every day. After all, you see only the outside of people and what they choose to reveal about what's happening on the inside, but in a well-written story you see what the characters are thinking and feeling as well.

When you read "Tuesday of the Other June," it is as if you are walking around inside June. You see her harried and sincere mother. You hear the words of the horrible Other June. You sense June's embarrassment when the Other June bullies her. You "overhear" June's thoughts as she waits for the next Tuesday and the dreaded swim class. After living so closely with June, you want to celebrate with her when she finally turns the tables on the Other June. You feel as if you've been through the ordeal yourself.

It is no accident that you identify so strongly with June. The writer has skillfully used certain techniques to make her come alive. You will learn more about those techniques throughout this unit.

In this unit, we will look at these ways in which author Norma Fox Mazer creates realistic, believable characters:

1. The author makes the characters come alive through dialogue.

2. She shows the characters in action.

3. She shows how the characters change and grow because of their experiences.

1 • Character and Dialogue

A good way to begin to describe a character is by telling what that person looks like. But to make a character seem real, a writer must go beyond simply telling whether the character is a boy or a girl, short or tall, athletic or delicate. The writer must find a way to let you get to know the character—how he or she thinks and feels and what the character is likely to do in any given situation.

A writer may describe the character directly. In a *direct description,* the writer just comes out and tells you about the character. For example, in "Tuesday of the Other June," the Other June is described in this way: "She had large square teeth, she was shorter than I was, but heavier, with bigger bones and square hands."

A writer may also describe a person indirectly by telling what he or she says. Read this passage from "Tuesday of the Other June" to learn about June and her mother and their relationship. Here June tells us about her mother.

> Every day when I went to school, she went to work. "Sometimes I stop what I'm doing," she said, "lay down my tools, and stop everything, because all I can think about is you. Wondering what you're doing and if you need me. Now, Junie, if anyone ever bothers you—"
>
> "—I walk away, run away, come on home as fast as my feet will take me," I recited.
>
> "Yes. You come to me. You just bring me your trouble, because I'm here on this earth to love you and take care of you."

When you read this dialogue, or conversation, you learn that June's mother loves June and is always thinking about her welfare. You learn that June knows the rules and tries to follow them, and you understand that their relationship is built on love and respect. As this conversation shows, June and her mother are so close that it is almost impossible for June to disobey her mother or to worry her with small problems such as the Other June.

Exercise 1

Read this passage in which the two Junes meet. Use what you have learned in this lesson to answer the questions that follow.

> "What's your name?" She had a deep growly voice.
> "June. What's yours?"
> She stared at me. "June."
> "We have the same name."
> "No we don't. June is *my* name, and I don't give you permission to use it. Your name is Fish Eyes." She pinched me hard. "Got it, Fish Eyes?"
> The next Tuesday, the Other June again stood next to me at the edge of the pool. "What's your name?"
> "June."
> "Wrong. Your—name—is—Fish—Eyes."
> "June."
> "Fish Eyes, you are really stupid." She shoved me into the pool.

1. What do you learn about the Other June in this passage? How would you describe her, based on what she has said so far?

2. June doesn't say much in this passage, but what she does say lets you know what kind of person she is, too. How is June different from the Other June, based on what she has said?

Check your answers with your teacher. Review this part of the lesson if you don't understand why an answer was incorrect.

Writing on Your Own 1

In this exercise, you will use what you have learned in the lesson to write a dialogue between the character you chose for Creating a Character on page 42 and another character. Follow these steps:

- Think of a character who might have a conversation with your chosen character. It could be a family member or friend, or it could be a stranger. List some possible characters who could take part in your dialogue.

- Decide what the characters will be talking about. Are they planning something? Are they telling jokes? Are they arguing? Choose one of these scenarios or make up one of your own.

- Divide a page into two columns. Label each column with the name of one of the characters. Write what the first character says and then write the other character's response beside the first character's words. Continue until each character has said at least five sentences. Try to make the conversation reveal something about each character's attitudes and feelings.

- Read over your dialogue. Look for ways to make it believable and natural sounding. Make sure it reveals something about both characters.

2 • Character and Action

How do you get to know new people? First, you probably look at them. You may get a quick impression this way, but you know that first impressions are often misleading. Then you listen to what they say. Are they funny or shy or intelligent or thoughtless? Their words soon give you a clearer picture of what they are really like inside.

Another way to learn about people is by observing what they do. Have you ever heard the saying, "Actions speak louder than words"? In the following passage from "Tuesday of the Other June," the Other June's actions speak loud and clear and what they say about the Other June is not complimentary.

After that, everyone called me Fish Eyes. And every Tuesday, wherever I was, there was also the Other June— at the edge of the pool, in the pool, in the locker room. In the water, she swam alongside me, blowing and huffing, knocking into me. In the locker room, she stepped on my feet, pinched my arms, hid my blouse, and knotted my braids together. She had large square teeth, she was shorter than I was, but heavier, with bigger bones and square hands. If I met her outside on the street, carrying her bathing suit and towel, she'd walk toward me, smiling a square, friendly smile. "Oh well, if it isn't Fish Eyes." Then she'd punch me, *blam!* her whole solid weight hitting me.

The Other June is not a kind person. She clearly enjoys taking advantage of June's meekness. Through her constant teasing, she is turning the other swimmers against June. She is not content with bullying her only in the pool, but she also follows June into the locker room, terrorizing her and making her life miserable. Being outside the building doesn't save June from the abuse either. The Other June is having a wonderful time taking the fun out of June's life. All the details the author includes make the situation clear to the reader.

What do you know about June from this passage? She doesn't seem to be fighting back in any way. She appears to be accepting the treatment silently. Because the author lets you in on June's thoughts, you find out that she is angry, but she is also confused about how to deal with this unwelcome attention.

Exercise 2

Read this passage and answer the questions about it using what you have learned in this lesson.

I didn't know what to do about her. She was training me like a dog. After a few weeks of this, she only had to look at me, only had to growl, "I'm going to get you, Fish Eyes," for my heart to slink like a whipped dog down into my stomach. My arms were covered with bruises. When my mother noticed, I made up a story about tripping on the sidewalk.

My weeks were no longer Tuesday, Wednesday, Thursday, and so on. Tuesday was Awfulday, Wednesday was Badday. (The Tuesday bad feelings were still there.) Thursday was Betterday and Friday was Safeday. Saturday was Goodday, but Sunday was Toosoonday, and Monday— Monday was nothing but the day before Awfulday.

I tried to slow down time. Especially on the weekends, I stayed close by my mother, doing everything with her, shopping, cooking, cleaning, going to the laundromat. "Aw, sweetie, go play with your friends."

"No, I'd rather be with you." I wouldn't look at the clock or listen to the radio (they were always telling you the date and the time). I did special magic things to keep the day from going away, rapping my knuckles six times on the bathroom door six time a day and never, ever touching the chipped place on my bureau. But always I woke up to the day before Tuesday, and always, no matter how many times I circled the worn spot in the living-room rug or counted twenty-five cracks in the ceiling, Monday disappeared and once again it was Tuesday.

1. What is June doing to protect herself against the Other June? What does the strange and pointless method of trying to keep Tuesday from coming show you about June's character?

2. How is June different from the Other June? Which of these two characters uses forceful action to get what she wants? Which of them pins her hopes on indirect action meant to prevent the other's actions?

Check your answers with your teacher. Review this part of the lesson if you don't understand why an answer was incorrect.

Writing on Your Own 2

In this exercise, you will write a paragraph about the character you chose for Creating a Character on page 42 to show what he or she does in a crisis situation. Follow these steps:

- Think about your chosen character. Would that person react to a problem forcefully, or would he or she be more thoughtful and slow to act? Decide on a crisis situation that the character would be likely to encounter. For example, if your character is a boater, how would he or she react to a storm on the lake? How would a character who is babysitting react to a medical emergency?

- Jot down some notes, first about the crisis and then about how your character would react.

- Use your notes to write a paragraph about the crisis and the character's actions in response to it. Be sure to let your readers know the nature of the problem. You can use either first-person or third-person point of view. As the character acts, let readers know what he or she is thinking and feeling.

- Read over your paragraph. Look for ways to make the description of the character's actions more realistic and detailed.

3 • Character and Change

You have probably changed in many ways since you were a small child. You are bigger and more mature. You have developed abilities and skills that are beyond the capabilities of little children. Not only have you changed, but all the people around you have changed too. It is a fact of life that everything and everyone changes.

In short stories, as in life, characters often change. Such characters are referred to as *dynamic characters*. Sometimes characters change as a result of lessons they learn through experience. Sometimes they change because they make decisions that demand new ways of acting. Sometimes they change because someone around them has changed and they must adapt to a new set of circumstances.

In "Tuesday of the Other June," June becomes painfully aware of her situation after she moves into the Other June's school class. Read the passage below to see the war that is raging in June's mind as she tries to decide what to do about this problem that just won't go away. See if you can trace the changes that are taking place within June.

Someone knocked on the door. Mr. Morrisey went out into the hall. Paper planes burst into the air, flying from desk to desk. Someone turned on a transistor radio. And the Other June, coming closer, smiled and licked her lips like a cat sleepily preparing to gulp down a mouse.

I remembered my dream of kicking her, punching, biting her like a dog.

Then my mother spoke quickly in my ear: *Turn the other cheek, my Junie, smile at the world and the world'll surely smile back.*

But I had turned the other cheek and it was slapped. I had smiled and the world hadn't smiled back. I couldn't run home as fast as my feet would take me, I had to stay in school—and in school there was the Other June. Every morning, there would be the Other June, and every afternoon, and every day, all day, there would be the Other June.

The writer is leading her readers to the only solution that can work against a character as unpleasant as the Other June. Although June wants to "turn the other cheek," and has tried to follow her mother's advice, that approach clearly has not worked. June is being irresistibly drawn to this conclusion: this situation cannot be allowed to continue. She must do something about it or face a nightmare every day of the year. By restating the familiar arguments for not resisting the Other June and showing them to be unworkable, the author sets the stage for the radical change that is about to come over June.

Exercise 3

Read this passage and answer the questions about it using what you have learned in this part of the lesson.

She frisked down the aisle, stabbing the pencils in the air toward me. A boy stood up on his desk and bowed. "My fans," he said, "I greet you." My arm twitched and throbbed, as if the Other June's pencils had already poked through the skin. She came closer, smiling her Tuesday smile.

"No," I whispered, *"no."* The word took wings and flew me to my feet, in front of the Other June. *"Noooooo."* It flew out of my mouth into her surprised face.

The boy on the desk turned toward us. "You said something, my devoted fans?"

"No," I said to the Other June. "Oh, no! No. No. No. No more." I pushed away the hand that held the pencils.

The Other June's eyes opened, popped wide like the eyes of somebody in a cartoon. It made me laugh. The boy on the desk laughed, and then the other kids were laughing too.

"No," I said again, because it felt so good to say it. "No, no, no, no." I leaned toward the Other June, put my finger against her chest. Her cheeks turned red, she squawked something—it sounded like "Eeeraaghyou!"—and she stepped back. She stepped away from me.

1. What change has taken place within June? How does June outwardly show that she has changed?

2. What is the Other June's reaction to the "new" June? How do you think their relationship will change as a result of the changes that have taken place in June?

Check your answers with your teacher. Review this part of the lesson if you don't understand why an answer was incorrect.

Writing on Your Own 3

Now write two or three paragraphs about your chosen character. Show a change that takes place in your character as the result of a decision. Follow these steps:

- Review the crisis situation that your character faced in the paragraph you wrote for Writing on Your Own 2. How did the character react to the crisis?

- Write two or three paragraphs. In the first paragraph, describe your character before the crisis that forced him or her to make an important decision. In the other paragraphs, describe the character after the change took place. Try to bring out the differences between the character "before" and "after."

- Reread your paragraphs. Look for more ways to show the changes in appearance, attitude, and feelings that have taken place in your character. Rewrite sentences to improve them.

Discussion Guides

1. June could have used some friendly advice when she was putting up with the Other June's teasing. Work with a small group to come up with at least three suggestions for making the Other June treat June with respect. Then make a list of three ways in which any students who are new to a class can make friends.

2. A character who changes during a story is called a dynamic character. Both June and the Other June are dynamic characters. Work with a partner to present two conversations between the two characters. The first conversation should take place just after they meet; the second conversation should take place the day after June finally stands up to the Other June. How will they both have changed in how they carry themselves, what they say, and how they treat each other?

3. Reading "Tuesday of the Other June," you see into June's mind as she moves from one Tuesday to the next. Work with several other students. Take seven index cards and label each one with one day of the week. Together, compose a sentence or paragraph that reflects June's feelings on that day about her weekly swimming class. Take turns recording the group's statements on the cards. Here is an example of what June might think on Wednesday: "Thank goodness! It's a whole week until I have to see HER again. I can breathe again for a while. I can't wait for this year to be finished." When your group is finished, share the paragraphs on your cards with the rest of the class.

Write a Character Sketch

Throughout the unit, you have been working on writing activities that help you create an interesting character. Now is the time to put all those parts together to write your own character sketch.

If you have any questions about the writing process, refer to Using the Writing Process, beginning on page 306.

- Assemble the writing you did for Creating a Character at the beginning of the unit and for each of the Writing on Your Own exercises.

- You should have four pieces of writing: *a)* a few sentences with rough ideas about the character, *b)* a dialogue between your character and another character, *c)* a paragraph that describes how the character acts in a crisis, and *d)* two paragraphs that describe the character before and after an important change. Reread these pieces of writing now to get ideas for the story you are about to write.

- Next, make a decision about how you will tell the story. Will you use the first person, using the words *I* and *me,* or will you use the third person, using the words *he, she,* and *they?*

- Begin by introducing the character. Use the character description you wrote earlier as a starting point. Continue by describing the crisis your character faces. Explain how he or she deals with the problem, using dialogue and actions to make the person seem real and believable. Finally, make it clear how your character has changed because of his or her experiences.

- Reread your character sketch to make sure that all the parts work together smoothly. Let a classmate read it to point out details that you might have missed. Revise your writing and proofread to find spelling, grammar, and punctuation errors. When you have finished, let others read your character sketch. Then save your work in your writing portfolio.

Unit 3   Setting

Almost a Whole Trickster
by Gerald Vizenor

About the Illustration

What does this illustration suggest about the story you are about to read? Use details from the illustration as clues to answer these questions. Give reasons for your answers.

These questions will help you begin to think about the story:

- Where does this scene take place?

- What might these people be doing here?

- Can you guess how these people are related to each other? Are they relatives? Are they friends?

- How do the people feel about being in this place? How can you tell? How would you feel if you were there?

Unit 3

Introduction

About the Story

The Leech Lake Indian reservation in northern Minnesota is home to a boy nicknamed Pincher, his mother, and his Uncle Clement, nicknamed Almost. Almost got his nickname because his favorite word to use in the stories he is always telling is *almost*. On a trip to town, Pincher and his uncle read a sign advertising an ice-sculpture contest to be held on July Fourth. They enlist the help of Black Ice, Pincher's cousin visiting from the city, to create an ice sculpture to enter in the contest. To find the block of ice, they travel to the island where Pig Foot, a friend of Almost's, keeps ice in a cold cave. There they carve a huge block of ice to look almost like a trickster—a funny, wise character from old stories. When it is time to take the huge statue to the contest, numerous adventures happen to the trickster and its creators along the way.

About the Author

Gerald Vizenor is a professor of Native American Studies at the University of California at Berkeley. He was born into the Chippewa tribe in Minnesota. Mr. Vizenor is known for a variety of works, including short stories, novels, memoirs, poems, and essays. Because of his cultural background, he is able to shed light on a way of life that is unknown to many of his readers. In his stories, Mr. Vizenor often shows the difficulties that Native Americans experience when they try to adjust to the demands of white America. In spite of the sometimes heavy subject matter of his writing, many of his characters are both good-humored and witty, as you will see when you read this story.

About the Lessons

The lessons that follow "Almost a Whole Trickster" focus on *setting*. Setting includes both where and when a story takes place. The setting of a story helps to determine what might happen in the story. It also affects how readers feel about what is happening in the story. Writers create the setting with care, using precise and realistic details to make readers feel that they can see, hear, and feel what it is like to be in this particular time and place.

Writing: Creating a Setting

In the course of this unit, you will create a setting and then write a story opener that takes place in that setting. Following are some suggestions to help you get started.

- Think about some settings you know and find interesting. Your school, a neighborhood in your town, or a place you have visited are possibilities. Choose several possible settings. Start a note card like the one on page 75 for each setting.

```
Setting: real

Time: Saturday afternoon; summer

Place: downtown city park

Details:




```

- Think of several imaginary settings that would be natural for
  fantasies or science fiction stories. Fill out a note card for each
  of these settings.

```
Setting: imaginary

Time: the future; the year 3004

Place: a strange new planet

Details:




```

- Look over your note cards. For each setting, list descriptive
  details about the time and about how the place looks, sounds,

smells, and feels. Choose one setting that you seem most comfortable describing. You will use that setting for the story opener you write at the end of this unit.

Before Reading

The following questions will help you see how Gerald Vizenor created the setting for "Almost a Whole Trickster" and how the setting affects the story. As you read, keep these questions in mind:

- Which details tell you about how each place in the story looks, sounds, and feels?

- How does the setting affect the action of the story?

- Do you get different feelings from the different settings of the story? How does each setting make you feel?

Vocabulary Tips

This story includes some words that may be unfamiliar to you but are useful for understanding the story. Below you will find some of these words, their definitions, and sentences that show how the words are used. Look over the words before you begin to read.

depot   a station. At Thanksgiving, the bus <u>depot</u> was crowded with travelers trying to get back home for the holidays.

prance   to move in a lively way with springs and bounds. The horse will <u>prance</u> happily through the fields when spring comes.

cloven   split into two parts. Cows, sheep, and pigs have <u>cloven</u> hoofs.

liberate   to set free. The soldiers <u>liberated</u> prisoners of war after they drove the enemy out of the city.

appeal   to ask for help or special favors. The politician <u>appealed</u> to voters to donate money to her campaign.

pedestal   a base to set objects on. The expensive vase teetered when someone bumped the <u>pedestal</u> it sat on.

Almost a Whole Trickster

Gerald Vizenor

Uncle Clement told me last night that he knows *almost* everything. Almost, that's his nickname and favorite word in stories, lives with me and my mother in a narrow house on the Leech Lake Chippewa Indian Reservation in northern Minnesota.

Last night, just before dark, we drove into town to meet my cousin at the bus depot and to buy rainbow ice cream in thick brown cones. Almost sat in the backseat of our old car and started his stories the minute we were on the dirt road around the north side of the lake to town. The wheels bounced and the car doors shuddered and raised thick clouds of dust. He told me about the time he almost started an ice cream store when he came back from the army. My mother laughed and turned to the side. The car rattled on the washboard road. She shouted, "I heard that one before!"

"Almost!" he shouted back.

"What almost happened?" I asked. My voice bounced with the car.

"Well, it was winter then," he said. Fine brown dust settled on his head and the shoulders of his overcoat. "Too cold for ice cream in the woods, but the idea came to mind in the summer, almost."

"Almost, you know almost everything about nothing," my mother shouted and then laughed, "or almost nothing about almost everything."

"Pincher, we're almost to the ice cream," he said, and brushed me on the head with his hard right hand. He did that to ignore what my mother said about what he knows. Clouds of dust covered the trees behind us on both sides of the road.

Almost is my great-uncle and he decides on our nicknames, even the nicknames for my cousins who live in the cities and visit the reservation in the summer. Pincher, the name he gave me, was natural because I pinched my way through childhood. I learned about the world between two fingers. I pinched everything, or almost everything as my uncle would say. I pinched animals, insects, leaves, water, fish, ice cream, the moist night air, winter breath, snow, and even words, the words I could see, or almost see. I pinched the words and learned how to speak sooner than my cousins. Pinched words are easier to remember. Some words, like *government* and *grammar,* are unnatural, never seen and never pinched. Who could pinch a word like grammar?

Almost named me last winter when my grandmother was sick with pneumonia and died on the way to the public health hospital. She had no teeth and covered her mouth when she smiled, almost a child. I sat in the backseat of the car and held her thin brown hand. Even her veins were hidden, it was so cold that night. On the road we pinched summer words over the hard snow and ice. She smiled and said *papakine, papakine,* over and over. That means cricket or grasshopper in our tribal language and we pinched that word together. We pinched *papakine* in the backseat of our cold car on the way to the hospital. Later she whispered *bisanagami sibi,* the river is still, and then she died. My mother straightened my grandmother's fingers, but later at the wake in our house, she'd pinched a summer word and we could see that. She was buried in the cold earth with a warm word between her fingers. That's when my uncle gave me my nickname.

Almost never told lies, but he used the word *almost* to stretch the truth like a tribal trickster, my mother told me. The trickster is a character in stories, an animal, or person, even a tree at times, who pretends the world can be stopped with words, and he frees the world in stories. Almost said the trickster is almost a man and almost a woman, and almost a child, a clown, who laughs and plays games with words in stories. The trickster is almost a free spirit. Almost told me about the trickster many times, and I think I almost understand his stories. He brushed my head with his hand and said, "The *almost* world is a better world, a sweeter dream than the world we are taught to understand in school."

"I understand, almost," I told my uncle.

"People are almost stories, and stories tell almost the whole truth," Almost told me last winter when he gave me my nickname. "Pincher is your nickname and names are stories too, *gega*." The word *gega* means almost in the Anishinaabe or Chippewa language.

"Pincher *gega*," I said, and then tried to pinch a tribal word I could not yet see clear enough to hold between my fingers. I could almost see *gega*.

Almost, no matter the season, wore a long dark overcoat. He bounced when he walked, and the thick bottom of the overcoat hit the ground. The sleeves were too short but he never minded that because he could eat and deal cards with no problems. So there he was in line for a rainbow ice cream cone dressed for winter, or almost winter he would say. My mother wonders if he wears that overcoat for the attention.

"*Gega, gega,*" an old woman called from the end of the line. "You spending some claims money on ice cream or a new coat?" No one ignored his overcoat.

"What's that?" answered Almost. He cupped his ear to listen because he knew the old woman wanted to move closer, ahead in the line. The claims money she mentioned is a measure of everything in the reservation. The federal government promised to settle a treaty over land with tribal people. Almost and thousands of others had been waiting for more than a century to be paid for land that was taken from them. There were rumors at least once a week that federal checks were in the mail, final payment for the broken treaties. When white people talk about a rain dance, tribal people remember the claims dancers who promised a federal check in every mailbox.

"Claims money," she whispered in the front of the line.

"Almost got a check this week," Almost said and smiled.

"Almost is as good as nothing," she said back.

"Pincher gets a bicycle when the claims money comes."

"My husband died waiting for the claims settlement," my mother said. She looked at me and then turned toward the ice cream counter to order. I held back my excitement about a new bicycle because the claims money might never come; no one was ever sure. Almost believed in rumors and he waited for a check to appear one morning in his mailbox on the reservation. Finally, my mother scolded him for wasting his time on promises made by the government. "You grow old too fast on government promises," she said. "Anyway, the government has nothing to do with bicycles." He smiled at me and we ate our rainbow ice cream cones at the bus depot. That was a joke because the depot is nothing more than a park bench in front of a restaurant. On the back of the bench there was a sign that announced an ice sculpture contest to be held in the town park on July Fourth.

"Ice cube sculpture?" asked my mother.

"No blocks big enough around here in summer," I said, thinking about the ice sold to tourists, cubes and small blocks for camp coolers.

"Pig Foot, he cuts ice from the lake in winter and stores it in a cave, buried in straw," my uncle whispered. He looked around, concerned that someone might hear about the ice cave. "Secret *mikwam,* huge blocks, enough for a great sculpture." The word *mikwam* means ice.

"Never mind," my mother said as she licked the ice cream on her fingers. The rainbow turned pink when it melted. The pink ran over her hand and under her rings.

We were going to pick up my cousin, Black Ice, from the bus station.

Black Ice was late but that never bothered her because she liked to ride in the back of buses at night. She sat in the dark and pretended that she could see the people who lived under the distant lights. She lived in a dark apartment building in Saint Paul with her mother and older brother and made the world come alive with light more than from sound or taste. She was on the reservation for more than a month last summer and we thought her nickname would be *light* or *candle* or something like that, even though she wore black clothes. Not so. Almost avoided one obvious name and chose another when she attended our grandmother's funeral. Black Ice had never been on the reservation in winter. She slipped and fell seven times on black ice near the church and so she got that as a nickname.

Black Ice was the last person to leave the bus. She held back, behind the darkened windows, as long as she could. Yes, she was shy, worried about being embarrassed in public. I might be that way too, if we lived in an apartment in the cities, but the only public on the reservation are the summer tourists. She was happier when we bought her a rainbow ice cream cone. She was dressed in black, black everything, even black canvas shoes, no almost black. The latest television style in the cities. Little did my uncle know that her reservation nickname would describe a modern style of clothes. We sat in the backseat on the way back to our house. We could smell the dust in the dark, in the tunnel of light through the trees. The moon was new that night.

"Almost said he would buy me my first bicycle when he gets his claims money," I told Black Ice. She brushed her clothes, there was too much dust.

"I should've brought my new mountain bike," she said. "I don't use it much though—too much traffic and you have to worry about it being stolen."

"Should we go canoeing? We have a canoe."

"Did you get television yet?" asked Black Ice.

"Yes," I boasted, "my mother won a big screen with a dish and everything at a bingo game on the reservation." We never watched much television though.

"Really?"

"Yes, we can get more than a hundred channels."

"On the reservation?"

"Yes, and bingo too."

"Well, here we are, paradise at the end of a dust cloud," my mother announced as she turned down the trail to our house on the lake. The headlights held the eyes of animals, a raccoon, and we could smell a skunk in the distance. Low branches brushed the side of the car and whipped through the open windows. The dogs barked and ran ahead of the car; we were home. We sat in the car for a few minutes and listened to the night. The dogs were panting. Mosquitoes, so big we called them the state bird, landed on our arms, bare knuckles, and warm shoulder blades. The water was calm and seemed to hold back a secret dark blue light from the bottom of the lake. One loon called and another answered. One thin wave rippled over the stones on the shore. We ducked mosquitoes and went into the house. We were tired, and too tired in the morning to appreciate the plan to carve a trickster from a block of ice.

Pig Foot lived alone on an island. He came down to the wooden dock to meet us in the morning. We were out on the lake before dawn, my uncle at the back of the canoe in his overcoat. We paddled and he steered us around the point of the island where bald eagles nested.

"Pig Foot?" questioned Black Ice.

"Almost gave him that nickname," I whispered to my cousin as we came closer to the dock. "Watch his little feet—he prances like a pig when he talks. The people in town swear his feet are hard and cloven."

"Are they?"

"No," I whispered as the canoe touched the dock.

"Almost," shouted Pig Foot.

"Almost," said Almost. "Pincher, you know him from the funeral, and this lady is from the city; we named her Black Ice."

"*Makate Mikwam*," said Pig Foot. "Black ice comes with the white man and roads. No black ice on the island." He tied the canoe to the dock and patted his thighs with his open hands. The words *makate mikwam* mean black ice.

Black Ice looked down at Pig Foot's feet when she stepped out of the canoe. He wore black overshoes. The toes were turned out. She watched him prance on the rough wooden dock when he talked about the weather and mosquitoes. The black flies and mosquitoes on the island, a special breed, were more vicious than anywhere else on the reservation. Pig Foot was pleased that no one camped on the island because of the black flies. Some people accused him of raising mean flies to keep the tourists away. "Not a bad idea, now that I think about it," said Pig Foot. He had a small bunch of black hair on his chin. He pulled the hair when he was nervous and revealed a row of short stained teeth. Black Ice turned toward the sunrise and held her laughter.

"We come to see the ice cave," said Almost. "We need a large block to win the ice sculpture contest in four days."

"What ice cave is that?" questioned Pig Foot.

"The almost secret one!" shouted Almost.

"That one, sure enough," said Pig Foot. He mocked my uncle and touched the lapel of his overcoat. "I was wondering about that contest—what does ice have to do with July Fourth?" He walked ahead as he talked and then every eight steps he would stop and turn to wait for us. But if you were too close you would bump into him when he stopped. Black Ice counted his steps and when we were near the entrance to the ice cave she imitated his prance, toes turned outward. She pranced seven steps and then waited for him to turn on the eighth.

Pig Foot stopped in silence on the shore, where the bank was higher and where several trees leaned over the water. There in the vines and boulders we could feel the cool air. A cool breath on the shore.

Pig Foot told us we could never reveal the location of the ice cave, but he said we could tell stories about ice and the great spirit of winter in summer. He said this because most tribal stories should be told in winter, not in summer when evil spirits could be about to listen and do harm to words and names. We agreed to the conditions and followed him over the boulders into the wide, cold cave. We could hear our breath, even a heartbeat. Whispers were too loud in the cave.

"Almost the scent of winter on July Fourth," whispered Almost. "In winter we overturn the ice in shallow creeks to smell the rich blue earth, and then in summer we taste the winter in this ice cave, almost."

"Almost, you're a poet, sure enough, but that's straw, not the smell of winter," said Pig Foot. He was hunched over where the cave narrowed at the back. Beneath the mounds of straw were huge blocks of ice, lake ice, blue and silent in the cave. Was that thunder, or the crack of winter ice on the lake? "Just me, dropped a block over the side." In winter he sawed blocks of ice in the bay where it was the thickest and towed the blocks into the cave on an aluminum slide. Pig Foot used the ice to cool his cabin in summer, but Almost warned us that there were other reasons. Pig Foot believes that the world is becoming colder and colder, the ice thicker and thicker. Too much summer in the blood would weaken him, so he rests on a block of ice in the cave several hours a week to stay in condition for the coming of the ice age on the reservation.

"Black Ice, come over here," said Almost. "Stretch out on this block." My cousin brushed the straw from the ice and leaned back on the block. "Almost, almost, now try this one, no this one, almost."

"Almost what?" asked Black Ice.

"Almost a whole trickster," whispered Almost. Then he told us what he had in mind. A trickster, Almost wanted us to carve a tribal trickster to enter in the ice sculpture contest.

"What does a trickster look like?" I asked. The trickster was a word I could not see, there was nothing to pinch. How could I know a trickster between my fingers?

"Almost like a person," he said, and brushed the straw from a block as large as me. "Almost in there, we have three days to find the trickster in the ice."

Early the next morning we paddled across the lake to the ice cave to begin our work on the ice trickster. We were dressed for winter. I don't think my mother believed us when we told her about the ice cave. "Almost," she said with a smile, "finally found the right place to wear his overcoat in the summer."

Pig Foot was perched on a block of ice when we arrived. We slid the block that held the trickster to the center of the cave and set to work with an axe and chisels. We rounded out a huge head, moved down the shoulders, and on the second day we freed the nose, ears, and hands of the trickster. I could see him in the dark blue ice, the trickster was almost free. I could almost pinch the word "trickster."

Almost directed us to carve the ice on the first and second days, but on the third and final day he surprised us. We were in the cave, dressed in winter coats and hats, ready to work when he told us to make the final touches on our own, to liberate the face of the trickster. That last morning he leaned back on a block of ice with Pig Foot; we were in charge of who the trickster would become in ice.

Black Ice wanted the trickster to look like a woman. I wanted the ice sculpture to look like a man. The trickster, we decided, would be both, one side a man and the other side a woman. The true trickster, almost a man and almost a woman.

It took us a few hours but in the end the ice trickster had features that looked like our uncle, our grandmother, and other members of our families. The trickster had small feet turned outward, he wore an overcoat, and she pinched her fingers on her female hand. He was ready for the contest—she was the ice trickster on the Fourth of July.

That same night we tied sheets around the ice trickster and towed her behind the canoe to the park on the other side of the lake. The ice floated and the trickster melted slower in the water. We rounded the south end of the island and headed to the park near the town, slow and measured like traders on a distant sea. The park lights reflected on the calm water. We tied the ice trickster to the end of the town dock and beached our canoe. We were very excited, but soon we were tired and slept on the grass in the park near the dock. The trickster was a liberator, she would win on Independence Day. Almost anyway.

"The trickster almost melted," shouted Almost the next morning. He stood on the end of the dock, a sad uncle in his overcoat, holding the rope and empty sheets. At first we thought he had tricked us, we thought the whole thing was a joke, from the beginning, so we laughed. We rolled around on the grass and laughed. Almost was not amused at first, he turned toward the lake to hide his face, but then he broke into wild laughter. He laughed so hard he almost lost his balance in that heavy overcoat. He almost fell into the lake.

"The ice trickster won the ice sculpture contest at last," said Black Ice.

"No, wait, she almost won. No ice trickster would melt that fast into the lake," he said, and ordered us to launch the canoe for a search. Overnight the trickster had slipped from the sheets and floated free from the dock, somewhere out in the lake. The ice trickster was free on July Fourth.

We paddled the canoe in circles and searched for hours and hours but we could not find the ice trickster. Later, my mother rented a motorboat and we searched in two circles.

Almost was worried about the time that the registration would close, so he abandoned the search and appealed to the people who organized the ice sculpture competition. They agreed to extend the time and they even invited other contestants to search for the ice trickster. The lake was crowded with motorboats.

"There she floats," a woman shouted from a fishing boat. The trickster was almost submerged, only a shoulder was above water. We paddled out and towed the trickster back to the dock. Then we hauled her up the bank to the park and a pedestal. We circled the pedestal and admired the ice trickster.

"Almost a trickster," said Almost. We looked over the other entries. There were more birds than animals, more heads than hips or hands, and the other ice sculptures were much smaller. Dwarfs next to the ice trickster. She had melted some overnight in the lake, but he was still head and shoulders above the other entries. The competition was about to close when we learned that there was a height restriction. Almost never read the rules. No entries over three feet and six inches in any direction. The other entries were much smaller, no one found large blocks of ice in town, so they were all within the restrictions. Our trickster was four feet tall, or at least she was that tall when we started out in the ice cave.

"No trickster that started out almost he or she can be too much of either," said Almost. We nodded in agreement but we were not certain what he meant.

"What now?" asked Black Ice.

"Get a saw," my mother ordered. "We can cut the trickster down a notch or two on the bottom." She held her hand about four inches from the base to see what a shorter trickster would look like.

"Almost short enough," said Almost. "He melted some, she needs to lose four more inches by my calculations. We should have left her in the lake for another hour."

Pig Foot turned the trickster on his side, but when we measured four inches from the bottom he protested. "Not the feet, not my feet, those are my feet on the trickster."

"Not my ear either."

"Not the hands," I pleaded.

"The shins," shouted Black Ice. No one had claimed the shins on the ice trickster so we measured and sawed four inches from his shins and then carved the knees to fit the little pig feet.

"Almost whole," announced Almost.

"What's a trickster?" asked the three judges who hurried down the line of pedestals before the ice sculptures melted beyond recognition.

"Almost a person," said Black Ice.

"What person?"

"My grandmother," I told the judges. "See how she pinched her fingers, she was a trickster, she pinched a cricket there." Pig Foot was nervous; he pranced around the pedestal.

The judges prowled back and forth, whispered here and there between two pedestals, and then they decided that there would be two winners because they could not decide on one. "The winners are the Boy and His Dog, and that ice trickster, Almost a Person," the judges announced.

The ice trickster won a bicycle, a large camp cooler, a dictionary, and twelve double rainbow cones. The other ice cave sculptors gave me the bicycle because I had never owned one before, and because the claims payment might be a bad promise. We divided the cones as best we could between five people, Almost, Pig Foot, Black Ice, me, and my mother.

Later, we packed what remained of the ice trickster, including the shin part, and took him back to the ice cave, where she lasted for more than a year. She stood in the back of the cave without straw and melted down to the last drop of a trickster. She was almost a whole trickster, almost.

Reviewing and Interpreting the Story

Record your answers to these comprehension questions in your personal literature notebook. Follow the directions for each part.

Reviewing Try to complete each of these sentences without looking back at the story.

Recalling Facts

1. A trickster is

   a. an evil god.

   b. a person with frightening powers.

   c. always a person, never an animal.

   d. a character who plays games with words.

Identifying Sequence

2. After Pincher sees the sign about the ice sculpture contest,

   a. he decides to ask his cousin to visit.

   b. Almost gives him his nickname.

   c. he and Almost visit Pig Foot at his cave.

   d. his grandmother dies of pneumonia.

Identifying Cause and Effect

3. Black Ice got her name because she

   a. always wears black.

   b. slipped and fell on the black ice many times at her grandmother's funeral.

   c. comes to the reservation only in the winter when there is ice on the roads.

   d. lives in a dark apartment in Saint Paul.

4. Almost helps Pincher and Black Ice with the ice sculpture because he

   a. wants them to become professional artists.

   b. feels sorry for the children.

   c. wants them to have fun, but also to learn about their culture.

   d. is paid by the government to work with local children.

Recognizing
Story Elements
(Character)

5. A good word to describe Almost is

   a. unusual.

   b. stubborn.

   c. impatient.

   d. curious.

Interpreting   To answer these questions, you may look back at the story if you like.

Making
Inferences

6. The fact that Pig Foot chooses to live on an island by himself probably means that he

   a. is very lonely and unhappy.

   b. likes to be by himself.

   c. was born on the island.

   d. has no friends.

Predicting
Outcomes

7. Now that the ice from Pig Foot's cave has been used to win a contest, Pig Foot will probably

   a. move to the mainland next year.

   b. advertise his ice in the local newspaper.

   c. make his island into a tourist attraction.

   d. go back to his usual quiet life.

Making
Generalizations

8. Choose the way the characters in this story would finish this sentence: If you don't have much money,

    a. life is not much fun.

    b. you can still have a happy life.

    c. you should make it your primary goal to get more.

    d. you can count on the government to give you more.

Analyzing

9. From what Pincher's mother says to and about Almost, you can tell that she

    a. likes Almost and enjoys his stories.

    b. wishes that he would start telling the truth.

    c. believes everything he says.

    d. finds him annoying much of the time.

Understanding
Story Elements
(Character)

10. How do you know that Almost has a good sense of humor?

    a. His favorite word is *almost*.

    b. He always wears a long black coat no matter what the weather is.

    c. He tells funny stories and laughs when people tease him.

    d. He knows all about tricksters.

Now check your answers with your teacher. Study the questions you answered incorrectly. What types of questions were they? Talk with your teacher about ways to work on those skills.

Setting

"Once upon a time in a kingdom far away" is a familiar introduction to many fairy tales. When you read this phrase you know when the story you are about to hear happens (once upon a time) and where it takes place (in a kingdom far away). You know that this is a different time and a different place from the one you live in today. This phrase begins to describe the *setting* of the story. The setting of any story is the time and the place in which the characters live, work, and resolve their problems. The time may be present, past, or future. The place may be real or imaginary.

Like character and plot, setting is an essential part of every story. The details the writer includes can make you feel as if you are in the same place at the same time as the characters. You can actually see, hear, and feel the things they do.

The setting also plays another role in stories. It determines what can or cannot happen to the characters. In a story set in the desert in summer, for example, it is not likely that the conflict the characters face will be surviving a blizzard. In a story set in the past, the characters will not be using computers to send e-mail.

Writers may also use the setting to create a mood, or a feeling, both in the characters and in the reader. Characters spending a sunny day at an amusement park will probably feel carefree and happy, and so will the reader.

In this unit, we will look at these ways in which author Gerald Vizenor uses setting to help tell his story:

1. Vizenor includes details that make you feel you are there, in the middle of the story's events.

2. He shows how the setting affects the action in the story.

3. He uses descriptive words and phrases about the setting to develop the mood of both the characters in the story and its readers.

1 • Understanding the Setting

The setting of the story takes you away from the world around you and into the world of the characters. Every detail that the writer includes helps you see, hear, and feel what the characters feel. These details make the setting seem real.

Read the passage below to see how Gerald Vizenor sets the scene in the second paragraph of "Almost a Whole Trickster."

> Last night, just before dark, we drove into town to meet my cousin at the bus depot and to buy rainbow ice cream in thick brown cones. Almost sat in the backseat of our old car and started his stories the minute we were on the dirt road around the north side of the lake to town. The wheels bounced and the car doors shuddered and raised thick clouds of dust. He told me about the time he almost started an ice cream store when he came back from the army. My mother laughed and turned to the side. The car rattled on the washboard road. She shouted, "I heard that one before!"

The writer doesn't just tell the reader about the setting. He lets you experience what the characters experience about the area they are driving through. What do you know so far about the place where Pincher lives? It must be pretty far from town because Pincher's mother is driving down a dirt road around a lake. The dirt road must not be traveled often because it is in bad shape with so many ruts that driving over it makes the car doors rattle. Finally, you know that the area must be dry because the car is raising clouds of dust.

All of these details help you feel that you are in the old car with Pincher and Almost. You can see the dark dirt road and the clouds of dust. You can feel the dry dust as it settles on the car and its passengers. You can feel the bumps in the road and you can hear the rattling of the car doors. The writer has skillfully used these details to pull readers into the story.

Exercise 1

Read this passage in which the family arrives at the house. Use what you have learned in this lesson to answer the questions that follow.

"Well, here we are, paradise at the end of a dust cloud," my mother announced as she turned down the trail to our house on the lake. The headlights held the eyes of animals, a raccoon, and we could smell a skunk in the distance. Low branches brushed the side of the car and whipped through the open windows. The dogs barked and ran ahead of the car; we were home. We sat in the car for a few minutes and listened to the night. The dogs were panting. Mosquitoes, so big we called them the state bird, landed on our arms, bare knuckles, and warm shoulder blades. The water was calm and seemed to hold back a secret dark blue light from the bottom of the lake. One loon called and another answered. One thin wave rippled over the stones on the shore. We ducked mosquitoes and went into the house.

1. Which details appeal to the sense of sight? Which appeal to the senses of smell and touch?

2. The family sat in the car for a few minutes listening to the night. Which details tell you what they were hearing?

Check your answers with your teacher. Review this part of the lesson if you don't understand why an answer was incorrect.

Writing on Your Own 1

In this exercise you will use what you have learned in the lesson to write a paragraph describing a setting you chose for Creating a Setting on page 74. Follow these steps:

• Review the list of details you made for your setting. Write headings for each of the five senses—Sight, Hearing, Touch, Taste, and Smell—on your note card. Remember that good descriptive details should appeal to at least one of these senses. Add one or more details that appeal to each sense on your list.

- Use these details to write a paragraph about the setting. Make sure that you appeal to at least three different senses.

- Reread your paragraph and look for ways to make the scene seem more realistic. Does it need any more details? Can you make the details more vivid? Make any necessary changes and additions.

2 • Setting and Action

Setting has a powerful effect on a story. The setting is not just a backdrop for the action; it also gets readers ready for what happens. For example, if a story is set in a jungle, readers immediately understand that the characters are probably not going to be concerned with choosing a restaurant for dinner. Readers also know that characters in downtown Manhattan are probably not going to be worried about running into a herd of wild elephants. Logically, readers know that certain story events are likely to go along with certain settings.

Gerald Vizenor's "Almost a Whole Trickster" is about a memorable event in a boy's life. Read this passage to see how Vizenor "sets the stage" for the happy and interesting events that are to come.

> . . . He smiled at me and we ate our rainbow ice cream cones at the bus depot. That was a joke because the depot is nothing more than a park bench in front of a restaurant. On the back of the bench there was a sign that announced an ice-sculpture contest to be held in the town park on July Fourth.

The relaxed atmosphere that the author creates gets you ready for the simple pleasures that will follow. By emphasizing the ordinariness of Pincher's life, he prepares you for the happiness that the creation of the ice sculpture and the ice competition are sure to bring the boy.

Exercise 2

Read this passage and answer the questions about it using what you have learned in this part of the lesson.

Black Ice looked down at Pig Foot's feet when she stepped out of the canoe. He wore black overshoes. The toes were turned out. She watched him prance on the rough wooden dock when he talked about the weather and mosquitoes. The black flies and mosquitoes on the island, a special breed, were more vicious than anywhere else on the reservation. Pig Foot was pleased that no one camped on the island because of the black flies. Some people accused him of raising mean flies to keep the tourists away.

1. What do you learn about Pig Foot's island? Is it likely that other people will bother Pig Foot and Pincher's family while they are in the cave? Why or why not?

2. Some people might feel that Pig Foot's island is not a pleasant place to live. What does Pig Foot's home show about his personality? What does his home suggest about how Pig Foot might act?

Check your answers with your teacher. Review this part of the lesson if you don't understand why an answer was incorrect.

Writing on Your Own 2

Now it's time to put some characters into your chosen setting and to think about problems they might face. Follow these steps:

- Decide on characters that might live in your chosen setting. Settle on one or two main characters.

- Think about the setting. What are some problems that might happen in this setting? Write down as many ideas as you can think of.

- Look over your list of possible problems. Choose the one that you feel will be most interesting to write about. Then write a paragraph in which your characters first encounter the problem.

- Read over your paragraph. Be sure that the setting works together with the problem to make a believable situation.

3 • Setting and Mood

The setting of a story can affect the feelings, or *moods,* of the characters and of the readers. For example, a character entering a house that is rumored to be haunted will be fearful and nervous. The writer can create that scary mood by adding details about the setting that would frighten the characters, such as creaking doors, chilly winds, and cobweb-covered walls. Anyone reading the scary story will also feel nervous and on edge.

Read the following passage from "Almost a Whole Trickster" and see how Gerald Vizenor creates a still, quiet mood that makes readers feel that the characters have entered a place set apart from the everyday world.

> Pig Foot stopped in silence on the shore, where the bank was higher and where several trees leaned over the water. There in the vines and boulders we could feel the cool air. A cool breath on the shore.
>
> Pig Foot told us we could never reveal the location of the ice cave, but he said we could tell stories about ice and the great spirit of winter in summer. He said this because most tribal stories should be told in winter, not in summer when evil spirits could be about to listen and do harm to words and names. We agreed to the conditions and followed him over the boulders into the wide, cold cave. We could hear our breath, even a heartbeat. Whispers were too loud in the cave.
>
> "Almost the scent of winter on July Fourth," whispered Almost. "In winter we overturn the ice in shallow creeks to smell the rich blue earth, and then in summer we taste the winter in this ice cave, almost."

Clearly, Pig Foot's cave is not an ordinary place. It has an otherworldly quality. It seems almost holy, set aside from normal life. The writer has established a reverential mood, and the reader begins to believe that something special will come of this visit to the ice cave.

Exercise 3

Read this passage and answer the questions about it using what you have learned in this part of the lesson.

> That same night we tied sheets around the ice trickster and towed her behind the canoe to the park on the other side of the lake. The ice floated and the trickster melted slower in the water. We rounded the south end of the island and headed to the park near the town, slow and measured like traders on a distant sea. The park lights reflected on the calm water. We tied the ice trickster to the end of the town dock and beached our canoe. We were very excited, but soon we were tired and slept on the grass in the park near the dock. The trickster was a liberator, she would win on Independence Day. Almost anyway.

1. What words or phrases in this description create a calm mood?

2. How would the mood have been different if Pincher and his family had traveled to the contest on a bus through busy city streets? Why would the mood have changed?

Check your answers with your teacher. Review this part of the lesson if you don't understand why an answer was incorrect.

Writing on Your Own 3

Now write a description of your setting using details that create a mood. Follow these steps:

- Decide how you feel about your setting. Think of details that will help to reflect that feeling. Make a list of at least six words or phrases that you can use to describe the feeling the setting gives you.

- Write a paragraph or two from the first-person point of view telling how the setting makes you feel. Use words and details to create the same mood in your readers.

- Let a partner read your description and describe the mood it creates for him or her. Then revise your description, changing words and adding more details if necessary.

Discussion Guides

1. Each character in "Almost a Whole Trickster" is referred to by a nickname. More than a name given at birth, the nickname fits that character's personality. If you could choose a nickname for yourself, what would it be? Decide on a nickname for yourself. Explain to the rest of the class why you chose it. Then work with your classmates to decide on a nickname for your class. Be ready to explain why you chose that nickname.

2. The reservation where Pincher and his family live may be very different from your home and neighborhood. Work with a group to make a chart like the one that follows comparing the reservation with your own neighborhood. Record details about what Pincher can see, hear, and smell on his reservation and details about what you see, hear, and smell in your neighborhood. Notice which things are the same and which are different. Then get together with other groups and combine your information on a class list.

	The Reservation	**Our Neighborhood**
Sights		
Sounds		
Smells		

3. Each place and time has its own advantages and disadvantages for those who live there. For example, one advantage of living in the mountains is seeing the beautiful scenery every day. A disadvantage might be the difficulty of traveling through the mountains in the heavy snows in winter. What would be the advantages of living on a reservation such as the one Pincher lives on? What would be the disadvantages of life there? Work with a small group to think of at least two advantages and two disadvantages of life on the reservation and record them in a chart like the one below.

	Advantages	Disadvantages
1.		
2.		

4. Make a chart like the one above showing the advantages and disadvantages of living in your neighborhood, a city, or a small town.

Write a Story Opener

Throughout the unit, you have been working on some elements of a story with an interesting setting. Now you can put all those parts together to write a one- to two-page story opener.

If you have any questions about the writing process, refer to Using the Writing Process, beginning on page 306.

- Assemble the writing you did for all the writing exercises in this unit. You should have four pieces of writing: *a)* a list of details about a chosen setting, *b)* a paragraph that describes the setting and makes it seem real, *c)* a paragraph that names one or two main characters and tells about a problem that could arise in that setting, *d)* a description written from the first-person point of view that explains how the speaker feels about the setting and creates a mood. Reread these pieces of writing now to get ideas for the story opener you are about to write.

- Use the paragraphs you wrote earlier for ideas as you write a rough draft of a story opener told from the first-person point of view.

  1) *Begin with a description of the setting.* Use specific words and vivid details about sights, sounds, and smells to set a mood.

2) *Introduce the characters.* Choose the character who will be the narrator. Be sure to show the narrator's feelings about the setting. Help your readers to share in the narrator's feelings.

3) *Introduce the problem.* Make this situation as interesting and exciting as you can. Get your readers hooked. Make them ask, "What happens next?"

- Read your draft to make sure that all the parts work together smoothly. Ask a partner to read your draft and give you feedback. Have her or him point out details that you might have missed. Then revise your opener, adding details and making sure your writing is clear and easy to follow.

- Proofread for spelling, grammar, and punctuation errors. Correct these errors and make a clean copy. You might also want to illustrate your opener with a picture of the setting.

- Share your story opener with your class. Keep a copy in your writing portfolio, and, if possible, complete the story at a later time.

Unit 4　Conflict

President Cleveland, Where Are You?
by Robert Cormier

About the Illustration

Describe the people in the scene and tell what they are doing. Talk about what might be happening here. Use details from the illustration as clues. Give reasons for your answer.

These questions will help you begin to think about the story:

- When and where do you think this action takes place?

- What do you suppose the boys are doing?

- Which of the boys seems to be having a problem with the others? What do you suppose the problem concerns?

Unit 4

Introduction

About the Story

"President Cleveland, Where Are You?" is set in the early 1930s, during the Great Depression. It is a time when admission to a movie is 10 cents and a man's tie costs 65 cents. It is also a time when an experienced, full-time office worker would be delighted to earn as much as thirty dollars a week—almost $1600 per year! So for Jerry, the narrator, and his friends in the Frenchtown neighborhood, spending a nickel on gum is a major purchase. However, when each package includes a trading card, the boys are willing to use whatever money they have to get that card.

Then a new candy comes out with a President card in each pack and the offer of a prize baseball glove to whoever can collect a complete set of cards. The competition is keen. The special glove is one thing that the rich boy in the neighborhood cannot buy; for once, all the boys have an equal chance. Jerry, however, discovers that there are more important things in life than trading cards, baseball gloves, and even the joy of showing up the rich kid.

About the Author

Robert Cormier says he never considered being anything but a writer. For thirty years he was a newspaper journalist and columnist in Leominster, Massachusetts, where he has lived since his birth there in 1925. He began writing fiction in the 1960s but did not switch from journalism to full-time fiction writing until his young adult novel *The Chocolate War,* published in 1974, became a bestseller. Some of his other popular books are *I Am the Cheese, After the First Death,* and *The Bumblebee Flies Anyway*. Cormier's short stories in the collection *Eight Plus One,* from which this selection is taken, are more family oriented and hopeful than his novels.

Cormier has won awards for both his journalism and his young-adult fiction. His books are often controversial because they focus on such real-life problems as evil, corruption, and the abuse of authority, and they rarely have happy endings. In one speech, Cormier stated that he hoped his books "show adolescents the bigness of what's out there and that happy endings are not our birthright. You have to do something to make them happen."

About the Lessons

The lessons that follow "President Cleveland, Where Are You?" focus on conflict, the heart of a short story. *Conflict* refers to a character's struggle with a problem (or problems). Like real people, characters can have problems with people and things around them, with forces of nature, and with themselves. We read a story to see its characters struggle against their problems and to discover whether they win out or are defeated by them. The end of the conflict brings an end to the story.

Writing: Developing Conflict

Conflict can be inside a character or between a character and the people or things around him or her. After you read this story, you will learn more about how to make different kinds of conflict work together to give a story strength. At this time, prepare by trying the following suggestions.

- Think of a character, setting, and problem that would make an interesting scene. Write a few sentences that tell who is in the scene and where and when the action happens. Here is an example:

    Lydia is a teenage couch potato. She impulsively joins some friends who are spending a summer weekend in a cabin in the woods. The group has to hike several miles to get to the cabin.

- Make notes about at least two types of conflict your character might face. Here are some types of conflict you could use.

    Conflict within oneself: Lydia doesn't like hiking, and she complains.
    Conflict between two or more people: Lydia blames her friends, lags behind, wants them to slow down; her friends consider Lydia lazy and leave her behind.
    Conflict with nature: It gets dark; the woods seem dangerous; Lydia is lost.

- For each conflict you thought of for your story, write a few sentences that describe what the conflict is about.

Before Reading

The questions below will help you see how the author develops and resolves the conflicts in "President Cleveland, Where Are You?" As you read the story, think about the answers to the following questions:

- What conflicts, or problems, does the narrator, Jerry, face? How do these conflicts make the story interesting?

- What does Jerry learn about himself and about life through his reaction to his problems?

- The moment of greatest intensity of the conflict is the climax of the plot. At what point do the conflict and story reach a climax?

Vocabulary Tips

This story includes some words that may be unfamiliar to you but are useful for understanding the story. Below you will find some of these words, their definitions, and sentences that show how the words are used. Look over the words before you begin to read.

serial
a story presented in a series of continuous parts at regular intervals. We went to the theater every Saturday to see the next part of our favorite serial.

disconsolately
in a sad and hopeless way. When their team lost the playoff by a single point, the fans left the arena disconsolately.

obsessed
taken over by an idea or emotion that cannot be gotten rid of by reasoning. Chicken Little was obsessed with the idea that the sky was falling.

compassion
deep sympathy. Photos of the flood victims inspired compassion in many viewers and raised donations.

dominant
ruling; most important. Betty's desire to see the midnight sun was the dominant influence in her decision to visit Alaska.

lethargy
the state of being without energy. I don't know whether to blame my lethargy on today's hot weather or yesterday's late hours.

President Cleveland, Where Are You?

Robert Cormier

That was the autumn of the cowboy cards—Buck Jones and Tom Tyler and Hoot Gibson and especially Ken Maynard. The cards were available in those five-cent packages of gum: pink sticks, three together, covered with a sweet white powder. You couldn't blow bubbles with that particular gum, but it couldn't have mattered less. The cowboy cards were important—the pictures of those rock-faced men with eyes of blue steel.

On those wind-swept, leaf-tumbling afternoons we gathered after school on the sidewalk in front of Lemire's Drugstore, across from St. Jude's Parochial School, and we swapped and bargained and matched for the cards. Because a Ken Maynard serial was playing at the Globe every Saturday afternoon, he was the most popular cowboy of all, and one of his cards was worth at least ten of any other kind. Rollie Tremaine had a treasure of thirty or so, and he guarded them jealously. He'd match you for the other cards, but he risked his Ken Maynards only when the other kids threatened to leave him out of the competition altogether.

You could almost hate Rollie Tremaine. In the first place, he was the only son of Auguste Tremaine, who operated the Uptown Dry Goods Store, and he did not live in a tenement but in a big white birthday cake of a house on

Laurel Street. He was too fat to be effective in the football games between the Frenchtown Tigers and the North Side Knights, and he made us constantly aware of the jingle of coins in his pockets. He was able to stroll into Lemire's and casually select a quarter's worth of cowboy cards while the rest of us watched, aching with envy.

Once in a while I earned a nickel or dime by running errands or washing windows for blind old Mrs. Belander, or by finding pieces of copper, brass, and other valuable metals at the dump and selling them to the junkman. The coins clutched in my hand, I would race to Lemire's to buy a cowboy card or two, hoping that Ken Maynard would stare boldly out at me as I opened the pack. At one time, before a disastrous matching session with Roger Lussier (my best friend, except where the cards were involved), I owned five Ken Maynards and considered myself a millionaire, of sorts.

One week I was particularly lucky; I had spent two afternoons washing floors for Mrs. Belander and received a quarter. Because my father had worked a full week at the shop, where a rush order for fancy combs had been received, he allotted my brothers and sisters and me an extra dime along with the usual ten cents for the Saturday-afternoon movie. Setting aside the movie fare, I found myself with a bonus of thirty-five cents, and I then planned to put Rollie Tremaine to shame the following Monday afternoon.

Monday was the best day to buy the cards because the candy man stopped at Lemire's every Monday morning to deliver the new assortments. There was nothing more exciting in the world than a fresh batch of card boxes. I rushed home from school that day and hurriedly changed my clothes, eager to set off for the store. As I burst through the doorway, letting the screen door slam behind me, my brother Armand blocked my way.

He was fourteen, three years older than I, and a freshman at Monument High School. He had recently become a stranger to me in many ways—indifferent to such matters as cowboy cards and the Frenchtown Tigers—and he carried himself with a mysterious dignity that was fractured now and then when his voice began shooting off in all directions like some kind of vocal fireworks.

"Wait a minute, Jerry," he said. "I want to talk to you." He motioned me out of earshot of my mother, who was busy supervising the usual after-school skirmish in the kitchen.

I sighed with impatience. In recent months Armand had become a figure of authority, siding with my father and mother occasionally. As the oldest son he sometimes took advantage of his age and experience to issue rules and regulations.

"How much money have you got?" he whispered.

"You in some kind of trouble?" I asked, excitement rising in me as I remembered the blackmail plot of a movie at the Globe a month before.

He shook his head in annoyance. "Look," he said, "it's Pa's birthday tomorrow. I think we ought to chip in and buy him something. . . ."

I reached into my pocket and caressed the coins. "Here," I said, carefully pulling out a nickel. "If we all give a nickel we should have enough to buy him something pretty nice."

He regarded me with contempt. "Rita already gave me fifteen cents, and I'm throwing in a quarter. Albert handed over a dime—all that's left of his birthday money. Is that all you can do—a nickel?"

"Aw, come on," I protested. "I haven't got a single Ken

Maynard left, and I was going to buy some cards this afternoon."

"Ken Maynard!" he snorted. "Who's more important—him or your father?"

His question was unfair because he knew that there was no possible choice—"my father" had to be the only answer. My father was a huge man who believed in the things of the spirit, although my mother often maintained that the spirits he believed in came in bottles. He had worked at the Monument Comb Shop since the age of fourteen; his booming laugh—or grumble—greeted us each night when he returned from the factory. A steady worker when the shop had enough work, he quickened with gaiety on Friday nights and weekends, a bottle of beer at his elbow, and he was fond of making long speeches about the good things in life. In the middle of the Depression, for instance, he paid cash for a piano, of all things, and insisted that my twin sisters, Yolande and Yvette, take lessons once a week.

I took a dime from my pocket and handed it to Armand.

"Thanks, Jerry," he said. "I hate to take your last cent."

"That's all right," I replied, turning away and consoling myself with the thought that twenty cents was better than nothing at all.

When I arrived at Lemire's I sensed disaster in the air. Roger Lussier was kicking disconsolately at a tin can in the gutter, and Rollie Tremaine sat sullenly on the steps in front of the store.

"Save your money," Roger said. He had known about my plans to splurge on the cards.

"What's the matter?" I asked.

"There's no more cowboy cards," Rollie Tremaine said. "The company's not making any more."

"They're going to have President cards," Roger said, his face twisting with disgust. He pointed to the store window. "Look!"

A placard in the window announced: "Attention, Boys. Watch for the New Series. Presidents of the United States. Free in Each 5-Cent Package of Caramel Chew."

"President cards?" I asked, dismayed.

I read on: "Collect a Complete Set and Receive an Official Imitation Major League Baseball Glove, Embossed with Lefty Grove's Autograph."

Glove or no glove, who could become excited about Presidents, of all things?

Rollie Tremaine stared at the sign. "Benjamin Harrison, for crying out loud," he said. "Why would I want Benjamin Harrison when I've got twenty-two Ken Maynards?"

I felt the warmth of guilt creep over me. I jingled the coins in my pocket, but the sound was hollow. No more Ken Maynards to buy.

"I'm going to buy a Mr. Goodbar," Rollie Tremaine decided.

I was without appetite, indifferent even to a Baby Ruth, which was my favorite. I thought of how I had betrayed Armand and, worst of all, my father.

"I'll see you after supper," I called over my shoulder to Roger as I hurried away toward home. I took the shortcut behind the church, although it involved leaping over a tall wooden fence, and I zigzagged recklessly through Mr. Thibodeau's garden, trying to outrace my guilt. I pounded up the steps and into the house, only to learn that Armand had already taken Yolande and Yvette uptown to shop for the birthday present.

I pedaled my bike furiously through the streets, ignoring the indignant horns of automobiles as I sliced through the traffic. Finally I saw Armand and my sisters emerge from the Monument Men's Shop. My heart sank when I spied the long, slim package that Armand was holding.

"Did you buy the present yet?" I asked, although I knew it was too late.

"Just now. A blue tie," Armand said. "What's the matter?"

"Nothing," I replied, my chest hurting.

He looked at me for a long moment. At first his eyes were hard, but then they softened. He smiled at me, almost sadly, and touched my arm. I turned away from him because I felt naked and exposed.

"It's all right," he said gently. "Maybe you've learned something." The words were gentle, but they held a curious dignity, the dignity remaining even when his voice suddenly cracked on the last syllable.

I wondered what was happening to me, because I did not know whether to laugh or cry.

Sister Angela was amazed when, a week before Christmas vacation, everybody in the class submitted a history essay worthy of a high mark—in some cases as high as A-minus. (Sister Angela did not believe that anyone in the world ever deserved an A.) She never learned— or at least she never let on that she knew—we all had become experts on the Presidents because of the cards we purchased at Lemire's. Each card contained a picture of a President, and on the reverse side, a summary of his career. We looked at those cards so often that the biographies imprinted themselves on our minds without effort. Even our street-corner conversations were filled with such information as the fact that James Madison was called "The Father of the Constitution," or that John Adams had intended to become a minister.

The President cards were a roaring success and the cowboy cards were quickly forgotten. In the first place we did not receive gum with the cards, but a kind of chewy caramel. The caramel could be tucked into a corner of your mouth, bulging your cheek in much the same manner as wads of tobacco bulged the mouths of baseball stars. In the second place the competition for collecting the cards was fierce and frustrating—fierce because everyone was intent on being the first to send away for a baseball glove and frustrating because although there were only thirty-two presidents, including Franklin Delano Roosevelt, the variety at Lemire's was at a minimum. When the deliveryman left the boxes of cards at the store each Monday, we often discovered that one entire box was devoted to a single President—two weeks in a row the boxes contained nothing but Abraham Lincolns. One week Roger Lussier and I were the heroes of Frenchtown. We journeyed on our bicycles to the North Side, engaged three boys in a matching bout, and returned with five new Presidents, including Chester Alan Arthur, who up to that time had been missing.

Perhaps to sharpen our desire, the card company sent a sample glove to Mr. Lemire, and it dangled, orange and sleek, in the window. I was half sick with longing, thinking of my old glove at home, which I had inherited from Armand. But Rollie Tremaine's desire for the glove outdistanced my own. He even got Mr. Lemire to agree to give the glove in the window to the first person to get a complete set of cards, so that precious time wouldn't be wasted waiting for the postman.

We were delighted at Rollie Tremaine's frustration, especially since he was only a substitute player for the

Tigers. Once after spending fifty cents on cards—all of which turned out to be Calvin Coolidge—he threw them to the ground, pulled some dollar bills out of his pocket and said, "The heck with it! I'm going to buy a glove!"

"Not that glove," Roger Lussier said. "Not a glove with Lefty Grove's autograph. Look what it says at the bottom of the sign."

We all looked, although we knew the words by heart: "This Glove Is Not For Sale Anywhere."

Rollie Tremaine scrambled to pick up the cards from the sidewalk, pouting more than ever. After that he was quietly obsessed with the Presidents, hugging the cards close to his chest and refusing to tell us how many more he needed to complete his set.

I too was obsessed with the cards, because they had become things of comfort in a world that had suddenly grown dismal. After Christmas a layoff at the shop had thrown my father out of work. He received no paycheck for four weeks, and the only income we had was from Armand's after-school job at the Blue and White Grocery Store—a job he lost finally when business dwindled as the layoff continued.

Although we had enough food and clothing—my father's credit had always been good, a matter of pride with him—the inactivity made my father restless and irritable. He did not drink any beer at all, and laughed loudly, but not convincingly, after gulping down a glass of water and saying, "Lent came early this year." The twins fell sick and went to the hospital to have their tonsils removed. My father was confident that he would return to work eventually and pay off his debts, but he seemed to age before our eyes.

When orders again were received at the comb shop and he returned to work, another disaster occurred, although I was the only one aware of it. Armand fell in love.

I discovered his situation by accident, when I happened to pick up a piece of paper that had fallen to the floor in the bedroom he and I shared. I frowned at the paper, puzzled.

"Dear Sally, When I look into your eyes the world stands still . . ."

The letter was snatched from my hands before I finished reading it.

"What's the big idea, snooping around?" Armand asked, his face crimson. "Can't a guy have any privacy?"

He had never mentioned privacy before. "It was on the floor," I said. "I didn't know it was a letter. Who's Sally?"

He flung himself across the bed. "You tell anybody and I'll muckalize you," he threatened. "Sally Knowlton."

Nobody in Frenchtown had a name like Knowlton.

"A girl from the North Side?" I asked, incredulous.

He rolled over and faced me, anger in his eyes, and a kind of despair too.

"What's the matter with that? Think she's too good for me?" he asked. "I'm warning you, Jerry, if you tell anybody . . ."

"Don't worry," I said. Love had no particular place in my life; it seemed an unnecessary waste of time. And a girl from the North Side was so remote that for all practical purposes she did not exist. But I was curious. "What are you writing her a letter for? Did she leave town or something?"

"She hasn't left town," he answered. "I wasn't going to send it. I just felt like writing to her."

I was glad that I had never become involved with love—love that brought desperation to your eyes, that caused you to write letters you did not plan to send.

Shrugging with indifference, I began to search in the closet for the old baseball glove. I found it on the shelf, under some old sneakers. The webbing was torn and the padding gone. I thought of the sting I would feel when a sharp grounder slapped into the glove, and I winced.

"You tell anybody about me and Sally and I'll —"

"I know. You'll muckalize me."

I did not divulge his secret and often shared his agony, particularly when he sat at the supper table and left my mother's special butterscotch pie untouched. I had never realized before how terrible love could be. But my compassion was short-lived because I had other things to worry about: report cards due at Eastertime; the loss of income from Mrs. Belander, who had gone to live with a daughter in Boston; and, of course, the Presidents.

Because a stalemate had been reached, the President cards were the dominant force in our lives—mine, Roger Lussier's, and Rollie Tremaine's. For three weeks, as the baseball season approached, each of us had a complete set—complete except for one President, Grover Cleveland. Each time a box of cards arrived at the store, we hurriedly bought them (as hurriedly as our funds allowed) and tore off the wrappers, only to be confronted by James Monroe or Martin Van Buren or someone else. But never Grover Cleveland, never the man who had been the twenty-second *and* the twenty-fourth President of the United States. We argued about Grover Cleveland. Should he be placed between Chester Alan Arthur and Benjamin Harrison as the twenty-second President or did he belong between Benjamin Harrison and William McKinley as the twenty-fourth president? Was the card company playing fair? Roger Lussier brought up a horrifying possibility— did we need *two* Grover Clevelands to complete the set?

Indignant, we stormed Lemire's and protested to the harassed storeowner, who had long since vowed never to stock a new series. Muttering angrily, he searched his bills and receipts for a list of rules.

"All right," he announced. "Says here you only need one Grover Cleveland to finish the set. Now get out, all of you, unless you've got money to spend."

Outside the store, Rollie Tremaine picked up an empty tobacco tin and scaled it across the street. "Boy," he said. "I'd give five dollars for a Grover Cleveland."

When I returned home, I found Armand sitting on the piazza steps, his chin in his hands. His mood of dejection mirrored my own, and I sat down beside him. We did not say anything for a while.

"Want to throw the ball around?" I asked.

He sighed, not bothering to answer.

"You sick?" I asked.

He stood up and hitched up his trousers, pulled at his ear and finally told me what the matter was—there was a big dance next week at the high school, the Spring Promenade, and Sally had asked him to be her escort.

I shook my head at the folly of love. "Well, what's so bad about that?"

"How can I take Sally to a fancy dance?" he asked desperately. "I'd have to buy her a corsage. . . . And my shoes are practically falling apart. Pa's got too many worries now to buy me new shoes or give me money for flowers for a girl."

I nodded in sympathy. "Yeah," I said. "Look at me. Baseball time is almost here, and all I've got is that old glove. And no Grover Cleveland card yet . . ."

"Grover Cleveland?" he asked. "They've got some of those up on the North Side. Some kid was telling me there's a store that's got them. He says they're looking for Warren G. Harding."

"Holy Smoke!" I said. "I've got an extra Warren G. Harding!" Pure joy sang in my veins. I ran to my bicycle, swung into the seat—and found that the front tire was flat.

"I'll help you fix it," Armand said.

Within half an hour I was at the North Side Drugstore, where several boys were matching cards on the sidewalk. Silently but blissfully I shouted: President Grover Cleveland, here I come!

After Armand had left for the dance, all dressed up as if it were Sunday, the small green box containing the corsage under his arm, I sat on the railing of the piazza, letting my feet dangle. The neighborhood was quiet because the Frenchtown Tigers were at Daggett's Field, practicing for the first baseball game of the season.

I thought of Armand and the ridiculous expression on his face when he'd stood before the mirror in the bedroom. I'd avoided looking at his new black shoes. "Love," I muttered.

Spring had arrived in a sudden stampede of apple blossoms and fragrant breezes. Windows had been thrown open and dust mops had banged on the sills all day long as the women busied themselves with housecleaning. I was puzzled by my lethargy. Wasn't spring supposed to make everything bright and gay?

I turned at the sound of footsteps on the stairs. Roger Lussier greeted me with a sour face.

"I thought you were practicing with the Tigers," I said.

"Rollie Tremaine," he said. "I just couldn't stand him." He slammed his fist against the railing. "Jeez, why did he have to be the one to get a Grover Cleveland? You should see him showing off. He won't let anybody even touch that glove . . ."

I felt like Benedict Arnold and knew that I had to confess what I had done.

"Roger," I said. "I got a Grover Cleveland card up on

the North Side. I sold it to Rollie Tremaine for five dollars."

"Are you crazy?" he asked.

"I needed that five dollars. It was an—an emergency."

"Boy!" he said, looking down at the ground and shaking his head. "What did you have to do a thing like that for?"

I watched him as he turned away and began walking down the stairs.

"Hey, Roger!" I called.

He squinted up at me as if I were a stranger, someone he'd never seen before.

"What?" he asked, his voice flat.

"I had to do it," I said. "Honest."

He didn't answer. He headed toward the fence, searching for the board we had loosened to give us a secret passage.

I thought of my father and Armand and Rollie Tremaine and Grover Cleveland and wished that I could go away someplace far away. But there was no place to go.

Roger found the loose slat in the fence and slipped through. I felt betrayed: weren't you supposed to feel good when you did something fine and noble?

A moment later two hands gripped the top of the fence, and Roger's face appeared. "Was it a real emergency?" he yelled.

"A real one!" I called. "Something important!"

His face dropped from sight and his voice reached me across the yard: "All right."

"See you tomorrow!" I yelled.

I swung my legs over the railing again. The gathering dusk began to soften the sharp edges of the fence, the rooftops, and the distant church steeple. I sat there a long time, waiting for the good feeling to come.

Reviewing and Interpreting the Story

Record your answers to these comprehension questions in your personal literature notebook. Follow the directions for each part.

Reviewing Try to complete each of these sentences without looking back at the story.

Recalling Facts

1. The cowboy card Jerry wanted badly was that of
   a. Buck Jones.
   b. Lefty Grove.
   c. Ken Maynard.
   d. Hoot Gibson.

Identifying Cause and Effect

2. Jerry doesn't want to give Armand much money for his father's birthday present because he
   a. doesn't like his father much.
   b. wants to use his money to buy cowboy trading cards.
   c. thinks Armand has poor taste.
   d. would rather buy a present by himself.

Recognizing Story Elements (Characters)

3. During the story, Jerry has a conflict with each of the following except
   a. his brother Armand.
   b. Rollie Tremaine.
   c. Roger Lussier.
   d. his mother.

4. Jerry discovers that Armand is in love

   a. before their father's birthday.

   b. before their father is laid off from his job.

   c. after Armand tells him where to find President Cleveland cards.

   d. after the boys' father has been recalled to work following a layoff.

5. At one point, Rollie throws all his Calvin Coolidge cards to the ground and says he will just buy a glove. When the other boys remind him that the special glove is not for sale, Rollie picks up the cards. This scene shows that Rollie

   a. is determined to have the glove the other boys desire.

   b. really hates to litter.

   c. would rather not spend the money on a glove, if he can avoid it.

   d. doesn't want to embarrass the other boys by treating the President cards rudely.

Interpreting To answer these questions, you may look back at the story if you like.

6. Clues in the story tell you that Jerry's age is

   a. about eight years.

   b. about eleven years.

   c. about fourteen years.

   d. There are not enough clues to guess his age.

7. Jerry sells the Grover Cleveland card to Rollie

   a. because he secretly likes Rollie.
   b. so that Rollie will be grateful and do nice things for Jerry in return.
   c. to get money for Armand's new shoes and corsage.
   d. so that he will have money for an emergency.

8. After the end of the story, Jerry will probably

   a. demand that Armand pay him back, with interest.
   b. tell everyone in the neighborhood about selling the glove to Rollie.
   c. repair the loose slat in the fence that Roger Lussier slipped through.
   d. feel that he has done the correct thing.

9. The saying that best describes Jerry's actions is

   a. "Never give a sucker an even break."
   b. "Do the right thing."
   c. "Love is blind."
   d. "Waste not, want not."

10. Which of these conflicts is least important
in the plot?

    a. Jerry's competition with Roger Lussier
    in matching cards

    b. Jerry's argument with himself about
    donating money for his father's gift

    c. the rivalry between Rollie Tremaine
    and the rest of the boys

    d. Jerry's struggle to obtain a full set of
    President cards

Now check your answers with your teacher. Study the questions you answered incorrectly. What types of questions were they? Talk with your teacher about ways to work on those skills.

Conflict

Every good story has a beginning, a middle, and an end. A poor story also has a beginning and a middle, but hardly anyone pays attention long enough to discover whether it has an end. What's the difference between the two? Conflict.

Conflict is any problem or struggle between characters or forces. The most important conflict in a story is a critical struggle involving the main character. This is the essential element that unites the pieces of a story and glues the audience to the story until the outcome of the struggle is known.

In a good story, the conflict often reminds readers of their own problems. A character's struggle may be more serious, or more exciting, or funnier than your own experience, but if you don't feel anything in common with the character, you won't understand his or her difficulties.

However, conflict in a story is more contained than conflict in the real world. Over the course of a story, the reader sees the central conflict begin, rise in intensity to a climax, and end. The character may bring the conflict to an end by solving his or her problems or by giving in to them. Or the character may learn to handle the situation in such a way that it is no longer a major problem. If the writer is skillful, you don't know which turn the conflict will take until the story reaches its climax. Even then your concern for the character and curiosity about the conflict prevent you from leaving the story until the outcome is clear.

In this lesson, we will look at these ways in which author Robert Cormier develops conflict in "President Cleveland, Where Are You?"

1. The author develops external conflict—the problems the main character has with people and things around him.

2. He develops internal conflict—the struggles the main character has within himself.

3. He blends and builds the different conflicts to create a plot that captures our interest.

1 • External Conflict

External means *outside*. External conflict refers to any struggle a character has with people or things outside his or her mind. Conflicts involving the main character are of major importance. Usually a character struggles against one or more of these opponents:

- another person or specific people
- society as a whole
- a force of nature, such as a storm or an animal

"President Cleveland, Where Are You?" includes examples of all three of these kinds of external conflict.

1. *Character against another person.*   The rivalry between Jerry and his friends, on one side, and Rollie Tremaine on the other is introduced early in the story.

> You could almost hate Rollie Tremaine. In the first place, he was the only son of Auguste Tremaine, who operated the Uptown Dry Goods Store, and he did not live in a tenement but in a big white birthday cake of a house on Laurel Street. He was too fat to be effective in the football games between the Frenchtown Tigers and the North Side Knights, and he made us constantly aware of the jingle of coins in his pockets. He was able to stroll into Lemire's and casually select a quarter's worth of cowboy cards while the rest of us watched, aching with envy.

> Although the other boys talk and play with Rollie, he constantly makes them aware of the differences between their circumstances and his. It's only natural that the other boys would love to turn the tables and make Rollie ache with envy for something one of them has.

2. *Character against society or circumstances.*   Jerry never mentions the name of the city or town he lives in; he simply identifies with his neighborhood, Frenchtown. He and his

friends, the Frenchtown Tigers, play against the North Side Knights; otherwise, he has little to do with that part of town. He seems to have accepted the attitude that Frenchtown and the North Side should be separate. Jerry's older brother Armand, however, dares to engage in conflict with society by dating a girl from the North Side.

He had never mentioned privacy before. "It was on the floor," I said. "I didn't know it was a letter. Who's Sally?"

He flung himself across the bed. "You tell anybody and I'll muckalize you," he threatened. "Sally Knowlton."

Nobody in Frenchtown had a name like Knowlton.

"A girl from the North Side?" I asked, incredulous.

He rolled over and faced me, anger in his eyes, and a kind of despair too.

"What's the matter with that? Think she's too good for me?" he asked. "I'm warning you, Jerry, if you tell anybody . . ."

3. *Character against a force of nature.* No one makes a conscious decision to have a particular assortment of President cards delivered to Lemire's Drugstore, and no one causes any particular customer to buy a specific package of candy there. Chance alone, a force of nature, determines which cards any boy in Frenchtown finds in his packs of candy. Each of the boys, then, is in conflict with chance in his desire to collect a complete set. Jerry and his friend Roger Lussier discover a way to win a small victory against this blind force in the universe.

. . . When the deliveryman left the boxes of cards at the store each Monday, we often discovered that one entire box was devoted to a single President—two weeks in a row the boxes contained nothing but Abraham Lincolns. One week Roger Lussier and I were the heroes of Frenchtown. We journeyed on our bicycles to the North Side, engaged three boys in a matching bout and returned with five new Presidents, including Chester Alan Arthur, who up to that time had been missing.

Exercise 1

Read this passage about Rollie's and Jerry's conflicts. Use what you have learned in this lesson to answer the questions that follow.

We were delighted at Rollie Tremaine's frustration, especially since he was only a substitute player for the Tigers. Once after spending fifty cents on cards—all of which turned out to be Calvin Coolidge—he threw them to the ground, pulled some dollar bills out of his pocket and said, "The heck with it. I'm going to buy a glove!"

"Not that glove," Roger Lussier said. "Not a glove with Lefty Grove's autograph. Look what it says at the bottom of the sign."

We all looked, although we knew the words by heart: "This Glove Is Not For Sale Anywhere."

Rollie Tremaine scrambled to pick up the cards from the sidewalk, pouting more than ever. After that he was quietly obsessed with the Presidents, hugging the cards close to his chest and refusing to tell us how many more he needed to complete his set.

I too was obsessed with the cards, because they had become things of comfort in a world that had suddenly grown dismal. After Christmas a layoff at the shop had thrown my father out of work. He received no paycheck for four weeks, and the only income we had was from Armand's after-school job at the Blue and White Grocery Store—a job he lost finally when business dwindled as the layoff continued.

1. The first part of this passage focuses on Rollie's conflicts. What problem does chance throw at him? How does he react? How does his reaction worsen the conflict between himself and the other boys?

2. In the final paragraph, Jerry describes his family's "dismal" situation. Is this situation a struggle between the family and other individuals, between the family and society in general, or between the family and a force of nature? What are some possible solutions to this conflict?

Check your answers with your teacher. Review this part of the lesson if you don't understand why an answer was incorrect.

Writing on Your Own 1

In this exercise you will use what you learned in the lesson to develop an external conflict and consider possible outcomes. Review the writing you did in Developing Conflict on pages 108–109. Then follow these steps:

• Choose the most interesting of the external conflicts you described. Think of a specific action that the character takes in this conflict, the reaction from the opposing person(s) or force, and the character's next move. Begin a chart like the one below to organize your thoughts. Show how the conflict becomes more intense at each stage.

Character's Action	Reaction	Character's Next Move

• Consider possible outcomes to the conflict. Try to think of at least two ways your character can overcome the problem. What must happen in the story to make your character's success possible? What might happen to bring about the character's failure? How can the character learn to cope with the problem? Write several sentences describing what might happen to your character.

2 • Internal Conflict

Internal conflict refers to a struggle that happens *inside* a character's mind. For example, a character may be confused about the correct way to act and unable to make up his mind. Another character may know how she should act but be reluctant to do what is difficult or unpopular.

Events outside the person lead the character to see the issue in a new, approachable way, or they force the character to behave differently. When characters like those described finally decide to take action, they change. They grow by meeting the challenge the conflict presents.

Many stories involve little or no internal conflict. In many adventure tales, for example, the hero is concerned only with choosing the most effective way to defeat the enemy; he or she is the same person at the end of the story as at the beginning. Characters that remain the same throughout a story are called static characters. A hero who must face personal fears as well as an outside enemy is a dynamic character, one who experiences internal conflict and changes as a result of that conflict.

In "President Cleveland, Where Are You?" Jerry deals with internal conflict when Armand asks him for money for a birthday gift for their father. He knows without hesitation what he should do, but that doesn't match what he wants to do. He has saved his thirty-five cents to buy himself cowboy cards. Notice how the word *caressed* stresses Jerry's greedy frame of mind. It doesn't take him long to make his decision.

> I reached into my pocket and caressed the coins. "Here," I said carefully, pulling out a nickel. "If we all give a nickel we should have enough to buy him something pretty nice."
>
> He regarded me with contempt. "Rita already gave me fifteen cents, and I'm throwing in a quarter. Albert handed over a dime—all that's left of his birthday money. Is that all you can do—a nickel?"
>
> "Aw, come on," I protested. "I haven't got a single Ken Maynard left, and I was going to buy some cards this afternoon."
>
> "Ken Maynard!" he snorted. "Who's more important—him or your father?"
>
> His question was unfair because he knew that there was no possible choice—"my father" had to be the only answer. . . .
>
> I took a dime from my pocket and handed it to Armand.
>
> "Thanks, Jerry," he said. "I hate to take your last cent."
>
> "That's all right," I replied, turning away and consoling myself with the thought that twenty cents was better than nothing at all.

Then Jerry hurries to the drugstore to buy the cowboy cards and discovers they are no longer available.

> I felt the warmth of guilt creep over me. I jingled the coins in my pocket, but the sound was hollow. No more Ken Maynards to buy.
> "I'm going to buy a Mr. Goodbar," Rollie Tremaine decided.
> I was without appetite, indifferent even to a Baby Ruth, which was my favorite. I thought of how I had betrayed Armand and, worst of all, my father.

Although Jerry has made the wrong decision, his bout of internal conflict has changed him. Earlier he objected to his brother's query "Who's more important—him [Ken Maynard] or your father?" because both he and his brother knew there was no possible choice—"my father" had to be the only answer. Yet until the baseball cards disappear at the whim of the manufacturer, Jerry doesn't truly understand how unimportant they are compared to his father. Now he recognizes his error and wishes he could change his actions. Armand is correct in pointing out to him shortly afterward, "Maybe you've learned something."

Exercise 2

Read this passage and answer the questions about it using what you have learned in this part of the lesson.

> After Armand had left for the dance, all dressed up as if it were Sunday, the small green box containing the corsage under his arm, I sat on the railing of the piazza, letting my feet dangle. . . .
> Spring had arrived in a sudden stampede of apple blossoms and fragrant breezes. Windows had been thrown open and dust mops had banged on the sills all day long as the women busied themselves with housecleaning. I was puzzled by my lethargy. Wasn't spring supposed to make everything bright and gay?
> I turned at the sound of footsteps on the stairs. Roger Lussier greeted me with a sour face.

"I thought you were practicing with the Tigers," I said.

"Rollie Tremaine," he said. "I just couldn't stand him." He slammed his fist against the railing. "Jeez, why did *he* have to be the one to get a Grover Cleveland? You should see him showing off. He won't let anybody even touch that glove. . ."

I felt like Benedict Arnold and knew that I had to confess what I had done.

"Roger," I said, "I got a Grover Cleveland card up on the North Side. I sold it to Rollie Tremaine for five dollars."

"Are you crazy?" he asked.

"I needed that five dollars. It was an—an emergency."

1. How can you tell Jerry is upset? Why does he say he feels like Benedict Arnold? Why do you suppose he confesses to Roger?

2. The story does not describe Jerry's thinking at the time he decides to sell his President Cleveland card to Rollie. The author expects the reader to fill in the scene. What reasons would Jerry have for keeping the card? What reasons would he have for selling it? What has he used the money for?

3. Was Jerry correct, strictly speaking, in saying he had to sell the card? How does his decision to sell the card indicate his victory in his internal conflict?

Check your answers with your teacher. Review this part of the lesson if you don't understand why an answer was incorrect.

Writing on Your Own 2

In this exercise you will use what you learned in this lesson to develop an internal conflict. Follow these steps:

- Decide whether the internal conflict you described for Developing Conflict on page 108 relates to the external conflicts you developed for Writing on Your Own 1. If not, or if you didn't think of an internal conflict earlier, think of one now that relates to the major external conflict you developed. Write a sentence or more describing the internal conflict your character experiences as he or she tries to resolve the external conflict.

- List arguments on both sides of the issue that the character must decide. Try to make both sides sound equally good or equally bad.

3 • Conflict and Plot

You may be familiar with television soap operas. During a half-hour segment, different scenes may feature half a dozen different groups of characters. That half hour does not present one story; it presents bits of six different stories. Each story involves its own conflict. Although the conflicts are developed in back-to-back scenes, they have little, if anything, to do with each other.

In a short story, on the other hand, all the internal and external conflicts must be related to the central plot. The conflict that the story begins with may cause additional conflicts or may be made more serious by other conflicts. The climax of the story often occurs when several conflicts reach points of crisis at the same time.

Let's look at how some of the conflicts in "President Cleveland, Where Are You?" develop during the rising action:

- Rivalry with Rollie Tremaine (external conflict) causes Jerry to choose to spend his money on cowboy cards rather than on his father (internal conflict). Regret for his choice leaves Jerry feeling guilty and more respectful of his brother Armand.

- The boys' father's layoff puts the family in poor financial shape (external conflict) about the time that Armand falls in love with a girl from a nicer neighborhood (external conflict).

- Jerry's friends struggle to collect sets of President cards, to win a prize baseball glove (external conflict). Rollie, who can afford to buy any other glove, offers five dollars for a President Cleveland card so that he can win the glove instead of poorer boys like Jerry, who has far too little money to buy a glove (external conflict).

These three conflict strands all come together in the following excerpt. Jerry, depressed about his chances to acquire the President Cleveland card, finds Armand equally depressed because the girl he loves wants him to take her to the high school dance.

I shook my head at the folly of love. "Well, what's so bad about that?"

"How can I take Sally to a fancy dance?" he asked desperately. "I'd have to buy her a corsage. . . . And my shoes are practically falling apart. Pa's got too many worries now to buy me new shoes or give me money for flowers for a girl."

I nodded in sympathy. "Yeah," I said. "Look at me. Baseball time is almost here, and all I've got is that old glove. And no Grover Cleveland card yet . . ."

"Grover Cleveland?" he asked. "They've got some of those up on the North Side. Some kid was telling me there's a store that's got them. He says they're looking for Warren G. Harding."

"Holy Smoke!" I said. "I've got an extra Warren G. Harding!" Pure joy sang in my veins. I ran to my bicycle, swung into the seat—and found that the front tire was flat.

"I'll help you fix it," Armand said.

Within half an hour I was at the North Side Drugstore, where several boys were matching cards on the sidewalk. Silently but blissfully I shouted: President Grover Cleveland, here I come!

This moment echoes the earlier time when Jerry was intent on getting a Ken Maynard card and Armand asked him to contribute to a gift for their father. Again Jerry has the means to get the card he wants. Again he learns that someone in his family is in need of a gift. And, as a reminder of how much he owes his brother, when Jerry discovers a flat tire on his bike, it is Armand who helps him fix it. If Jerry has learned anything from the earlier episode and his wrong choice, then he must face a similar internal conflict now. This is the climax of the plot, when Jerry's decision will determine his future and the outcome of the story.

Exercise 3

Read this passage. Jerry has seen his brother go to the dance, wearing new shoes and carrying a corsage, and has just confessed to Roger Lussier that he sold a President Cleveland card to Rollie

Tremaine. Use what you have learned in this lesson to answer the questions below.

> Roger found the loose slat in the fence and slipped through. I felt betrayed: weren't you supposed to feel good when you did something fine and noble?
>
> A moment later two hands gripped the top of the fence and Roger's face appeared. "Was it a real emergency?" he yelled.
>
> "A real one!" I called. "Something important!"
>
> His face dropped from sight and his voice reached me across the yard: "All right."
>
> "See you tomorrow!" I yelled.
>
> I swung my legs over the railing again. The gathering dusk began to soften the sharp edges of the fence, the rooftops, the distant church steeple. I sat there a long time, waiting for the good feeling to come.

1. Jerry has already faced up to his internal conflict over the best use of the President Cleveland card. What external conflict is developed and quickly resolved in this part of the falling action? Which existing external conflict has Jerry decided he can live with?

2. Although Jerry is concerned about Roger's reaction, he has no doubt that he did the correct thing. Find the narrator's statement that proves this observation.

Check your answers with your teacher. Review this part of the lesson if you don't understand why an answer was incorrect.

Writing on Your Own 3

In this exercise you will decide on your scene's climax and develop the falling action. Follow these steps:

- Re-evaluate the conflict you chose to be your most important one in Writing On Your Own 2. Do you still think it is strong enough to be a major problem? Does it lead to complications and rise in intensity up to a turning point for the main character? Decide on your scene's climax. Add notes to your original plans to suggest additions or corrections you could make to ensure that the climax is the most exciting point in the scene.

- Decide how you will handle the falling action. Will it explain everything that happens during and after the climax? Or will it follow the climax with only a clue as to how characters or the situation changes? Write several sentences that summarize the events and information you will include in your falling action and resolution.

Discussion Guides

1. How do you suppose Armand reacted to Jerry's offer of a gift of five dollars? Did he accept it as a gift or insist the money was a loan to be repaid? Work with a partner to develop a dialogue between these two characters. Then present your dialogue to your class or another group.

2. Imagine that the setting of this story is this year in your town. What activity would replace collecting President cards? What prize would boys and girls in your neighborhood work hard for? How much money would Rollie have to offer to make Jerry think of giving up his prize to Rollie? With a small group, discuss these issues and any other changes that you think must be made to bring the story up to date. Make a chart comparing Then and Now—describe the item in the existing story in the first column and your group's version in the second column. Compare your chart with those of other groups.

3. In writing about this story, the author, Robert Cormier, discussed the problems of having a young narrator like Jerry describe Rollie's expensive house. One problem was that a long, detailed description of the house would get in the way of the story. Another problem was that a boy of Jerry's age wouldn't know much about architecture, so such a description could not come from him anyway. Cormier's solution was the phrase "a big white birthday cake of a house." Do you agree that this is the way an eleven-year-old boy might describe a fine house? What are some other ways he might describe the house?

4. Review the story to find another passage in which the author was careful to limit the information to what Jerry would know or understand. In a large-group or class discussion, point out the passage you found and explain why you think it sounds like the words of a young boy. Suggest how the passage might be different if the narrator were an adult.

Write a Scene with Conflict

Throughout this unit, you have been developing the conflict of an original scene. In your previous writing assignments, you have seen how the conflict is crucial to every stage of the plot. Now it is time to put the pieces together and make any changes needed to make them fit.

If you have questions about the writing process, refer to Using the Writing Process beginning on page 306.

- Assemble the writing you did for Developing Conflict at the beginning of the unit and for each of the Writing on Your Own exercises.

- Review and compare these assignments: *a)* your ideas about the setting, character, external conflicts, and events that show how the conflict grows, *b)* your description of a related internal conflict, *c)* your explanation of how conflict leads to a climax, and how the clearing away of the conflict is shown in your scene's falling action and resolution. Also review any notes you made after Exercises 2 and 3 about reworking earlier stages to make them mesh better with later developments.

- Write the scene you have outlined. Pay particular attention to the rising action to show how more than one conflict comes into play at various stages. However, be sure to keep the focus on the most important conflict, the one that is crucial to the climax. Make sure the falling action and resolution satisfactorily show how that conflict is cleared up.

- Read your scene to one or more classmates. Ask them to point out passages that should be improved. Make any revisions you agree with.

- Proofread your writing for errors in spelling, grammar, and punctuation. Make a corrected copy and save it in a portfolio of your writing.

Unit 5   The Narrator

The Tell-Tale Heart
by Edgar Allan Poe

Catch the Moon
by Judith Ortiz Cofer

About the Illustration

This picture gives you clues about what will happen in one of the stories you are about to read. The following questions will help you begin to think about the story. Use details from the illustration to answer the questions. Give reasons for your answers.

- Look at the clothes of the old man in bed. When and where do you think this event takes place?

- Look at the old man's face. What might he be feeling? Why might he feel that way?

- Why is the light shining only on the old man's face? Who do you think is shining the light? What might that person be thinking or planning to do?

Unit 5

Introduction

About the Story: The Tell-Tale Heart

A madman who believes he is perfectly sane decides to kill an old man because he cannot stand looking at the old man's eye. For seven nights, he cautiously looks in on the old man as he sleeps and shines his lantern on the man's closed eye. On the last night, the old man hears his intruder and sits up in his bed, waiting in terror to find out what will happen next. Eventually, the madman, who has been motionless for almost an hour, shines the lantern beam directly on the old man's eye and then goes berserk, killing the old man according to plan. Read to find out what happens when police officers come to check on the strange noises coming from the house.

About the Author

Edgar Allan Poe was born in 1809 in Boston, Massachusetts. Orphaned at an early age, he was raised by a wealthy tobacco exporter named John Allan in Richmond, Virginia. Allan wanted him to become a lawyer, but Poe decided to write for a living. Although he was a successful writer, he never earned enough to support his family. His young wife died at a very early age, and he died in poverty at the age of forty. His works include poems such as the haunting "The Raven," short stories such as "The Masque of the Red Death," detective stories such as "The Gold Bug," and criticisms of other people's writing. Among his other talents, Poe is known for his ability to throw light on the processes of diseased and clever minds in his tales of terror and his detective stories.

About the Story: Catch the Moon

Luis Cintrón has been released into his father's custody after serving time in juvenile hall for breaking and entering. Luis resents having to help his father in his auto parts salvage yard. His only desire is to reunite with the other members of his "social club," the same group that got him into trouble earlier. Luis's mother died three years ago, and neither Luis nor his father has gotten over her death. When the beautiful daughter of the funeral home's owner comes to the yard to find a hubcap, memories of his mother and her funeral come flooding back. How might this chance visit change Luis's life? Read the story to find out.

About the Author

Judith Ortiz Cofer was born in Puerto Rico but moved to Paterson, New Jersey, at a very early age. At age six, she and her mother and brother moved back to Puerto Rico to live with her grandmother while her father served in the U.S. Navy in Europe. Later, she moved back to Paterson. For twenty years, she split her time between New Jersey and Puerto Rico. Her childhood experiences have given Ms. Cofer a sensitivity for the difficulties of trying to live in two different cultures. She has written a critically acclaimed novel and a number of essays, poems, and short stories. "Catch the Moon" first appeared in a collection of short stories called *An Island Like You: Stories of the Barrio*.

About the Lessons

The lessons that follow "The Tell-Tale Heart" and "Catch the Moon" focus on the role of the narrator in a short story. The *narrator* is the person who is telling the story. A narrator may be either a character in the story or someone outside the story, looking at the action. Another name for the narrator is the speaker.

The narrator is the eyes and ears of the reader. Sometimes the narrator lets the reader in on the secret thoughts of the characters and at other times he or she can report the story only as an outsider. Either way, the writer uses the narrator to reveal story events, to create moods, and to bring the reader into the story.

Writing: Using a Narrator

Writers are careful when they choose the narrators to tell their stories. A story will unfold in certain ways, depending on who is telling it. In the course of this unit, you will get experience in writing from different points of view, using different narrators. Finally, you will write about an event from a point of view that you choose. The following suggestions will help you get started.

- Everyone has been to a gathering of friends or family members. Think back to such a party that you attended.

- Write some notes about the get-together. Who was there? How did you feel while you were getting ready for the party and while you were there? How did the guests act? What was said? What was done? What was the mood of the party?

- If you prefer, you can make up a party with imaginary guests. Answer the same questions for your imaginary get-together.

- Save your notes to use later in the unit.

Before Reading

The following questions will help you see how the writers of both stories have created effective narrators to help them tell their stories. Keep these questions in mind as you read the stories.

- Is the narrator a character taking part in the story or someone outside the story?

- What do you know about the narrator in each story? How has the author revealed this information?

- What is the mood of each story? What feelings do you get from the thoughts, attitudes, and feelings the narrator shares?

Vocabulary Tips

These stories include some words that may be unfamiliar to you but are useful for understanding the story. Below, you will find some of these words, their definitions, and sentences that show how the words are used. Look over the words before you begin to read.

The Tell-Tale Heart

dissimulation   the act of hiding one's true feelings or plans. The crooked politician, an expert in <u>dissimulation,</u> convinced voters that he was trustworthy.

sagacity   shrewdness and intelligence. The lawyer was known for her <u>sagacity</u> in thinking of winning arguments.

tattoo   a steady beating or tapping. The drum <u>tattoo</u> was a signal to the soldiers to return to quarters.

scantlings   small, upright pieces of wood used in the frame of a building. The <u>scantlings</u> that support a floor should be made of sturdy wood.

suavity   smoothness and refinement in social situations. The ambassador's <u>suavity</u> at parties and meetings gained him many admirers.

gesticulations   gestures; motions made to accompany or substitute for words. When she talks, her hands and arms move in constant <u>gesticulations</u>.

mockery   ridicule and scorn. The class clown tried to get laughs by making a <u>mockery</u> of the teacher's words.

dissemble   to pretend. Kwok liked Penny, but he <u>dissembled</u> by acting silly around her.

Catch the Moon

harassing   bothering repeatedly. The man was charged with <u>harassing</u> his former boss with angry phone calls.

decapitate   to cut off the head. During the French Revolution, those in power <u>decapitated</u> their enemies.

The Tell-Tale Heart

Edgar Allan Poe

True!—nervous—very, very dreadfully nervous I had been and am; but why *will* you say that I am mad? The disease had sharpened my senses—not destroyed—not dulled them. Above all was the sense of hearing acute. I heard all things in the heaven and in the earth. I heard many things in hell. How, then, am I mad? Hearken! and observe how healthily—how calmly I can tell you the whole story.

It is impossible to say how first the idea entered my brain; but once conceived, it haunted me day and night. Object there was none. Passion there was none. I loved the old man. He had never wronged me. He had never given me insult. For his gold I had no desire. I think it was his eye! Yes, it was this! He had the eye of a vulture—a pale blue eye, with a film over it. Whenever it fell upon me, my blood ran cold; and so by degrees—very gradually—I made up my mind to take the life of the old man, and thus rid myself of the eye forever.

Now this is the point. You fancy me mad. Madmen know nothing. But you should have seen *me*. You should have seen how wisely I proceeded—with what caution—with what foresight—with what dissimulation I went to work! I was never kinder to the old man than during the whole week before I killed him. And every night, about midnight, I turned the latch of his door and opened it—oh, so gently! And then, when I had made an opening sufficient for my head, I put in a dark lantern, all closed, closed, so that no light shone out, and then I thrust in my head. Oh, you would have laughed to see how cunningly I thrust it in! I moved it slowly—very, very slowly, so that I might not disturb the old man's sleep. It took me an hour to place my whole head within the opening so far that I could see him as he lay upon his bed. Ha!—would a madman have been so wise as this? And then, when my head was well in the room, I undid the lantern cautiously—oh, so cautiously—cautiously (for the hinges creaked)—I undid it just so much that a single, thin ray fell upon the vulture eye. And this I did for seven long nights—every night just at midnight—but I found the eye always closed; and so it was impossible to do the work; for it was not the old man who vexed me, but his Evil Eye. And every morning, when the day broke, I went boldly into the chamber, and spoke courageously to him, calling him by name in a hearty tone, and inquiring how he had passed the night. So you see he would have been a very profound old man, indeed, to suspect that every night, just at twelve, I looked in upon him while he slept.

Upon the eighth night I was more than usually cautious in opening the door. A watch's minute hand moves more quickly than did mine. Never before that night, had I *felt* the extent of my own powers—of my sagacity. I could scarcely contain my feelings of triumph. To think that there I was, opening the door, little by little, and he not even to dream of my secret deeds or thoughts. I fairly chuckled at the idea; and perhaps he heard me; for he moved on the bed suddenly, as if startled. Now you may think that I drew back—but no. His room was as black as pitch with the thick darkness (for the shutters were close fastened, through fear of robbers), and so I knew that he could not see the opening of the door, and I kept pushing it on steadily, steadily.

I had my head in, and was about to open the lantern, when my thumb slipped upon the tin fastening, and the old man sprang up in bed, crying out—"Who's there?"

I kept quite still and said nothing. For a whole hour I did not move a muscle, and in the meantime I did not hear him lie down. He was still sitting up in the bed listening, just as I have done, night after night, hearkening to the death watches in the wall.

Presently I heard a slight groan, and I knew it was the groan of mortal terror. It was not a groan of pain or of grief—oh, no!—it was the low, stifled sound that arises from the bottom of the soul when overcharged with awe. I knew the sound well. Many a night, just at midnight, when all the world slept, it has welled up from my own bosom, deepening, with its dreadful echo, the terrors that distracted me. I say I knew it well. I knew what the old man felt, and pitied him, although I chuckled at heart. I knew that he had been lying awake ever since the first slight noise, when he had turned in the bed. His fears had been ever since growing upon him. He had been trying to fancy them causeless, but could not. He had been saying to himself—"It is nothing but the wind in the chimney—it is only a mouse crossing the floor," or "it is merely a cricket which has made a single chirp." Yes, he had been trying to comfort himself with these suppositions: but he had found all in vain. *All in vain;* because Death, in approaching him, had stalked with his black shadow before him, and enveloped the victim. And it was the mournful influence of the unperceived shadow that caused him to feel—although he neither saw nor heard—to *feel* the presence of my head within the room.

When I had waited a long time, very patiently, without hearing him lie down, I resolved to open a little, a very, very little crevice in the lantern. So I opened it—you cannot imagine how stealthily, stealthily—until at length a single dim ray, like the thread of the spider, shot from out the crevice and fell full upon the vulture eye.

It was open—wide, wide open—and I grew furious as I gazed upon it. I saw it with perfect distinctness—all a dull blue, with a hideous veil over it that chilled the very marrow in my bones; but I could see nothing else of the old man's face or person; for I had directed the ray, as if by instinct, precisely upon the damned spot.

And have I not told you that what you mistake for madness is but over-acuteness of the senses?—now, I say, there came to my ears a low, dull, quick sound, such as a watch makes when enveloped in cotton. I knew *that* sound well, too. It was the beating of the old man's heart. It increased my fury, as the beating of a drum stimulates the soldier into courage.

But even yet I refrained and kept still. I scarcely breathed. I held the lantern motionless. I tried how steadily I could maintain the ray upon the eye. Meantime the hellish tattoo of the heart increased. It grew quicker and quicker, and louder and louder every instant. The old man's terror *must* have been extreme! It grew louder, I say, louder every moment!—do you mark me well? I have told you that I am nervous; so I am. And now at the dead hour of the night, amid the dreadful silence of that old house, so strange a noise as this excited me to uncontrollable terror. Yet, for some minutes longer I refrained and stood still. But the beating grew louder, louder! I thought the heart must burst. And now a new anxiety seized me—the sound would be heard by a neighbor! The old man's hour had come! With a loud yell, I threw open the lantern and leaped into the room. He shrieked once—once only. In an instant I dragged him to the floor, and pulled the heavy bed over him. I then smiled gaily, to find the deed so far done. But, for many minutes, the heart beat on with a muffled sound. This, however, did not vex me; it would not be heard through the wall. At length it ceased. The old man was dead. I removed the bed and examined the corpse. Yes, he was stone, stone dead. I placed my hand upon the heart and held it there many minutes. There was no pulsation. He was stone dead. His eye would trouble me no more.

If still you think me mad, you will think so no longer when I describe the wise precautions I took for the concealment of the body. The night waned, and I worked hastily, but in silence. First of all I dismembered the corpse. I cut off the head and the arms and the legs.

I then took up three planks from the flooring of the chamber, and deposited all between the scantlings. I then replaced the boards so cleverly, so cunningly, that no human eye—not even *his*—could have detected anything wrong. There was nothing to wash out—no stain of any kind—no bloodspot whatever. I had been too wary for that. A tub had caught all—ha! ha!

When I had made an end of these labors, it was four o'clock—still dark as midnight. As the bell sounded the hour, there came a knocking at the street door. I went down to open it with a light heart,—for what had I now to fear? There entered three men, who introduced themselves, with perfect suavity, as officers of the police. A shriek had been heard by a neighbor during the night;

suspicion of foul play had been aroused; information had been lodged at the police office, and they (the officers) had been deputed to search the premises.

I smiled,—for *what* had I to fear? I bade the gentlemen welcome. The shriek, I said, was my own in a dream. The old man, I mentioned, was absent in the country. I took my visitors all over the house. I bade them search—search *well*. I led them, at length, to *his* chamber. I showed them his treasures, secure, undisturbed. In the enthusiasm of my confidence, I brought chairs into the room, and desired them *here* to rest from their fatigues, while I myself, in the wild audacity of my perfect triumph, placed my own seat upon the very spot beneath which reposed the corpse of my victim.

The officers were satisfied. My *manner* had convinced them. I was singularly at ease. They sat, and while I answered cheerily, they chatted of familiar things. But, ere long, I felt myself getting pale and wished them gone. My head ached, and I fancied a ringing in my ears: but still they sat and still chatted. The ringing became more distinct;—it continued and became more distinct; I talked more freely to get rid of the feeling; but it continued and gained definiteness—until, at length, I found that the noise was *not* within my ears.

No doubt I now grew *very* pale;—but I talked more fluently, and with a heightened voice. Yet the sound increased—and what could I do? It was *a low, dull, quick sound—much such a sound as a watch makes when enveloped in cotton.* I gasped for breath—and yet the officers heard it not. I talked more quickly—more vehemently; but the noise steadily increased. I arose and argued about trifles, in a high key and with violent gesticulations; but the noise steadily increased. Why *would* they not be gone? I paced the floor to and fro with heavy strides, as if excited to fury by the observations of the men—but the noise steadily increased. Oh God; what *could* I do? I foamed—I raved—I swore! I swung the chair upon which I had been sitting, and grated it upon the boards, but the noise arose over all and continually increased. It grew louder—louder—*louder!* And still the men chatted pleasantly, and smiled. Was it possible they heard not? Almighty God!— no, no! They heard!—they suspected!—they *knew!*—they were making a mockery of my horror!—this I thought, and this I think. But anything was better than this agony! Anything was more tolerable than this derision! I could bear those hypocritical smiles no longer! I felt that I must scream or die! and now—again!—hark! louder! louder! louder! *louder!*

"Villains!" I shrieked, "dissemble no more! I admit the deed!—tear up the planks! here, here!—it is the beating of his hideous heart!"

Reviewing and Interpreting the Story

Record your answers to these comprehension questions in your personal literature notebook. Follow the directions for each part.

Reviewing   Try to complete each of these sentences without looking back at the story.

Recalling Facts

1. For seven nights, the narrator enters the old man's room carrying a

   a. knife.
   b. pillow.
   c. lantern.
   d. mirror.

Understanding Main Ideas

2. What enrages the narrator the most about the old man is his

   a. cruelty.
   b. sense of humor.
   c. voice.
   d. eye.

Identifying Cause and Effect

3. The old man wakes up one night because

   a. the narrator calls his name.
   b. the narrator's hand slips on the lantern and makes a noise.
   c. the light from the lantern wakes him.
   d. he always has trouble sleeping.

4. After the narrator shines the light on the old man's face, the

    a. old man's heart begins to beat loudly.

    b. old man sits up in bed and waits.

    c. narrator sticks his head into the room.

    d. clock strikes twelve.

5. Most of this story is taken up by

    a. the introduction.

    b. rising action.

    c. the climax.

    d. falling action and conclusion.

Interpreting   To answer these questions, you may look back at the story if you like.

6. The narrator probably hears the beating heart while the police officers do not because

    a. he feels guilty.

    b. his hearing is better than average.

    c. he knows what to listen for.

    d. he is sitting directly over the body.

7. Which of these statements would the narrator most likely make at his trial?

    a. I liked everything about the old man.

    b. I had no choice; his evil eye was driving me mad.

    c. I didn't really kill the old man. He died a natural death.

    d. I killed the old man in self-defense. He was trying to kill me.

8. Based on his actions, the narrator would probably agree with this statement:

    a. All's well that ends well.

    b. A friend in need is a friend indeed.

    c. The eye is the window of the soul.

    d. A thing of beauty is a joy forever.

9. In the end, the narrator is not able to get away with his crime because he is

    a. a good person at heart.

    b. too intelligent.

    c. an unstable person.

    d. not careful enough.

10. The climax occurs when the

    a. narrator pulls the old man to the floor.

    b. police officers enter the house.

    c. old man groans in terror.

    d. narrator kills the old man.

Now check your answers with your teacher. Study the questions you answered incorrectly. What types of questions were they? Talk with your teacher about ways to work on those skills.

Catch the Moon

Judith Ortiz Cofer

Luis Cintrón sits on top of a six-foot pile of hubcaps and watches his father walk away into the steel jungle of his car junkyard. Released into his old man's custody after six months in juvenile hall—for breaking and entering—and he didn't even take anything. He did it on a dare. But the old lady with the million cats was a light sleeper, and good with her aluminum cane. He has a scar on his head to prove it.

Now Luis is wondering whether he should have stayed in and done his full time. Jorge Cintrón of Jorge Cintrón & Son, Auto Parts and Salvage, has decided that Luis should wash and polish every hubcap in the yard. The hill he is sitting on is only the latest couple of hundred wheel covers that have come in. Luis grunts and stands up on top of his silver mountain. He yells at no one, "Someday, son, all this will be yours," and sweeps his arms like the Pope blessing a crowd over the piles of car sandwiches and mounds of metal parts that cover this acre of land outside the city. He is the "Son" of Jorge Cintrón & Son, and so far his father has had more than one reason to wish it was plain Jorge Cintrón on the sign.

Luis has been getting in trouble since he started high school two years ago, mainly because of the "social group" he organized—a bunch of guys who were into harassing the local authorities. Their thing was taking something to the limit on a dare or, better still, doing something dangerous, like breaking into a house, not to steal, just to prove that they could do it. That was Luis's specialty, coming up with very complicated plans, like military strategies, and assigning the "jobs" to guys who wanted to join the Tiburones.

Tiburón means "shark," and Luis had gotten the name from watching an old movie about a Puerto Rican gang called the Sharks with his father. Luis thought it was one of the dumbest films he had ever seen. Everybody sang their lines, and the guys all pointed their toes and leaped in the air when they were supposed to be slaughtering each other. But he liked their name, the Sharks, so he made it Spanish and had it air-painted on his black T-shirt with a killer shark under it, jaws opened wide and dripping with blood. It didn't take long for other guys in the barrio to ask about it.

Man, had they had a good time. The girls were interested too. Luis outsmarted everybody by calling his organization a social club and registering it at Central High. That meant they were legal, even let out of last-period class on Fridays for their "club" meetings. It was just this year, after a couple of botched jobs, that the teachers had started getting suspicious. The first one to go wrong was when he sent Kenny Matoa to *borrow* some "souvenirs" out of Anita Robles's locker. He got caught. It seems that Matoa had been reading Anita's diary and didn't hear her coming down the hall. Anita was supposed to be in the gym at that time but had copped out with the usual female excuse of cramps. You could hear her screams all the way to Market Street.

She told the principal all she knew about the Tiburones, and Luis had to talk fast to convince old Mr. Williams that the club did put on cultural activities such as the Save the Animals talent show. What Mr. Williams didn't know was that the animal that was being "saved" with the ticket sales was Luis's pet boa, which needed quite a few live mice to stay healthy and happy. They kept E.S. (which stood for "Endangered Species") in Luis's room, but she belonged to the club and it was the members' responsibility to raise the money to feed their mascot. So last year they had sponsored their first annual Save the Animals talent show, and it had been a great success. The Tiberones had come dressed as Latino Elvises and did a grand finale to "All Shook Up" that made the audience go wild. Mr. Williams had smiled while Luis talked, maybe remembering how the math teacher, Mrs. Laguna, had dragged him out in the aisle to rock-and-roll with her. Luis had gotten out of that one, but barely.

His father was a problem too. He objected to the T-shirt logo, calling it disgusting and vulgar. Mr. Cintrón prided himself on his own neat, elegant style of dressing after work, and on his manners and large vocabulary, which he picked up by taking correspondence courses in just about everything. Luis thought that it was just his way of staying busy since Luis's mother had died, almost three years ago, of cancer. He had never gotten over it.

All this was going through Luis's head as he slid down the hill of hubcaps. The tub full of soapy water, the can of polish, and the bag of rags had been neatly placed in front of a makeshift table made from two car seats and a piece of plywood. Luis heard a car drive up and someone honk their horn. His father emerged from inside a new red Mustang that had been totaled. He usually dismantled every small feature by hand before sending the vehicle into the *cementerio,* as he called the lot. Luis watched as the most beautiful girl he had ever seen climbed out of a vintage white Volkswagen Bug. She stood in the sunlight in her white sundress waiting for his father, while Luis stared. She was like a smooth wood carving. Her skin was mahogany, almost black, and her arms and legs were long and thin, but curved in places so that she did not look bony and hard—more like a ballerina. And her ebony hair was braided close to her head. Luis let his breath out, feeling a little dizzy. He had forgotten to breathe. Both the girl and his father heard him. Mr. Cintrón waved him over.

"Luis, the señorita here has lost a wheel cover. Her car is twenty-five years old, so it will not be an easy match. Come look on this side."

Luis tossed a wrench he'd been holding into a toolbox like he was annoyed, just to make a point about slave labor. Then he followed his father, who knelt on the gravel and began to point out every detail of the hubcap. Luis was hardly listening. He watched the girl take a piece of paper from her handbag.

"Señor Cintrón, I have drawn the hubcap for you, since I will have to leave soon. My home address and telephone number are here, and also my parents' office number." She handed the paper to Mr. Cintrón, who nodded.

"Sí, señorita, very good. This will help my son look for it. Perhaps there is one in that stack there." He pointed to the pile of caps that Luis was supposed to wash and polish. "Yes, I'm almost certain that there is a match there. Of course, I do not know if it's near the top or the bottom. You will give us a few days, yes?

Luis just stared at his father like he was crazy. But he didn't say anything because the girl was smiling at him with a funny expression on her face. Maybe she thought he had X-ray eyes like Superman, or maybe she was mocking him.

"Please call me Naomi, Señor Cintrón. You know my mother. She is the director of the funeral home. . . ." Mr. Cintrón seemed surprised at first; he prided himself on having a great memory. Then his friendly expression changed to one of sadness as he recalled the day of his wife's burial. Naomi did not finish her sentence. She reached over and placed her hand on Mr. Cintrón's arm for a moment. Then she said "Adiós" softly, and got in her shiny white car. She waved to them as she left, and her gold bracelets flashing in the sun nearly blinded Luis.

Mr. Cintrón shook his head. "How about that," he said as if to himself. "They are the Dominican owners of Ramirez Funeral Home." And, with a sigh, "She seems like such a nice young woman. Reminds me of your mother when she was her age."

Hearing the funeral parlor's name, Luis remembered too. The day his mother died, he had been in her room at the hospital while his father had gone for coffee. The alarm had gone off on her monitor and nurses had come running in, pushing him outside. After that, all he recalled was the anger that had made him punch a hole in his bedroom wall. And afterward he had refused to talk to anyone at the funeral. Strange, he did see a black girl there who didn't try like the others to talk to him, but actually ignored him as she escorted family members to the viewing room and brought flowers in. Could it be that the skinny girl in a frilly white dress had been Naomi? She didn't act like she had recognized him today, though. Or maybe she thought that he was a jerk.

Luis grabbed the drawing from his father. The old man looked like he wanted to walk down memory lane. But Luis was in no mood to listen to the old stories about his falling in love on a tropical island. The world they'd lived in before he was born wasn't his world. No beaches and palm trees here. Only junk as far as he could see. He climbed back up his hill and studied Naomi's sketch. It had obviously been done very carefully. It was signed "Naomi Ramirez" in the lower right-hand corner. He memorized the telephone number.

Luis washed hubcaps all day until his hands were red and raw, but he did not come across the small silver bowl that would fit the VW. After work he took a few practice Frisbee shots across the yard before showing his father what he had accomplished: rows and rows of shiny rings drying in the sun. His father nodded and showed him the bump on his temple where one of Luis's flying saucers had gotten him. "Practice makes perfect, you know. Next time you'll probably decapitate me." Luis heard him struggle with the word *decapitate*, which Mr. Cintrón pronounced in syllables. Showing off his big vocabulary again, Luis thought. He looked closely at the bump, though. He felt bad about it.

"They look good, hijo." Mr. Cintrón made a sweeping gesture with his arms over the yard. "You know, all this will have to be classified. My dream is to have all the parts divided by year, make of car, and condition. Maybe now that you are here to help me, this will happen."

"Pop . . ." Luis put his hand on his father's shoulder. They were the same height and build, about five foot six and muscular. "The judge said six months of free labor for you, not life, okay?" Mr. Cintrón nodded, looking distracted. It was then that Luis suddenly noticed how gray his hair had turned—it used to be shiny black like his own—and that there were deep lines in his face. His father had turned into an old man and he hadn't even noticed.

"Son, you must follow the judge's instructions. Like she said, next time you get in trouble, she's going to treat you like an adult, and I think you know what that means. Hard time, no breaks."

"Yeah, yeah. That's what I'm doing, right? Working my hands to the bone instead of enjoying my summer. But listen, she didn't put me under house arrest, right? I'm going out tonight."

"Home by ten. She did say something about a curfew, Luis." Mr. Cintrón had stopped smiling and was looking upset. It had always been hard for them to talk more than a minute or two before his father got offended at something Luis said, or at his sarcastic tone. He was always doing something wrong.

Luis threw the rag down on the table and went to sit in his father's ancient Buick, which was in mint condition. They drove home in silence.

After sitting down at the kitchen table with his father to eat a pizza they had picked up on the way home, Luis asked to borrow the car. He didn't get an answer then, just a look that meant "Don't bother me right now."

Before bringing up the subject again, Luis put some ice cubes in a Baggie and handed it to Mr. Cintrón, who had made the little bump on his head worse by rubbing it. It had GUILTY written on it, Luis thought.

"Gracias, hijo." His father placed the bag on the bump and made a face as the ice touched his skin.

They ate in silence for a few minutes more; then Luis decided to ask about the car again.

"I really need some fresh air, Pop. Can I borrow the car for a couple of hours?"

"You don't get enough fresh air at the yard? We're lucky that we don't have to sit in a smelly old factory all day. You know that?"

"Yeah, Pop. We're real lucky." Luis always felt irritated that his father was so grateful to own a junkyard, but he held his anger back and just waited to see if he'd get the keys without having to get in an argument.

"Where are you going?"

"For a ride. Not going anywhere. Just out for a while. Is that okay?"

His father didn't answer, just handed him a set of keys, as shiny as the day they were manufactured. His father polished everything that could be polished: doorknobs, coins, keys, spoons, knives, and forks, like he was King Midas counting his silver and gold. Luis thought his father must be really lonely to polish utensils only he used anymore. They had been picked out by his wife, though, so they were like relics. Nothing she had ever owned could be thrown away. Only now the dishes, forks, and spoons were not used to eat the yellow rice and red beans, the fried chicken, or the mouth-watering sweet plantains that his mother had cooked for them. They were just kept in the cabinets that his father had turned into a museum for her. Mr. Cintrón could cook as well as his wife, but he didn't have the heart to do it anymore. Luis thought that maybe if they ate together once in a while things might get better between them, but he always had something to do around dinnertime and ended up at a hamburger joint. Tonight was the first time in months they had sat down at the table together.

Luis took the keys. "Thanks," he said, walking out to take his shower. His father kept looking at him with those sad, patient eyes. "Okay, I'll be back by ten, and keep the ice on that egg," Luis said without looking back.

He had just meant to ride around his old barrio, see if any of the Tiburones were hanging out at El Building, where most of them lived. It wasn't far from the single-family home his father had bought when the business had started paying off: a house that his mother lived in for three months before she took up residence at St. Joseph's Hospital. She never came home again. These days Luis wished he still lived in that tiny apartment where there was always something to do, somebody to talk to.

Instead Luis found himself parked in front of the last place his mother had gone to: Ramirez Funeral Home. In the front yard was a huge oak tree that Luis remembered having climbed during the funeral to get away from people. The tree looked different now, not like a skeleton, as it had then, but green with leaves. The branches reached to the second floor of the house, where the family lived.

For a while Luis sat in the car allowing the memories to flood back into his brain. He remembered his mother before the illness changed her. She had not been beautiful, as his father told everyone; she had been a sweet lady, not pretty but not ugly. To him, she had been the person who always told him that she was proud of him and loved him. She did that every night when she came to his bedroom door to say good-night. As a joke he would sometimes ask her, "Proud of what? I haven't done anything." And she'd always say, "I'm just proud that you are my son." She wasn't perfect or anything. She had bad days when nothing he did could make her smile, especially after she got sick. But he never heard her say anything negative about anyone. She always blamed *el destino*, fate, for what went wrong. He missed her. He missed her so much. Suddenly a flood of tears that had been building up for almost three years started pouring from his eyes. Luis sat in his father's car, with his head on the steering wheel, and cried, "Mami, I miss you."

When he finally looked up, he saw that he was being watched. Sitting at a large window with a pad and a pencil on her lap was Naomi. At first Luis felt angry and embarrassed, but she wasn't laughing at him. Then she told him with her dark eyes that it was okay to come closer. He walked to the window, and she held up the sketch pad on which she had drawn him, not crying like a baby, but sitting on top of a mountain of silver disks, holding one up over his head. He had to smile.

The plate-glass window was locked. It had a security bolt on it. An alarm system, he figured, so nobody would steal the princess. He asked her if he could come in. It was soundproof too. He mouthed the words slowly for her to read his lips. She wrote on the pad, "I can't let you in. My mother is not home tonight." So they looked at each other and talked through the window for a little while. Then Luis got an idea. He signed to her that he'd be back, and drove to the junkyard.

Luis climbed up on his mountain of hubcaps. For hours he sorted the wheel covers by make, size, and condition, stopping only to call to his father and tell him where he was and what he was doing. The old man did not ask him for explanations, and Luis was grateful for that. By lamp-post light, Luis worked and worked, beginning to understand a little why his father kept busy all the time. Doing something that had a beginning, a middle, and an end did something to your head. It was like the satisfaction Luis got out of planning "adventures" for his Tiburones, but there was another element involved here that had nothing to do with showing off for others. This was a treasure hunt. And he knew what he was looking for.

Finally, when it seemed that it was a hopeless search, when it was almost midnight and Luis's hands were cut and bruised from his work, he found it. It was the perfect match for Naomi's drawing, the moon-shaped wheel cover for her car, Cinderella's shoe. Luis jumped off the small mound of disks left under him and shouted, "Yes!" He looked around and saw neat stacks of hubcaps that he would wash the next day. He would build a display wall for his father. People would be able to come into the yard and point to whatever they wanted.

Luis washed the VW hubcap and polished it until he could see himself in it. He used it as a mirror as he washed his face and combed his hair. Then he drove to the Ramirez Funeral Home. It was almost pitch-black, since it was a moonless night. As quietly as possible, Luis put some gravel in his pocket and climbed the oak tree to the second floor. He knew he was in front of Naomi's window—he could see her shadow through the curtains. She was at a table, apparently writing or drawing, maybe waiting for him. Luis hung the silver disk carefully on a branch near the window, then threw the gravel at the glass. Naomi ran to the window and drew the curtains aside while Luis held on to the thick branch and waited to give her the first good thing he had given anyone in a long time.

Reviewing and Interpreting the Story

Record your answers to these comprehension questions in your personal literature notebook. Follow the directions for each part.

Reviewing   Try to complete each of these sentences without looking back at the story.

Recalling Facts

1. Before the story begins, Luis got into trouble with his "social club" called the

    a. Mustangs.
    b. Tigers.
    c. Cougars.
    d. Sharks.

Understanding Main Ideas

2. In the beginning of the story, working for his father gives Luis a feeling of

    a. resentment and anger.
    b. pride.
    c. closeness with his father.
    d. confusion.

Identifying Cause and Effect

3. Luis probably became involved with the Tiburones because

    a. his father was abusive.
    b. they put on cultural activities.
    c. he was lonely.
    d. he wanted to hurt his father.

4. Just after Luis first meets the girl from the funeral home, he

   a. punches a hole in his bedroom wall.
   b. immediately starts to search for the needed hubcap.
   c. washes hubcaps for hours.
   d. starts to cry.

5. Most of the action in this story takes place in

   a. the auto salvage yard.
   b. a funeral parlor.
   c. Luis's high school.
   d. the family's kitchen.

Interpreting   To answer these questions, you may look back at the story if you like.

6. From the way that Luis treats his father, you know that he

   a. blames his father for his mother's death.
   b. really loves his father.
   c. wants to leave home as soon as possible.
   d. thinks his father is foolish.

7. Based on the way Naomi has acted in the story, now that Luis has given her the gift of a hubcap, she will probably

   a. thank him and become more friendly.
   b. make fun of him for crying.
   c. pay him but refuse to see him again.
   d. ignore his gift.

Making
Generalizations

8. The most important lesson this story teaches you is that

   a. unless you cry, you can't get over the death of someone close to you.

   b. friends can't be counted on when you are in trouble.

   c. when something sad happens, you should try to ignore it.

   d. doing something positive for someone else will help you face your problems and feel good about yourself.

Analyzing

9. From the beginning to the end of the story, Luis changes from

   a. happy to sad.

   b. angry to hopeful.

   c. silly to serious.

   d. relieved to confused.

Understanding
Story Elements
(Plot)

10. The turning point, or climax, occurs when

    a. Luis hangs the hubcap on the tree branch.

    b. Luis finally finds the hubcap.

    c. Naomi communicates to him through her window.

    d. Luis cries and admits that he misses his mother.

Now check your answers with your teacher. Study the questions you answered incorrectly. What types of questions were they? Talk with your teacher about ways to work on those skills.

Role of the Narrator

Suppose there is a traffic accident; perhaps one car bumps into another at an intersection. When the police come, they try to get statements from the drivers of both cars about what caused the accident. If possible, they take statements from witnesses who saw the action. Why do they get so many statements? You have probably guessed the answer. It's because people see events from different points of view. Each driver may believe that different details are important. An interested witness may see details that neither driver could see. Each person involved has a different way of looking at the event.

Like the people who give statements at the scene of an accident, narrators in stories let you know what has happened as they see it. It is important to identify the narrator so you can evaluate the trustworthiness and accuracy of the account. Just as the person who caused the accident may be slightly biased, so too the narrator in a story may not be able to tell the whole truth. Writers are careful to let readers know as much as they need to know about the narrator.

Since you see events through the eyes of the narrator, he or she has the power to influence not only what you know but also how you feel about people, places, and events in the story. The attitude of the narrator is crucial in determining your reaction to the story's action.

In these lessons, we will pay special attention to the role of the narrator. You will learn more about the following ways in which Edgar Allan Poe and Judith Ortiz Cofer make use of the narrator:

1. Each author chooses the narrator's point of view.

2. The authors let you know something about the narrator.

3. They communicate tone and create mood through the words of the narrator.

1 • Point of View

The author is the person who writes a story, but the *narrator,* or speaker, is the one who tells the story. When the narrator uses first-person pronouns, such as *I, me, we, us,* and *our,* we say that the story is being told from the *first-person point of view.* In such stories, the narrator may be a major or minor character in the story. If the narrator is a major character, the events may be happening to him or her. Not only do readers know what the narrator knows, but they also can "listen in" on the narrator's thoughts and feelings. By using this point of view, the author can write a very personal story.

In other stories written from the first-person point of view, the narrator is a minor character. He or she relates what is happening, but can't tell how other characters feel or what they are thinking. By choosing a minor character as the narrator, the author pulls readers away from the intense emotions of the main characters.

Some stories are told best from the *third-person point of view.* When the narrator uses third-person pronouns such as *he, she, they,* and *them,* the story is written from the third-person point of view. A story told from the third-person *limited* point of view tells only about what one character sees and feels. Readers experience only what that character experiences. In a story told from the third-person *omniscient* (om nish' ǝnt) point of view, the narrator can see into every character's mind and can travel through time and space to tell the story. It is as if the narrator is hovering above the action, knowing and understanding everything and everyone.

Read this passage from "The Tell-Tale Heart." From which point of view is it written? Why do you think the author chose that point of view?

> True!—nervous—very, very dreadfully nervous I had been and am; but why *will* you say that I am mad? The disease had sharpened my senses—not destroyed—not dulled them. Above all was the sense of hearing acute. I heard all things in the heaven and in the earth. I heard many things in hell. How, then, am I mad? Hearken! and observe how healthily—how calmly I can tell you the whole story.

In this powerful introduction to the story, the first-person point of view becomes clear immediately. The narrator is a person who is probably going to be a major character. He is highly emotional and perhaps even mad, as it seems that someone has accused him of being. Edgar Allan Poe wants us to be able to enter the mind of this madman, so he chooses the first-person point of view.

Exercise 1

Read this passage from "Catch the Moon." Use what you have learned in this lesson to answer the questions that follow.

Luis Cintrón sits on top of a six-foot pile of hubcaps and watches his father walk away into the steel jungle of his car junkyard. Released into his old man's custody after six months in juvenile hall—for breaking and entering—and he didn't even take anything. He did it on a dare. But the old lady with the million cats was a light sleeper, and good with her aluminum cane. He has a scar on his head to prove it.

Now Luis is wondering whether he should have stayed in and done his full time. Jorge Cintrón of Jorge Cintrón & Son, Auto Parts and Salvage, has decided that Luis should wash and polish every hubcap in the yard. The hill he is sitting on is only the latest couple of hundred wheel covers that have come in. Luis grunts and stands up on top of his silver mountain. He yells at no one, "Someday, son, all this will be yours," and sweeps his arms like the Pope blessing a crowd over the piles of car sandwiches and mounds of metal parts that cover this acre of land outside the city. He is the "Son" of Jorge Cintrón & Son, and so far his father has had more than one reason to wish it was plain Jorge Cintrón on the sign.

1. From which point of view is this story told, first-person or third-person? How do you know?

2. In these first paragraphs in the story, you learn about Luis's past and present. How does the point of view from which the story is told help you to understand Luis?

Check your answers with your teacher. Review this part of the lesson if you don't understand why an answer was incorrect.

Writing on Your Own 1

In this exercise you will use what you have learned in the lesson to write a diary entry and a paragraph about the get-together you chose for Using a Narrator on page 147. Follow these steps:

- Review your notes from the first assignment. Add any other details that occur to you at this time.

- Use your notes to write a diary entry about the party. Tell about what you saw, heard, and felt from the first-person point of view.

- Now suppose you are writing about the party for the school newspaper. Write a paragraph or two from the third-person point of view. Since it is a news article, remember not to include a description of people's feelings, except for the ones they reveal to others.

- Reread the two pieces of writing. Did you maintain the same point of view from beginning to end in each piece? If you need to make any changes, make them now.

2 • Getting to Know the Narrator

When narrators talk, they reveal much about themselves. Especially when the story is written from the first-person point of view, a careful reader will soon understand the narrator well. The narrator gives the reader clues about his or her level of intelligence, likes and dislikes, beliefs, and fears.

When a story is written from the third-person point of view, you know less about the narrator. Usually, all you know is whether the narrator can report on the thoughts and actions of only one person or can see into the minds of many people.

Read this passage from "Catch the Moon" and see what you can learn about the narrator:

Tiburón means "shark," and Luis had gotten the name from watching an old movie about a Puerto Rican gang called the Sharks with his father. Luis thought it was one of the dumbest films he had ever seen. Everybody sang their lines, and the guys all pointed their toes and leaped in the air when they were supposed to be slaughtering each other. But he liked their name, the Sharks, so he made it Spanish and had it air-painted on his black T-shirt with a killer shark under it, jaws opened wide and dripping with blood. It didn't take long for other guys in the barrio to ask about it.

Man, had they had a good time. The girls were interested too. Luis outsmarted everybody by calling his organization a social club and registering it at Central High. That meant they were legal, even let out of last-period class on Fridays for their "club" meetings. It was just this year, after a couple of botched jobs, that the teachers had started getting suspicious.

This passage is written from the third-person point of view. The narrator, who is outside the story, knows about events in Luis's past life. In addition, the narrator seems to have a direct connection to Luis's mind and is able to report on Luis's thoughts and feelings, now and in the past. In sentences such as "Man, had they had a good time," the narrator almost seems to be reading Luis's mind. Words and phrases such as "guys," "one of the dumbest films he had ever seen," "supposed to be slaughtering each other," and "a couple of botched jobs" suggest that the narrator is repeating Luis's thoughts. The narrator uses the same casual, conversational way of speaking that Luis himself would use.

Exercise 2

Read this passage from "The Tell-Tale Heart." It describes what happens after the old man is killed. Then answer the questions about the passage using what you have learned in this part of the lesson.

. . . The old man was dead. I removed the bed and examined the corpse. Yes, he was stone, stone dead. I placed my hand upon the heart and held it there many minutes. There was no pulsation. He was stone dead. His eye would trouble me no more.

If still you think me mad, you will think so no longer when I describe the wise precautions I took for the concealment of the body. The night waned, and I worked hastily, but in silence. First of all I dismembered the corpse. I cut off the head and the arms and the legs.

I then took up three planks from the flooring of the chamber, and deposited all between the scantlings. I then replaced the boards so cleverly, so cunningly, that no human eye—not even *his*—could have detected anything wrong. There was nothing to wash out—no stain of any kind—no bloodspot whatever. I had been too wary for that. A tub had caught all—ha! ha!

1. List at least three things you know about the personality of the narrator based on what he says in this passage and how he says it.

2. Does the narrator feel any sorrow for his crime? Give evidence to prove your answer.

Check your answers with your teacher. Review this part of the lesson if you don't understand why an answer was incorrect.

Writing on Your Own 2

In this exercise you will write a paragraph describing a chance meeting between you and another person. Follow these steps:

- Choose one of the following people to be the person you meet. This person will also be the narrator in your paragraph: a six-year-old boy; a grandparent; a teenaged girl; the principal of your school.

- Write a paragraph describing your meeting. Write it from the first-person point of view, but don't write it as yourself.

Instead, write it from the point of view of the person you have chosen to meet. Include details about how the person views you and what his or her thoughts and feelings are.

- Make sure that your readers can guess which of the characters listed above is your narrator. Let your word choices, thoughts, and details give clues about the narrator's identity. For example, your grandmother might think, "My grandson is growing up so fast. It's been too long since I've seen him."

- Share your description with a partner. Ask your partner to identify the narrator you have chosen. If it isn't clear who the narrator is, revise your description to make the choice clearer.

3 • The Narrator and Tone and Mood

When someone speaks to you, you can tell by the tone of voice how that person is feeling toward you. Your response depends on what you learn from the tone of voice. The tone of spoken words communicates the speaker's attitude toward his or her subject or audience. This is true of writing as well. In all kinds of writing, the writer's attitudes come through and set a tone. In a short story, the tone is created by the author's careful attention to detail.

Tone and mood often go together. Mood is the feeling a writer or speaker creates in a reader or listener. For example, if the tone in your mother's voice is excited or pleased, your mood becomes happy too. The mood of a story might be humorous, suspenseful, or sad.

Writers often get across the tone of a piece by having their narrators express a certain attitude toward people, places, and events. When you read the narrator's words, you share in these feelings. Your mood changes to match the narrator's tone.

Read this passage from "The Tell-Tale Heart." Try to identify the narrator's tone. Is it angry, sarcastic, kind, realistic, or cold? Or is it a combination of some of these tones?

It was impossible to say how first the idea entered my brain; but once conceived, it haunted me day and night. Object there was none. Passion there was none. I loved the old man. He had never wronged me. He had never given me insult. For his gold I had no desire. I think it was his eye! Yes, it was this! He had the eye of a vulture—a pale blue eye, with a film over it. Whenever it fell upon me, my blood ran cold; and so by degrees—very gradually—I made up my mind to take the life of the old man, and thus rid myself of the eye forever.

In this passage, the narrator is analyzing the reasons why he committed a hideous crime. In reality, there is no good reason to explain this deed. However, the narrator coldly, logically describes his feelings and seems to expect the reader to understand and agree with him. The narrator is clearly out of his mind. As you read his cruel, chilling words, you begin to be nervous about what this person might do. The narrator's tone creates a mood of fear and anxiety in the reader.

Exercise 3

Read these passages from "Catch the Moon" and answer the questions about them using what you have learned in this part of the lesson.

Luis washed hubcaps all day until his hands were red and raw, but he did not come across the small silver bowl that would fit the VW. After work he took a few practice Frisbee shots across the yard before showing his father what he had accomplished: rows and rows of shiny rings drying in the sun. His father nodded and showed him the bump on his temple where one of Luis's flying saucers had gotten him. "Practice makes perfect, you know. Next time you'll probably *decapitate* me." Luis heard him struggle with the word decapitate, which Mr. Cintrón pronounced in syllables. Showing off his big vocabulary again, Luis thought. He looked closely at the bump, though. He felt bad about it. . . .

Before bringing up the subject again, Luis put some ice cubes in a Baggie and handed it to Mr. Cintrón, who had made the little bump on his head worse by rubbing it. It had GUILTY written on it, Luis thought.

1. How does the narrator feel about Luis? How would you describe the tone of these passages—sympathetic or disapproving?

2. The mood of the story before these events was one of hopelessness. Luis was angry and resentful—a troublemaker. How does Luis's concern for his father begin to change the mood? How do you feel about Luis now?

Check your answers with your teacher. Review this part of the lesson if you don't understand why an answer was incorrect.

Writing on Your Own 3

In this exercise you will write two paragraphs in which you create two different moods. Follow these steps:

- Imagine you are a guest at two different parties. One is a fancy party where you don't know many people and the other is a casual party with good friends and close family members. How will you feel about attending each kind of party? Jot down some notes about what you would see, hear, and feel at each. Review your writing from earlier in this unit for ideas.

- Write a paragraph about each party from the first-person point of view. In the first paragraph, describe the fancy party. If you enjoy this kind of party, make it clear in your paragraph. If you don't, make that clear too. In the second paragraph, describe the casual party. Let your attitude toward the parties come through in your word choice, thoughts, and details. Make sure that readers can share in your mood at each party.

- Read your paragraphs to one or more classmates. Discuss the mood of each paragraph— exciting, tense, warm, happy, quiet, or boring, for example. If your listeners have trouble identifying the mood you intended to create, ask them to suggest changes and improvements you can make.

- Revise each paragraph until you are satisfied that it expresses the mood you intended.

Discussion Guides

1. It is interesting to read Edgar Allan Poe's story "The Tell-Tale Heart" aloud. Get together with a group of four or five class-mates. Divide the story into parts. Look up the pronunciation of difficult words. Practice reading your part aloud. Be sure to put emotion and drama into your reading. Practice reading the whole story with your group, then tape it. Share your tape with the class.

2. In "Catch the Moon," how do you think Luis and his father's lives will change now? How will Luis's new ability to give of himself change their relationship? Discuss with a partner what changes might occur. Then create a dialogue that could take place between Luis and his father in about a year. How do they treat each other? What have they accomplished together? What plans are they making? Present your dialogue to the class.

3. Edgar Allan Poe created a scary, creepy mood in "The Tell-Tale Heart." Together with a few other students, make a list of the words and phrases that helped to create the frightening mood. After you finish, compare your list with other groups' lists. Did you include the same words and phrases or have other groups identified some that you overlooked? Make a class list of the words and phrases that create the story's mood.

4. With a group of classmates, compare the tone and mood of the beginning of "Catch the Moon" with its tone and mood at the end. How does the author feel about Luis at both times? What is your mood as you read each part? Find words and phrases that create the mood in each part. You may want to use a chart like the following to record your thoughts.

	Tone and Mood	Words and Phrases
Beginning		
End		

Write About an Event

You have been writing paragraphs and descriptions from different points of view throughout the unit. Now is the time to use what you have learned and practiced. Suppose that you are writing a story in which a party takes place. Write a page or two describing the party and what happens there.

If you have any questions about the writing process, refer to Using the Writing Process beginning on page 306.

- You should have four completed writing assignments for this unit: *a)* notes about what you see and feel at a party, *b)* two descriptions of a party from the first- and third-person points of view, *c)* a paragraph written from the first-person point of view with someone besides you as the narrator, and *d)* two descriptions of parties with different moods. Reread these pieces of writing now. Jot down ideas about your thoughts and feelings about parties and family get-togethers.

- Decide on your narrator. Will it be someone in the story telling about the event from the first-person point of view? Or will the narrator be someone outside the story who can see into everyone's mind? Will the event be described from the third-person limited point of view, with the narrator seeing and reporting on what only one person sees and thinks?

- Decide who the characters will be. Think about what will happen at the party. Write a simple outline of the events.

- Think about what mood you want to create and what the narrator's tone will be. Then write your account of the party. Make sure your narrator is clear and consistent in reporting what is happening.

- Reread what you have written to make sure that all the parts work together smoothly. Share your writing with a partner for feedback. Ask your partner to point out details that you might have missed.

- Revise your writing. Proofread for spelling, grammar, and punctuation errors. Share your writing with the class or continue writing, making the party one event in a longer story. Keep a corrected copy of your work in your writing portfolio.

Unit 6 Theme

Many Moons
by James Thurber

The Richer, the Poorer
by Dorothy West

About the Illustration

Describe these two scenes from "Many Moons" and the people who appear in them. Talk about what might be happening here. Use details from the illustration as clues. Give reasons for your answers.

These questions will help you begin to think about the story.

- Where do you think this action takes place? How might the characters be related?

- Why do you suppose the man on the throne looks worried?

- Do you think this story is about the real world? Why or why not?

- Do you expect this story to be serious or funny? What hints in the illustration make you think as you do?

Unit 6

Introduction

About the Story: Many Moons

In a fairy-tale land, the princess is sick and says she must have the moon in order to get well. The king calls on his Lord High Chamberlain, Royal Wizard, and Royal Mathematician for advice on how to obtain the moon. His advisors claim nobody can get it from the sky. His Court Jester, however, goes to the princess for a solution. She describes the moon as a gold object the size of a necklace charm. The Jester has such a charm made and the princess gets well. However, as the next night approaches, the king worries about how the princess will react to seeing the moon in the sky once more. Will she think her "moon" is a fake and get sick again? Read the story to find out who, if anyone, can relieve the king's worries.

About the Author

James Thurber (1894–1961) was one of the most famous American humor writers of the twentieth century, noted for both his comic writing and cartoonlike drawings. He was born in Columbus, Ohio, and worked there as a newspaper reporter before moving to New York and being hired by *The New Yorker* magazine in 1927. It was in *The New Yorker* that many of his short stories, fables, and cartoons first appeared. During the last fifteen years of his life, Thurber was almost blind.

Thurber's favorite theme was the anxieties of the average person in modern society. Usually, the men in his tales are dominated by their wives and children, and they escape their frustrations through daydreams. Perhaps his most famous short story is "The Secret Life of Walter Mitty," about a henpecked man who has persistent fantasies about being a hero in thrilling adventures. Thurber also wrote several books, a play, and the autobiographical *My Life and Hard Times*.

About the Story: The Richer, the Poorer

Two sisters, Lottie and Bess, grow up with different attitudes toward life. Practical Lottie takes on paying jobs as a child, gets a part-time job in high school, and dedicates the next forty or more years to doing her job. She lives in a miserly way, saving for her old age. Bess has a good time in school and marries her high-school boyfriend right after graduation. She travels with her musician husband from city to city as he plays in various bands until his death. Then, penniless, she accepts Lottie's grudging offer to take her in. As Lottie prepares a room, and then her whole house, for Bess's arrival, she makes a startling discovery about which of the two is richer and which is poorer.

About the Author

Dorothy West (1909–   ) is the last surviving member of the Harlem Renaissance, a great flowering of African American art and literature of the 1920s and 1930s. Her friends included such great writers as Langston Hughes and Zora Neale Hurston. West was born in Boston and attended Boston University and the Columbia University School of Journalism. During the time she lived in New York, she edited two African American literary magazines and worked as a relief investigator in Harlem. In time, she was able to earn enough money from her short stories to become a full-time writer. For the past fifty years, she has lived in Martha's Vineyard, an island off Massachusetts.

West frequently writes about the problems of class and race, especially for middle class African Americans. In addition to her short stories, she has written two novels: *The Living Is Easy,* published in 1948, and *The Wedding,* published in 1995. In 1995, she also published a collection called *The Richer, the Poorer: Stories, Sketches, and Reminiscences.*

About the Lessons

The lessons that follow "Many Moons" and "The Richer, the Poorer" focus on the theme in a short story.

In addition to the specific actions in a story, a writer usually presents certain ideas, feelings, or messages about life or human nature. These ideas or attitudes are called *themes.* A theme may be described in a phrase, such as "the importance of family," or in a sentence, such as "Family ties give family members strength." Often, the writer has one or more themes in mind from the time he or she begins to develop a story. The writer consciously uses many techniques to bring out these ideas or feelings.

Writing: Developing a Theme

After you read the two stories in this unit, you will learn how to use story elements and various writers' techniques to develop themes in your own writing. The following suggestions will help you start thinking about themes that are important to you.

1. Think of moments that have been memorable to you—a joyful reunion with a friend, your first scary night at home alone, or

disappointment with something that you worked hard to get. What did you learn about life from that experience? Try to state that lesson or idea in a general way, so that another person will understand what you mean. Here are some examples:

- It takes effort to make and keep friends, but they're worth it.

- Growing up is not always a pleasant experience.

- Be careful about what you wish for, because you may get it.

2. Write the titles of two or three of your favorite stories. What do you like about each story? What do you think its theme might be—what message do you get from it? Beside each title, write a sentence that expresses its theme. Compare your titles and themes with those of others who have read the same stories.

3. Brainstorm some ideas about life that you consider important. You might feel strongly that music is a source of great joy or that the destruction caused by misuse of natural resources is a serious problem. List at least six possible themes that you might write about.

Before Reading

The questions below will help you see how the authors have developed the themes in "Many Moons" and "The Richer, the Poorer." As you read each story, keep these questions in mind:

- What aspect of life is highlighted by the conflict in the story?

- What message about life do you learn from what the characters say and do?

- How do the story's tone and mood reinforce the theme?

Vocabulary Tips

These stories include some words that may be unfamiliar to you but are useful for understanding the story. Below, you will find some of these words, their definitions, and sentences that show how the words are used. Look over the words before you begin to read.

Many Moons

surfeit   too much of anything, especially food and drink. Many children at the party had stomachaches from a <u>surfeit</u> of sweets.

compound to mix various parts to make something. We <u>compounded</u> modeling clay from flour, salt, and water.

cascade   a small waterfall or something looking like a waterfall. The skirt of the bridal gown was made of <u>cascades</u> of silk cloth.

The Richer, the Poorer

miserly   stingy; having the characteristic of storing money. Frankie had <u>miserly</u> habits, never spending a penny that he wasn't forced to spend.

frugally in a thrifty, not wasteful manner. The large family lived <u>frugally</u> but comfortably on Mr. Smith's small income.

dowdy   shabby; not stylish. I wouldn't be seen dead in that <u>dowdy</u> dress I found at the back of my closet!

dismal   gloomy. It was such a <u>dismal</u> day that we never saw the sun at all.

giddy   dizzy; lightheaded. Many people enjoy the <u>giddy</u> feeling they get from amusement park rides.

Many Moons

James Thurber

ONCE UPON A TIME, in a kingdom by the sea, there lived a little Princess named Lenore. She was ten years old, going on eleven. One day Lenore fell ill of a surfeit of raspberry tarts and took to her bed.

The Royal Physician came to see her and took her temperature and felt her pulse and made her stick out her tongue. The Royal Physician was worried. He sent for the King, Lenore's father, and the King came to see her.

"I will get you anything your heart desires," the King said. "Is there anything your heart desires?"

"Yes," said the Princess. "I want the moon. If I can have the moon, I will be well again."

Now the King had a great many wise men who always got for him anything he wanted, so he told his daughter that she could have the moon. Then he went to the throne room and pulled a bell cord, three long pulls and a short pull, and presently the Lord High Chamberlain came into the room.

The Lord High Chamberlain was a large, fat man who wore thick glasses which made his eyes seem twice as big as they really were. This made the Lord High Chamberlain seem twice as wise as he really was.

"I want you to get the moon," said the King. "The Princess Lenore wants the moon. If she can have the moon, she will get well again."

"The moon?" exclaimed the Lord High Chamberlain, his eyes widening. This made him look four times as wise as he really was.

"Yes, the moon," said the King. "M-o-o-n, moon. Get it tonight, tomorrow at the latest."

The Lord High Chamberlain wiped his forehead with a handkerchief and then blew his nose loudly. "I have got a great many things for you in my time, your Majesty," he said. "It just happens that I have with me a list of the things I have got for you in my time." He pulled a long scroll of parchment out of his pocket. "Let me see, now." He glanced at the list, frowning. "I have got ivory, apes, and peacocks, rubies, opals, and emeralds, black orchids, pink elephants, and blue poodles, gold bugs, scarabs, and flies in amber, hummingbirds' tongues, angels' feathers, and unicorns' horns, giants, midgets, and mermaids, frankincense, ambergris, and myrrh, troubadours, minstrels, and dancing women, a pound of butter, two dozen eggs, and a sack of sugar—sorry, my wife wrote that in there."

"I don't remember any blue poodles," said the King.

"It says blue poodles right here on the list, and they are checked off with a little check mark," said the Lord High Chamberlain. "So there must have been blue poodles. You just forget."

"Never mind the blue poodles," said the King. "What I want now is the moon."

"I have sent as far as Samarkand and Araby and Zanzibar to get things for you, your Majesty," said the Lord High Chamberlain. "But the moon is out of the question. It is 35,000 miles away and it is bigger than the room the Princess lies in. Furthermore, it is made of molten copper. I cannot get the moon for you. Blue poodles, yes; the moon, no."

The King flew into a rage and told the Lord High Chamberlain to leave the room and to send the Royal Wizard to the throne room.

The Royal Wizard was a little, thin man with a long face. He wore a high red peaked hat covered with silver stars, and a long blue robe covered with golden owls. His face grew very pale when the King told him that he wanted the moon for his little daughter, and that he expected the Royal Wizard to get it.

"I have worked a great deal of magic for you in my time, your Majesty," said the Royal Wizard. "As a matter of fact, I just happen to have in my pocket a list of the wizardries I have performed for you." He drew a paper from a deep pocket of his robe. "It begins: 'Dear Royal Wizard: I am returning herewith the so-called philosopher's stone which you claimed—' no, that isn't it." The Royal Wizard brought a long scroll of parchment from another pocket of his robe. "Here it is," he said. "Now, let's see. I have squeezed blood out of turnips for you, and turnips out of blood. I have produced rabbits out of silk hats, and silk hats out of rabbits. I have conjured up flowers, tambourines, and doves out of nowhere, and nowhere out of flowers, tambourines, and doves. I have brought you divining rods, magic wands, and crystal spheres in which to behold the future. I have compounded philters, unguents, and potions, to cure heartbreak, surfeit, and ringing in the ears. I have made you my own special mixture of wolfbane, nightshade, and eagles' tears, to ward off witches, demons, and things that go bump in the night. I have given you seven-league boots, the golden touch, and a cloak of invisibility—"

"It didn't work," said the King. "The cloak of invisibility didn't work."

"Yes, it did," said the Royal Wizard.

"No, it didn't," said the King. "I kept bumping into things, the same as ever."

"The cloak is supposed to make you invisible," said the Royal Wizard. "It is not supposed to keep you from bumping into things."

"All I know is, I kept bumping into things," said the King.

The Royal Wizard looked at his list again. "I got you," he said, "horns from Elfland, sand from the Sandman, and gold from the rainbow. Also a spool of thread, a paper of needles, and a lump of beeswax—sorry, those are things my wife wrote down for me to get her."

"What I want you to do now," said the King, "is to get me the moon. The Princess Lenore wants the moon, and when she gets it, she will be well again."

"Nobody can get the moon," said the Royal Wizard. "It is 150,000 miles away, and it is made of green cheese, and it is twice as big as this palace."

The King flew into another rage and sent the Royal Wizard back to his cave. Then he rang a gong and summoned the Royal Mathematician.

The Royal Mathematician was a bald-headed, near-sighted man, with a skullcap on his head and a pencil behind each ear. He wore a black suit with white numbers on it.

"I don't want to hear a long list of all the things you have figured out for me since 1907," the King said to him. "I want you to figure out right now how to get the moon for the Princess Lenore. When she gets the moon, she will be well again."

"I am glad you mentioned all the things I have figured out for you since 1907," said the Royal Mathematician. "It so happens that I have a list of them with me."

He pulled a long scroll of parchment out of a pocket and looked at it. "Now let me see. I have figured out for you the distance between the horns of a dilemma, night and day, and A and Z. I have computed how far is Up, how long it takes to get to Away, and what becomes of Gone. I have discovered the length of the sea serpent, the price of the priceless, and the square of the hippopotamus. I know where you are when you are at Sixes and Sevens, how much Is you have to have to make an Are, and how many birds you can catch with the salt in the ocean—187,796,132, if it would interest you to know."

"There aren't that many birds," said the King.

"I didn't say there were," said the Royal Mathematician. "I said if there were."

"I don't want to hear about seven hundred million imaginary birds," said the King. "I want you to get the moon for the Princess Lenore."

"The moon is 300,000 miles away," said the Royal Mathematician. "It is round and flat like a coin, only it is made of asbestos, and it is half the size of this kingdom. Furthermore, it is pasted on the sky. Nobody can get the moon."

The King flew into still another rage and sent the Royal Mathematician away. Then he rang for the Court Jester. The Jester came bounding into the throne room in his motley and his cap and bells, and sat at the foot of the throne.

"What can I do for you, your Majesty?" asked the Court Jester.

"Nobody can do anything for me," said the King mournfully. "The Princess Lenore wants the moon, and she cannot be well till she gets it, but nobody can get it for her. Every time I ask anybody for the moon, it gets larger and farther away. There is nothing you can do for me except play on your lute. Something sad."

"How big do they say the moon is," asked the Court Jester, "and how far away?"

"The Lord High Chamberlain says it is 35,000 miles away, and bigger than the Princess Lenore's room," said the King. "The Royal Wizard says it is 150,000 miles away, and twice as big as this palace. The Royal Mathematician says it is 300,000 miles away, and half the size of this kingdom."

The Court Jester strummed on his lute for a little while. "They are all wise men," he said, "and so they must all be right. If they are all right, then the moon must be just as large and as far away as each person thinks it is. The thing to do is find out how big the Princess Lenore thinks it is, and how far away."

"I never thought of that," said the King.

"I will go and ask her, your Majesty," said the Court Jester. And he crept softly into the little girl's room.

The Princess Lenore was awake, and she was glad to see the Court Jester, but her face was very pale and her voice very weak.

"Have you brought the moon to me?" she asked.

"Not yet," said the Court Jester, "but I will get it for you right away. How big do you think it is?"

"It is just a little smaller than my thumbnail," she said, "for when I hold my thumbnail up at the moon, it just covers it."

"And how far away is it?" asked the Court Jester.

"It is not as high as the big tree outside my window," said the Princess, "for sometimes it gets caught in the top branches."

"It will be very easy to get the moon for you," said the Court Jester. "I will climb the tree tonight when it gets caught in the top branches and bring it to you."

Then he thought of something else. "What is the moon made of, Princess?" he asked.

"Oh," she said, "it's made of gold, of course, silly."

The Court Jester left the Princess Lenore's room and went to see the Royal Goldsmith. He had the Royal Goldsmith make a tiny round golden moon, just a little smaller than the thumbnail of the Princess Lenore. Then he had him string it on a golden chain so the Princess could wear it around her neck.

"What is this thing I have made?" asked the Royal Goldsmith when he had finished it.

"You have made the moon," said the Court Jester. "That is the moon."

"But the moon," said the Royal Goldsmith, "is 500,000 miles away and is made of bronze and is round like a marble."

"That's what you think," said the Court Jester as he went away with the moon.

The Court Jester took the moon to the Princess Lenore, and she was overjoyed. The next day she was well again and could get up and go out in the gardens to play.

But the King's worries were not yet over. He knew that the moon would shine in the sky again that night, and he did not want the Princess Lenore to see it. If she did, she would know that the moon she wore on a chain around her neck was not the real moon.

So the King sent for the Lord High Chamberlain and said, "We must keep the Princess Lenore from seeing the moon when it shines in the sky tonight. Think of something."

The Lord High Chamberlain tapped his forehead with his fingers thoughtfully and said, "I know just the thing. We can make some dark glasses for the Princess Lenore. We can make them so dark that she will not be able to see anything at all through them. Then she will not be able to see the moon when it shines in the sky."

This made the King very angry, and he shook his head from side to side. "If she wore dark glasses, she would bump into things," he said, "and then she would be ill again." So he sent the Lord High Chamberlain away and called the Royal Wizard.

"We must hide the moon," said the King, "so that the Princess Lenore will not see it when it shines in the sky tonight. How are we going to do that?"

The Royal Wizard stood on his hands and then he stood on his head and then he stood on his feet again. "I know what we can do," he said. "We can stretch some black velvet curtains on poles. The curtains will cover all the palace gardens like a circus tent, and the Princess Lenore will not be able to see through them, so she will not see the moon in the sky."

The King was so angry at this that he waved his arms around. "Black velvet curtains would keep out the air," he said. "The Princess Lenore would not be able to breathe, and she would be ill again." So he sent the Royal Wizard away and summoned the Royal Mathematician.

"We must do something," said the King, "so that the Princess Lenore will not see the moon when it shines in the sky tonight. If you know so much, figure out a way to do that."

The Royal Mathematician walked around in a circle, and then he walked around in a square, and then he stood still. "I have it!" he said. "We can set off fireworks in the gardens every night. We will make a lot of silver fountains and golden cascades, and when they go off they will fill the sky with so many sparks that it will be as light as day and the Princess Lenore will not be able to see the moon."

The King flew into such a rage that he began jumping up and down. "Fireworks would keep the Princess Lenore awake," he said. "She would not get any sleep at all and she would be ill again." So the King sent the Royal Mathematician away.

When he looked up again, it was dark outside and he saw the bright rim of the moon just peeping over the horizon. He jumped up in a great fright and rang for the Court Jester. The Court Jester came bounding into the room and sat down at the foot of the throne.

"What can I do for you, your Majesty?" he asked.

"Nobody can do anything for me," said the King mournfully. "The moon is coming up again. It will shine into the Princess Lenore's bedroom, and she will know it is still in the sky and that she does not wear it on a golden chain around her neck. Play me something on your lute, something very sad, for when the Princess sees the moon, she will be ill again."

The Court Jester strummed on his lute. "What do your wise men say?" he asked.

"They can think of no way to hide the moon that will not make the Princess Lenore ill," said the King.

The Court Jester played another song, very softly. "Your wise men know everything," he said, "and if they cannot hide the moon, then it cannot be hidden."

The King put his head in his hands again and sighed. Suddenly he jumped up from his throne and pointed to the windows. "Look!" he cried. "The moon is already shining into the Princess Lenore's bedroom. Who can explain how the moon can be shining in the sky when it is hanging on a golden chain around her neck?"

The Court Jester stopped playing on his lute. "Who could explain how to get the moon when your wise men said it was too large and too far away? It was the Princess Lenore. Therefore, the Princess Lenore is wiser than your wise men and knows more about the moon than they do. So I will ask *her*." And before the King could stop him, the Court Jester slipped quietly out of the throne room and up the wide marble staircase to the Princess Lenore's bedroom.

The Princess was lying in bed, but she was wide awake and she was looking out the window at the moon shining in the sky. Shining in her hand was the moon the Court Jester had got for her. He looked very sad, and there seemed to be tears in his eyes.

"Tell me, Princess Lenore," he said mournfully, "how can the moon be shining in the sky when it is hanging on a golden chain around your neck?"

The Princess looked at him and laughed. "That is easy, silly," she said. "When I lose a tooth, a new one grows in its place, doesn't it?"

"Of course," said the Court Jester. "And when the unicorn loses his horn in the forest, a new one grows in the middle of his forehead."

"That is right," said the Princess. "And when the Royal Gardener cuts the flowers in the garden, other flowers come to take their place."

"I should have thought of that," said the Court Jester, "for it is the same way with the daylight."

"And it is the same way with the moon," said the Princess Lenore. "I guess it is the same way with everything." Her voice became very low and faded away, and the Court Jester saw that she was asleep. Gently he tucked the covers in around the sleeping Princess.

But before he left the room, he went over to the window and winked at the moon, for it seemed to the Court Jester that the moon had winked at him.

Reviewing and Interpreting the Story

Record your answers to these comprehension questions in your personal literature notebook. Follow the directions for each part.

Reviewing Try to complete each of these sentences without looking back at the story.

Recalling Facts

1. The King was disappointed in the cloak of invisibility because

    a. it cost more than his seven-league boots.

    b. he bumped into things when he wore it.

    c. it didn't make him invisible.

    d. it didn't fit him.

Understanding Main Ideas

2. The King wants the moon for his daughter because

    a. he wants to keep his advisors busy.

    b. no other king's daughter has one.

    c. she has asked for it.

    d. he wants to impress his subjects.

Recognizing Story Elements (Conflict)

3. The King's major worry in this story is

    a. ruling his country fairly.

    b. finding reliable advisors.

    c. keeping his daughter well and happy.

    d. paying for nightly fireworks.

4. The King asks the Court Jester for a sad
   song immediately after

   a. the Princess falls ill.

   b. the Lord High Chamberlain tells the
      King the Princess cannot have the
      moon.

   c. all three advisors give the King answers
      he dislikes.

   d. the Court Jester talks with the
      Princess.

5. The Princess thinks the moon is small
   because

   a. she herself is small.

   b. when she looks at it through her win-
      dow, she can cover it with her thumb-
      nail.

   c. the Lord High Chamberlain and the
      Royal Wizard told her that it is small.

   d. she knows it is far away.

Interpreting   To answer these questions, you may look back at the
story if you like.

6. Which of these phrases most clearly tells
   the reader that the setting is imaginary?

   a. "once upon a time"

   b. "a surfeit of raspberry tarts"

   c. "wore a high red peaked hat covered
      with silver stars"

   d. "wiped his forehead with a handker-
      chief"

7. Which of these statements about the Court
Jester is most likely false?

    a. He wants the Lord High Chamberlain's
    job.

    b. He knows that criticizing the King's
    advisors will get him into trouble.

    c. He sincerely likes the King.

    d. He is very wise.

8. The next time the King tells the Court
Jester his problems, the Court Jester will
probably

    a. go to the Princess for her ideas.

    b. point out that the King's advisors aren't
    doing their job.

    c. recommend that the King give up the
    throne.

    d. have a sensible suggestion to offer.

9. A real-life truth that this story illustrates
is that

    a. nobody knows what the moon is made
    of.

    b. little girls are generally smarter than
    everyone else.

    c. government officials are never right.

    d. not everyone sees a problem the same
    way.

10. The climax of this story occurs when the

a. Court Jester winks at the moon.

b. Court Jester asks the Princess how the moon can be in the sky and on a chain, too.

c. King flies into a rage with the Royal Mathematician for suggesting that fireworks be set off every night.

d. King sees that it is dark outside and he knows that the Princess will see the moon.

Now check your answers with your teacher. Study the questions you answered incorrectly. What types of questions were they? Talk with your teacher about ways to work on those skills.

The Richer, the Poorer

Dorothy West

Over the years Lottie had urged Bess to prepare for her old age. Over the years Bess had lived each day as if there were no other. Now they were both past sixty, the time for summing up. Lottie had a bank account that had never grown lean. Bess had the clothes on her back, and the rest of her worldly possessions in a battered suitcase.

Lottie had hated being a child, hearing her parents' skimping and scraping. Bess had never seemed to notice. All she ever wanted was to go outside and play. She learned to skate on borrowed skates. She rode a borrowed bicycle. Lottie couldn't wait to grow up and buy herself the best of everything.

As soon as anyone would hire her, Lottie put herself to work. She minded babies, she ran errands for the old.

She never touched a penny of her money, though her child's mouth watered for ice cream and candy. But she could not bear to share with Bess, who never had anything to share with her. When the dimes began to add up to dollars, she lost her taste for sweets.

By the time she was twelve, she was clerking after school in a small variety store. Saturdays she worked as long as she was wanted. She decided to keep her money for clothes. When she entered high school, she would wear a wardrobe that neither she nor anyone else would be able to match.

But her freshman year found her unable to indulge so frivolous a whim, particularly when her admiring instructors advised her to think seriously of college. No one in her family had ever gone to college, and certainly Bess would never get there. She would show them all what she could do, if she put her mind to it.

She began to bank her money, and her bank became her most private and precious possession.

In her third year high she found a job in a small but expanding restaurant, where she cashiered from the busy hour until closing. In her last year high the business increased so rapidly that Lottie was faced with the choice of staying in school or working full time.

She made her choice easily. A job in hand was worth two in the future.

Bess had a beau in the school band, who had no other ambition except to play a horn. Lottie expected to be settled with a home and family while Bess was still waiting for Harry to earn enough to buy a marriage license.

That Bess married Harry straight out of high school was not surprising. That Lottie never married at all was not really surprising either. Two or three times she was halfway persuaded, but to give up a job that paid well for a homemaking job that paid nothing was a risk she was incapable of taking.

Bess's married life was nothing for Lottie to envy. She and Harry lived like gypsies, Harry playing in second-rate bands all over the country, even getting himself and Bess stranded in Europe. They were often in rags and never in riches.

Bess grieved because she had no child, not having sense enough to know she was better off without one.

Lottie was certainly better off without nieces and nephews to feel sorry for. Very likely Bess would have dumped them on her doorstep.

That Lottie had a doorstep they might have been left on was only because her boss, having bought a second house, offered Lottie his first house at a price so low and terms so reasonable that it would have been like losing money to refuse.

She shut off the rooms she didn't use, letting them go to rack and ruin. Since she ate her meals out, she had no food at home, and did not encourage callers, who always expected a cup of tea.

Her way of life was mean and miserly, but she did not know it. She thought she lived frugally in her middle years so that she could live in comfort and ease when she most needed peace of mind.

The years, after forty, began to race. Suddenly Lottie was sixty, and retired from her job by her boss's son, who had no sentimental feeling about keeping her on until she was ready to quit.

She made several attempts to find other employment, but her dowdy appearance made her look old and inefficient. For the first time in her life Lottie would gladly have worked for nothing, to have some place to go, something to do with her day.

Harry died abroad, in a third-rate hotel, with Bess weeping as hard as if he had left her a fortune. He had left her nothing but his horn. There wasn't even money for her passage home.

Lottie, trapped by the blood tie, knew she would not only have to send for her sister, but take her in when she returned. It didn't seem fair that Bess should reap the harvest of Lottie's lifetime of self-denial.

It took Lottie a week to get a bedroom ready, a week

of hard work and hard cash. There was everything to do, everything to replace or paint. When she was through the room looked so fresh and new that Lottie felt she deserved it more than Bess.

She would let Bess have her room, but the mattress was so lumpy, the carpet so worn, the curtains so threadbare that Lottie's conscience pricked her. She supposed she would have to redo that room, too, and went about doing it with an eagerness that she mistook for haste.

When she was through upstairs, she was shocked to see how dismal downstairs looked by comparison. She tried to ignore it, but with nowhere to go to escape it, the contrast grew more intolerable.

She worked her way from kitchen to parlor, persuading herself she was only putting the rooms to right to give herself something to do. At night she slept like a child after a long and happy day of playing house. She was having more fun than she had ever had in her life. She was living each hour for itself.

There was only a day now before Bess would arrive. Passing her gleaming mirrors, at first with vague awareness, then with painful clarity, Lottie saw herself as others saw her, and could not stand the sight.

She went on a spending spree from specialty shops to beauty salon, emerging transformed into a woman who believed in miracles.

She was in the kitchen basting a turkey when Bess rang the bell. Her heart raced, and she wondered if the heat from the oven was responsible.

She went to the door, and Bess stood before her. Stiffly she suffered Bess's embrace, her heart racing harder, her eyes suddenly smarting from the onrush of cold air.

"Oh, Lottie, it's good to see you," Bess said, but saying

nothing about Lottie's splendid appearance. Upstairs Bess, putting down her shabby suitcase, said, "I'll sleep like a rock tonight," without a word of praise for her lovely room. At the lavish table, top-heavy with turkey, Bess said, "I'll take light and dark both," with no marveling at the size of the bird, or that there was turkey for two elderly women, one of them too poor to buy her own bread.

With the glow of good food in her stomach, Bess began to spin stories. They were rich with places and people, most of them lowly, all of them magnificent. Her face reflected her telling, the joys and sorrows of her remembering, and above all, the love she lived by that enhanced the poorest place, the humblest person.

Then it was that Lottie knew why Bess had made no mention of her finery, or the shining room, or the twelve-pound turkey. She had not even seen them. Tomorrow she would see the room as it really looked, and Lottie as she really looked, and the warmed-over turkey in its second-day glory. Tonight she saw only what she had come seeking, a place in her sister's home and heart.

She said, "That's enough about me. How have the years used you?"

"It was me who didn't use them," said Lottie wistfully. "I saved for them. I forgot the best of them would go without my ever spending a day or a dollar enjoying them. That's my life story in those few words, a life never lived.

"Now it's too near the end to try."

Bess said, "To know how much there is to know is the beginning of learning to live. Don't count the years that are left us. At our time of life it's the days that count. You've too much catching up to do to waste a minute of a waking hour feeling sorry for yourself."

Lottie grinned, a real wide open grin, "Well, to tell the truth I felt sorry for you. Maybe if I had any sense I'd feel sorry for myself, after all. I know I'm too old to kick up my heels, but I'm going to let you show me how. If I land on my head, I guess it won't matter. I feel giddy already, and I like it."

Reviewing and Interpreting the Story

Record your answers to these comprehension questions in your personal literature notebook. Follow the directions for each part.

Reviewing   Try to complete each of these sentences without looking back at the story.

Recalling Facts

1. The first day that Bess was in Lottie's home, she

   a. complained about her loneliness.

   b. argued with Lottie.

   c. praised Lottie for the fine way she had decorated the house.

   d. didn't even notice the rooms and furnishings.

Recognizing Story Elements (Language)

2. The crucial difference between Lottie and Bess is that

   a. Lottie has always been happy and Bess has always been unhappy.

   b. Lottie is rich and Bess is poor.

   c. Lottie saves for her life in the future and Bess spends her life in the present.

   d. Lottie stays single and Bess gets married.

Identifying Cause and Effect

3. Lottie didn't go to college because

   a. she wasn't very smart.

   b. she didn't want to give up her job at the restaurant.

   c. nobody else in her family had ever gone to college.

   d. her clothes weren't nice enough.

4. During the years Lottie worked at the
restaurant, she

   a. was popular with her coworkers.
   b. was intensely disliked by her coworkers.
   c. was easily frightened by other people.
   d. had few friends.

5. The last thing Lottie did before Bess
arrived was

   a. improve her own appearance.
   b. redecorate a bedroom for Bess.
   c. redecorate the downstairs of the house.
   d. polish her mirrors.

Interpreting   To answer these questions, you may look back at the
story if you like.

6. This story is told from the third-person
point of view, that is, using *she* instead of
I, but the facts and opinions it states come
from

   a. Lottie.
   b. Bess.
   c. one of Lottie's neighbors.
   d. an all-knowing narrator.

7. From the fact that Lottie spent money freely to fix up her house and then go on "a spending spree," you can tell that she

    a. expected to die soon and, therefore, didn't need to save her money any longer.

    b. didn't care if she went into debt.

    c. had saved far more for her old age than she needed.

    d. figured Bess would eventually pay her back.

8. After the end of the story, Lottie will probably

    a. go back to her old miserly ways.

    b. enjoy life far more than before.

    c. make sure Bess doesn't spend too much.

    d. apply for Social Security.

9. Before Lottie's change of heart, she believed that

    a. a person's first duty is to take care of herself financially.

    b. you get out of life only what you put in.

    c. it's important to live each day to the fullest.

    d. a thing of beauty is a joy forever.

Understanding
Story Elements
(Author's
Purpose)

10. The author never specifically states what either sister looks like so that

   a. she could write the story quickly.

   b. readers would more easily recognize that the story can apply to everyone.

   c. no one would discover that she couldn't write exact descriptions.

   d. readers could imagine that the two women are identical twins.

Now check your answers with your teacher. Study the questions you answered incorrectly. What types of questions were they? Talk with your teacher about ways to work on those skills.

Theme

You have probably read or heard many fables. One fable, for example, tells about a father who gives his sons a bundle of sticks and asks them to break the sticks. The sons try, but they cannot break the sticks. Then the father separates the bundle into single sticks, and the sons break them easily. This fable ends with a statement of its moral, or theme, "In unity there is strength." The theme is not about sticks at all; the sticks simply illustrate the lesson the storyteller wanted to teach.

Like a fable, a story usually has one or more ideas or messages underlying the action. Most stories, however, do not state their themes directly. Instead, writers use events, characters, and all the other elements of a good story to lead the reader to recognize the message or lesson. The most important theme of a story is not necessarily obvious. A reader may need to complete the story and then reflect on it before deciding why the writer chose to develop the story as he or she did.

In this lesson, we will look at the themes of "Many Moons" and "The Richer, the Poorer" and some techniques that authors James Thurber and Dorothy West use to develop their themes:

1. The author stresses themes through the conflicts that he or she develops in a story.

2. He or she uses the character's words and actions to suggest themes.

3. He or she reinforces themes by using the appropriate tone and mood in the story.

1 • Theme and Conflict

James Thurber's favorite themes include the confusion and frustration a person experiences in dealing with everyday life. The person's family, job, or encounters with technology can produce this frustration. Notice how these themes are brought out in "Many Moons" through the conflicts the king experiences.

First, the king wants to please his daughter, so he promises her the moon. However, he is totally at a loss as to how he will fulfill this promise. Then the advisors upon whom he relies for help give him no satisfaction.

> "I want you to get the moon," said the King. "The Princess Lenore wants the moon. If she can have the moon, she will get well again."
>
> "The moon?" exclaimed the Lord High Chamberlain, his eyes widening. This made him look four times as wise as he really was.
>
> "Yes, the moon," said the King. "M-o-o-n, moon. Get it tonight, tomorrow at the latest."
>
> The Lord High Chamberlain wiped his forehead with a handkerchief and then blew his nose loudly. "I have got a great many things for you in my time, your Majesty," he said. . . .
>
> "But the moon is out of the question. It is 35,000 miles away and it is bigger than the room the Princess lies in. Furthermore, it is made of molten copper. I cannot get the moon for you. Blue poodles, yes; the moon, no."
>
> The King flew into a rage and told the Lord High Chamberlain to leave the room and to send the Royal Wizard to the throne room.

An important theme in the story is the idea that wisdom is found in unexpected places. It is not the advisors with all their titles who discover the answer to the King's problems; it is the supposed fool, the Court Jester. He has the intelligence to go to the same child who started the king's problems. Lenore sees what the adults overlooked.

> "Tell me, Princess Lenore," he said mournfully, "how can the moon be shining in the sky when it is hanging on a golden chain around your neck?"

The Princess looked at him and laughed. "That is easy, silly," she said. "When I lose a tooth, a new one grows in its place, doesn't it?"

Exercise 1

Read this passage from "The Richer, the Poorer," about Lottie after her forced retirement and the death of Bess's husband. Use what you have learned in this lesson to answer the questions that follow.

> She made several attempts to find other employment, but her dowdy appearance made her look old and inefficient. For the first time in her life Lottie would gladly have worked for nothing, to have some place to go, something to do with her day. . . .
>
> Lottie, trapped by the blood tie, knew she would not only have to send for her sister, but take her in when she returned. It didn't seem fair that Bess should reap the harvest of Lottie's lifetime of self-denial.
>
> It took Lottie a week to get a bedroom ready, a week of hard work and hard cash. There was everything to do, everything to replace or paint. When she was through the room looked so fresh and new that Lottie felt she deserved it more than Bess.

1. Why is Lottie so unhappy when she has free time? Is she in need of the money she would earn at a job? What feelings is she in conflict with? Does this conflict have more to do with the wise use of money or the wise use of time?

2. In the last two paragraphs, with whom does Lottie think she is in conflict? With whom or what is she actually in conflict? Does Lottie have a good reason for never giving herself a nice room earlier? Does this conflict suggest that it is right or wrong to enjoy what you have?

Check your answers with your teacher. Review this part of the lesson if you don't understand why an answer was incorrect.

Writing on Your Own 1

In this exercise you will use what you learned in the lesson to write a story beginning based on a theme you choose. Review your ideas for Developing a Theme on pages 191–192. Follow these steps:

- Choose one of the themes you listed. Think of a combination of conflict and characters that reflects the theme. For example, the difficulties of growing up could be brought out in a story about a girl dealing with dares by her friends, or one about a boy facing and accepting responsibilities at home. A story about the importance of music might involve humans resisting an invasion by space aliens who banish music. Write a brief paragraph describing the theme, the conflict, and the major characters.

- Write a story beginning that introduces the characters and gets the conflict under way. Include details or observations that support the theme you selected.

- You may want to change and rewrite your story beginning several times to make sure the events bring attention to your theme.

2 • Theme and Character

The actions and words of characters in a story often suggest important themes. From the first lines of "The Richer, the Poorer," for example, Lottie and Bess illustrate two different ways of looking at life:

> Over the years Lottie had urged Bess to prepare for her old age. Over the years Bess had lived each day as if there were no other. Now they were both past sixty, the time for summing up. Lottie had a bank account that had never grown lean. Bess had the clothes on her back, and the rest of her worldly possessions in a battered suitcase.

This introduction to the two sisters suggests that Lottie is not only more practical but also more sensible than Bess. But the following paragraphs, which detail Lottie's actions from childhood to the present, bring out another feeling.

As soon as anyone would hire her, Lottie put herself to work. She minded babies, she ran errands for the old.

She never touched a penny of her money, though her child's mouth watered for ice cream and candy. But she could not bear to share with Bess, who never had anything to share with her. When the dimes began to add up to dollars, she lost her taste for sweets.

. . . She decided to keep her money for clothes. When she entered high school, she would wear a wardrobe that neither she nor anyone else would be able to match.

But her freshman year found her unable to indulge so frivolous a whim, particularly when her admiring instructors advised her to think seriously of college. . . .

In her last year high the business increased so rapidly that Lottie was faced with the choice of staying in school or working full-time.

She made her choice easily. A job in hand was worth two in the future.

Time after time Lottie tells herself she is saving for a worthy goal, yet time after time, as soon as the goal is within her reach, she loses interest. Nothing is important to Lottie except acquiring money—not sweets, not clothes, not even learning and proving her abilities in college! Even her plans for entering college are dropped and forgotten when Lottie realizes that she must give up her job to attend classes. By the time the story turns to Bess's life, the reader realizes that Lottie's life has no particular direction or attraction. Lottie may be more practical, but it's difficult to see her as more sensible than Bess.

There is little dialogue in "The Richer, the Poorer," and the few speeches focus on the theme of enjoying life while you can.

"It was me who didn't use them [the years]," said Lottie wistfully. "I saved for them. I forgot the best of them would go without my ever spending a day or a dollar enjoying them. That's my life story in those few words, a life never lived.

"Now it's too near the end to try."

Bess said, "To know how much there is to know is the beginning of learning to live. Don't count the years that are left us. At our time of life it's the days that count. You've too much catching up to do to waste a minute of a waking hour feeling sorry for yourself."

Exercise 2

Read this passage from "Many Moons." It follows the king's complaint about how his three advisors disagree on how big and how far away the moon is. Use what you have learned in this lesson to answer the questions that follow.

The Court Jester strummed on his lute for a little while. "They are all wise men," he said, "and so they must all be right. If they are all right, then the moon must be just as large and as far away as each person thinks it is. The thing to do is find out how big the Princess Lenore thinks it is, and how far away."

"I never thought of that," said the King.

"I will go and ask her, your Majesty," said the Court Jester. And he crept softly into the little girl's room.

1. Can the Court Jester really believe that all three conflicting statements about the moon are correct? Or does he mean that, for all practical purposes, the question really doesn't matter? What attitude toward self-important thinkers do the Court Jester's words suggest?

2. Unlike the advisors, the Court Jester makes no mention of his past services to the king. He wastes no time in talk at all, but immediately puts his plan into effect. Keeping in mind that the Jester's plan is successful, what theme does the author suggest about these differing approaches to planning and taking action?

Check your answers with your teacher. Review this part of the lesson if you don't understand why an answer was incorrect.

Writing on Your Own 2

Now use what you have learned in this lesson to write some dialogue to support a story's theme and to add to your own story. Review your notes and writing for all the exercises in this unit. Then follow these steps:

- Think about how the characters communicate through dialogue in the two stories you've read. "Many Moons" is full of dialogue. The dialogue creates the characters and moves the plot along. The amount of dialogue also indirectly supports the theme, which, ironically, stresses the importance of action over talking.

  In "The Richer, the Poorer," there is no dialogue between the main characters until the end of the story, when the dialogue expresses the theme directly. How do you think the lack of frequent dialogue between the main characters in that story adds to its theme?

  Try writing a dialogue between the two sisters when they were children, teenagers, or young adults. Note where you would place your dialogue within the story. Then reread the story with your dialogue in place and compare the change in the story.

- Write a paragraph describing a block of dialogue you might use in the story beginning you wrote for Writing on Your Own 1. Which characters will be involved? What do they have to say to each other?

- Now write the dialogue you described. Add it to your story beginning. Does the dialogue support your theme directly or indirectly?

3 • Theme, Tone, and Mood

With most themes, the author has a good deal of choice concerning how to focus the theme. Consider, for example, the theme

"There's no place like home." In the movie *The Wizard of Oz,* this theme is brought out in a life-and-death conflict, but the scriptwriter's tone is lighthearted and the story's mood is generally cheerful. In the musical *Fiddler on the Roof,* in which the main characters are driven from their homes forever, the playwright's tone is more serious and the mood, at the end, is sorrowful. Although they use the same general theme, the writers of these two stories develop it in distinctive ways that are appropriate to their audiences and their own purposes.

What tone and mood are developed in "Many Moons"? Read the following passage to discover Thurber's attitude toward his characters. The Royal Wizard is reminding the king of his past services.

> . . . "I have given you seven-league boots, the golden touch, and a cloak of invisibility—"
>
> "It didn't work," said the King. "The cloak of invisibility didn't work."
>
> "Yes, it did," said the Royal Wizard.
>
> "No, it didn't," said the King. "I kept bumping into things, the same as ever."
>
> "The cloak is supposed to make you invisible," said the Royal Wizard. "It is not supposed to keep you from bumping into things."
>
> "All I know is, I kept bumping into things," said the King.

The king's objection to the cloak of invisibility stresses the theme of frustration with technology. At the same time, it makes the humorous point that not even the technology of magic is idiot-proof. The king's silliness, however, is matched by the Royal Wizard, as the two argue "Yes, it did" and "No, it didn't" like children. Clearly, the author thinks these two characters are funny. He encourages the reader to smile at their argument.

Exercise 3

Read the following passage from "The Richer, the Poorer." Use what you have learned in this lesson to answer the questions.

Bess grieved because she had no child, not having sense enough to know she was better off without one. Lottie was certainly better off without nieces and nephews to feel sorry for. Very likely Bess would have dumped them on her doorstep.

That Lottie had a doorstep they might have been left on was only because her boss, having bought a second house, offered Lottie his first house at a price so low and terms so reasonable that it would have been like losing money to refuse.

She shut off the rooms she didn't use, letting them go to rack and ruin. Since she ate her meals out, she had no food at home, and did not encourage callers, who always expected a cup of tea.

1. It is Lottie, not the author, who thinks that Bess is better off without children and that the only feeling Lottie would have toward nieces and nephews is pity. What other shortsighted opinions of Lottie's are brought out in this excerpt?

2. Who suffers as a result of Lottie's opinions? Does the narrator regard Lottie as evil or simply as foolish? How would you describe the narrator's tone, or attitude?

3. What feeling, or mood, do you experience while reading about Lottie—admiration, sympathy, anger, frustration, or some other feeling?

Check your answers with your teacher. Review this part of the lesson if you don't understand why an answer was incorrect.

Writing on Your Own 3

Review your notes and writing for this unit. Then follow these steps:

- Reread the theme statement you chose for Writing on Your Own 1. Write a list of adjectives that describe your feelings as you read. Then write a list of adjectives that describe how you want your readers to feel as *they* read your theme statement.

- Suppose that each of the characters you identified for your story beginning is reading your theme statement. How might each character feel about the theme? Write a list of adjectives to describe how each character would respond.

- All of these feelings—between you and your audience, between you and your characters, and between your characters—should be revealed in your story. These feelings will add to your story's tone and mood. Do you think the characters' feelings about a theme might change over the course of a story? If so, you would have to revise your list as your characters change. You can use such lists as you write stories to ensure consistency of tone and mood.

Discussion Guides

1. Were the king and Court Jester right to let Princess Lenore think she had the moon, or should they have forced her to live with reality? How will she react when she discovers that her father and her friend lied to her? What evidence, including personal experience, can you use to back up your opinions? Present your view in a group discussion and respond to the opinions stated by others. The group should come to a consensus on what advice to give the king and Court Jester if the Princess makes any further unrealistic demands.

2. The story "The Richer, the Poorer" is critical of Lottie for not using her time to live her life more fully. Was Bess blameless in her use of time, or should she have made at least some small effort to think ahead? After all, what would have happened to her if she had had no sister to call on? With a partner, discuss what either woman did that was right, and what was wrong. Make up a list of at least four guidelines for living that would help young people avoid the mistakes the sisters made.

3. In many ways, "Many Moons" is like a fairy tale. With a group of other students, compare "Many Moons" to fairy tales in such aspects as setting, characters, items mentioned by various characters, and wording. Make a list of the similarities. Then share your list with other groups. Did different groups notice different elements?

4. Imagine Bess and Lottie as high-school students invited to a graduation pizza party. Imagine the two sisters as they receive the invitation. How would their responses differ? Work with a partner to develop and act out a scene in which the sisters receive the invitation. If you like, follow it up with other scenes during or after the party.

Write a Short Story

In this unit, you have practiced writing theme statements and completed writing exercises demonstrating how the theme of a short story determines the development of conflict, characters, tone, and mood. If you'd like to build on what you've done to write an entire short story, follow the steps outlined below.

If you have questions about the writing process, refer to Using the Writing Process (page 306).

- Assemble the writing you did for Developing a Theme at the beginning of the unit and for each of the Writing on Your Own exercises. You should have the following pieces of writing: a) a list of your favorite stories and their themes, b) a list of possible themes that you might write about, c) a story beginning that introduces characters and possible conflicts, d) a dialogue between the two sisters in "The Richer, the Poorer," e) a block of dialogue for your own story beginning, and f) lists of adjectives that you can use to establish tone, mood, and the theme of your story.

- Decide whether you want to continue with the story for which you have already written a beginning or work with a new plot. For a new story, write sentences identifying the major theme or themes you intend to bring out. Then outline your story by writing one or more sentences about each of the stages: introduction, rising action, climax, falling action, and resolution.

- Write your complete story. You will need to vary the tone and mood according to the events in any given scene.

- Read your story to one or more classmates who can point out passages that should be improved. Make any revisions you agree with.

- Proofread your story for errors in spelling, grammar, and punctuation. Make a clean copy and save it in a portfolio of your writing.

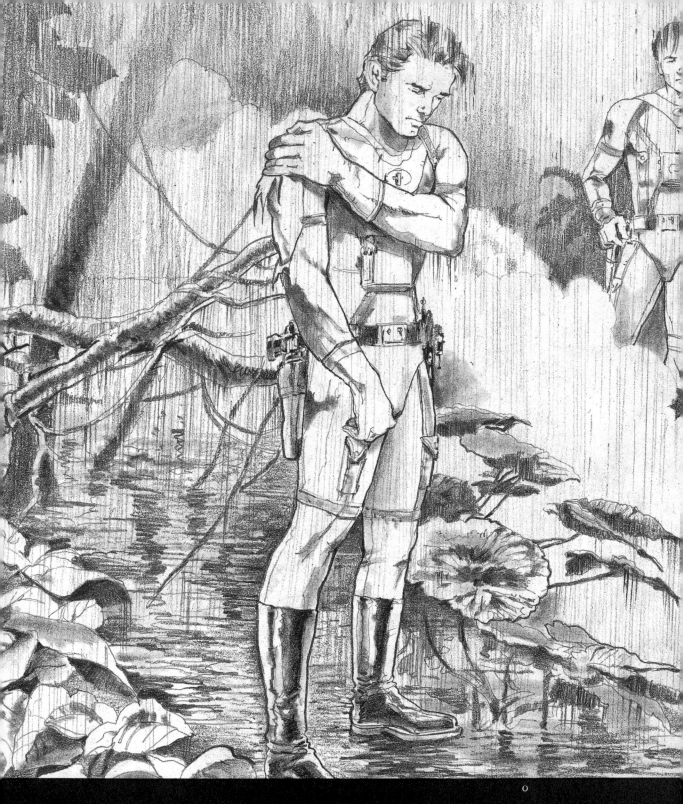

Unit 7 Descriptive Language

The Long Rain
by Ray Bradbury

About the Illustration

This picture illustrates a scene from the story you are about to read. Following are some questions that will help you begin to think about the story. Use details from the illustration as clues to answer the questions. Give reasons for your answers.

- Where and when do you think this story takes place?

- Who are these people? Why are they in this place?

- Read the expressions on the men's faces. What are they feeling? Why?

- What will the men do next?

Unit 7

Introduction

About the Story

When their rocket ship crashes on Venus, four men face a struggle for survival. The main danger on Venus is its constant rain, a downpour that eventually drives people mad. The men's only hope is to find one of the Sun Domes that Earth people have built on the planet's surface. Each Sun Dome houses an artificial sun. It is dry, warm, and supplied with fresh food. The men begin to search for a dome, only to find that they have circled around, back to their own ship. Disappointed, they travel on, finally finding the nearest Sun Dome, which unfortunately has been destroyed by angry Venusians. Can all four men stay sane long enough to reach the next Sun Dome? Will the next Sun Dome have been destroyed, just as this one has been? Read the story to find out.

About the Author

Ray Bradbury, born in 1920 in Waukegan, Illinois, is recognized as one of the major fantasy and science fiction writers in the United States. He has written several collections of short stories, including *The Martian Chronicles; I Sing the Body Electric;* and *R Is for Rocket,* from which this story is taken. He has also written novels, such as *Fahrenheit 451* about a future society in which books are forbidden. In addition, Bradbury has been nominated for both an Academy Award and an Emmy Award for his playwriting. His latest collection of short stories is called *Quicker Than the Eye.*

About the Lessons

The lessons that follow "The Long Rain" focus on the author's use of language. Words are writers' most valuable tools; words allow writers to share their feelings and to put new ideas into readers' minds. Writers work very hard to select the exact words to express themselves. Sometimes the words they choose have the power to picture a place or to express a feeling so accurately that readers respond, "I know just what you mean!" Sometimes their words show familiar places and situations in a new light, so readers respond, "I never thought of it in quite that way before."

Writing: Using Descriptive Language

In the course of this unit, you will learn to write a vivid description of a sport or game. The suggestions below will help you get started.

- Which games or sports do you like best? Make a list of your favorites. Choose the one about which you know the most.

- Try to picture a typical game or sports session—how it looks, sounds, smells, and feels. Jot down any ideas or details that are associated with your chosen activity. You will use these notes in later writing activities.

Before Reading

The questions below will help you see how Ray Bradbury has made use of the powerful tool of words in "The Long Rain." As you read the story, keep these questions in mind:

- Which descriptions help you see the characters and the setting most clearly?

- Which words are most effective in creating a mental picture?

- In which passages does the author compare things in a new way?

- What figures of speech does the author use? What does the narrator's unusual way of speaking add to the story?

Vocabulary Tips

This story includes a few words that may be unfamiliar to you but are useful for understanding the story. Below, you will find some of these words and their definitions, as well as sentences that show how the words are used. Look over these words before you begin to read.

cynic   a person who feels that people act only in their own self-interest. If I were a <u>cynic</u>, I'd say that you're only being nice to me because you know I have an extra ticket to the concert.

Camembert   a soft yellow cheese with a gray-white rind. Which cheese do you prefer—<u>Camembert</u> or Cheddar?

exterminator   one who destroys or kills in order to get rid of completely. The <u>exterminator</u> sprayed our house for termites.

synthetic   artificial; not natural. I can taste the difference between real sugar and <u>synthetic</u> sweetener.

dismantle   to take apart into pieces. We will <u>dismantle</u> the display and put it away until next year.

amber   a hard yellow fossil resin that can be used in jewelry. The fly had been stuck in <u>amber</u> for thousands of years.

flounder   to struggle to stand or move. I watched the little dog <u>flounder</u> in the deep snow.

bole   the trunk of a tree. Deer rubbing their antlers against the tree <u>bole</u> had worn away much of the bark.

The Long Rain

Ray Bradbury

The rain continued. It was a hard rain, a perpetual rain, a sweating and steaming rain; it was a mizzle, a downpour, a fountain, a whipping at the eyes, an undertow at the ankles; it was a rain to drown all rains and the memory of rains. It came by the pound and the ton, it hacked at the jungle and cut the trees like scissors and shaved the grass and tunneled the soil and molted the bushes.

It shrank men's hands into the hands of wrinkled apes; it rained a solid glassy rain, and it never stopped.

"How much farther, Lieutenant?"

"I don't know. A mile, ten miles, a thousand."

"Aren't you sure?"

"How can I be sure?"

"I don't like this rain. If we only knew how far it is to the Sun Dome, I'd feel better."

"Another hour or two from here."

"You really think so, Lieutenant?"

"Of course."

"Or are you lying to keep us happy?"

"I'm lying to keep you happy. Shut up!"

The two men sat together in the rain. Behind them sat two other men who were wet and tired and slumped like clay that was melting.

The lieutenant looked up. He had a face that once had been brown and now the rain had washed it pale, and the rain had washed the color from his eyes and they were white, as were his teeth, and as was his hair. He was all white. Even his uniform was beginning to turn white, and perhaps a little green with fungus.

The lieutenant felt the rain on his cheeks. "How many million years since the rain stopped raining here on Venus?"

"Don't be crazy," said one of the two other men. "It never stops raining on Venus. It just goes on and on. I've lived here for ten years and I never saw a minute, or even a second, when it wasn't pouring."

"It's like living under water," said the lieutenant, and rose up, shrugging his guns into place. "Well, we'd better get going. We'll find that Sun Dome yet."

"Or we won't find it," said the cynic.

"It's an hour or so."

"Now you're lying to me, Lieutenant."

"No, now I'm lying to myself. This is one of those times when you've got to lie. I can't take much more of this."

They walked down the jungle trail, now and then looking at their compasses. There was no direction anywhere, only what the compass said. There was a gray sky and rain falling and jungle and a path, and, far back behind them somewhere, a rocket in which they had ridden and fallen. A rocket in which lay two of their friends, dead and dripping rain.

They walked in single file, not speaking. They came to a river which lay wide and flat and brown, flowing down to the great Single Sea. The surface of it was stippled in a billion places by the rain.

"All right, Simmons."

The lieutenant nodded and Simmons took a small packet from his back which, with a pressure of hidden chemical, inflated into a large boat. The lieutenant directed the cutting of wood and the quick making of paddles and they set out into the river, paddling swiftly across the smooth surface in the rain.

The lieutenant felt the cold rain on his cheeks and on his neck and on his moving arms. The cold was beginning to seep into his lungs. He felt the rain on his ears, on his eyes, on his legs.

"I didn't sleep last night," he said.

"Who could? Who has? When? How many nights have we slept? Thirty nights, thirty days! Who can sleep with rain slamming their head, banging away. . . . I'd give anything for a hat. Anything at all, just so it wouldn't hit my head any more. I get headaches. My head is sore; it hurts all the time."

"I'm sorry I came to China," said one of the others.

"First time I ever heard Venus called China."

"Sure, China. Chinese water cure. Remember the old torture? Rope you against a wall. Drop one drop of water on your head every half-hour. You go crazy waiting for the next one. Well, that's Venus, but on a big scale. We're not made for water. You can't sleep, you can't breathe right, and you're crazy from just being soggy. If we'd been ready for a crash, we'd have brought waterproofed uniforms and hats. It's this beating rain on your head gets you, most of all. It's so heavy. It's like BB shot. I don't know how long I can take it."

"Boy, me for the Sun Dome! The man who thought them up, thought of something."

They crossed the river, and in crossing they thought of the Sun Dome, somewhere ahead of them, shining in the jungle rain. A yellow house, round and bright as the sun. A house forty feet high by one hundred feet in diameter, in which was warmth and quiet and hot food and freedom from rain. And in the center of the Sun

Dome, of course, was a sun. A small floating free globe of yellow fire, drifting in a space at the top of the building where you could look at it from where you sat, smoking or reading a book or drinking your hot chocolate crowned with marshmallow dollops or drinking something else. There it would be, the yellow sun, just the size of the Earth sun, and it was warm and continuous, and the rain world of Venus would be forgotten as long as you stayed in that house and idled your time.

The lieutenant turned and looked back at the three men using their oars and gritting their teeth. They were as white as mushrooms, as white as he was. Venus bleached everything away in a few months. Even the jungle was an immense cartoon nightmare, for how could the jungle be green with no sun, with always rain falling and always dusk? The white, white jungle with the pale cheese-colored leaves, and the earth carved of wet Camembert, and the tree boles like immense toadstools—everything black and white. And how often could you see the soil itself? Wasn't it mostly a creek, a stream, a puddle, a pool, a lake, a river, and then, at last, the sea?

"Here we are!"

They leaped out on the farthest shore, splashing and sending up showers. The boat was deflated and stored in a cigar-box packet. Then, standing on the rainy shore, they tried to light up a few smokes for themselves, and it was five minutes or so before, shuddering, they worked the inverted lighter and, cupping their hands, managed a few drags upon cigarettes that all too quickly were limp and beaten away from their lips by a sudden slap of rain.

They walked on.

"Wait just a moment," said the lieutenant. "I thought I saw something ahead."

"The Sun Dome?"

"I'm not sure. The rain closed in again."

Simmons began to run. "The Sun Dome!"

"Come back, Simmons!"

"The Sun Dome!"

Simmons vanished in the rain. The others ran after him.

They found him in a little clearing, and they stopped and looked at him and what he had discovered.

The rocket ship.

It was lying where they had left it. Somehow they had circled back and were where they had started. In the ruin of the ship green fungus was growing out of the mouths of the two dead men. As they watched, the fungus took flower, the petals broke away in the rain, and the fungus died.

"How did we do it?"

"An electrical storm must be nearby. Threw our compasses off. That explains it."

"You're right."

"What'll we do now?"

"Start out again."

"Good Lord, we're not any closer to anywhere!"

"Let's try to keep calm about it, Simmons."

"Calm, calm! This rain's driving me wild!"

"We've enough food for another two days if we're careful."

The rain danced on their skin, on their wet uniforms; the rain streamed from their noses and ears, from their fingers and knees. They looked like stone fountains frozen in the jungle, issuing forth water from every pore.

And, as they stood, from a distance they heard a roar.

And the monster came out of the rain.

The monster was supported upon a thousand electric blue legs. It walked swiftly and terribly. It struck down a leg with a driving blow. Everywhere a leg struck a tree fell and burned. Great whiffs of ozone filled the rainy air, and smoke blew away and was broken up by the rain. The monster was a half mile wide and a mile high and it felt of the ground like a great blind thing. Sometimes, for a moment, it had no legs at all. And then, in an instant, a thousand whips would fall out of its belly, white-blue whips, to sting the jungle.

"There's the electrical storm," said one of the men. "There's the thing ruined our compasses. And it's coming this way."

"Lie down, everyone," said the lieutenant.

"Run!" cried Simmons.

"Don't be a fool. Lie down. It hits the highest points. We may get through unhurt. Lie down about fifty feet from the rocket. It may very well spend its force there and leave us be. Get down!"

The men flopped.

"Is it coming?" they asked each other, after a moment.

"Coming."

"Is it nearer?"

"Two hundred yards off."

"Nearer?"

"Here she is!"

The monster came and stood over them. It dropped down ten blue bolts of lightning which struck the rocket. The rocket flashed like a beaten gong and gave off a metal ringing. The monster let down fifteen more bolts which danced about in ridiculous pantomime, feeling of the jungle and the watery soil.

"No, no!" One of the men jumped up.

"Get down, you fool!" said the lieutenant.

"No!"

The lightning struck the rocket another dozen times. The lieutenant turned his head on his arm and saw the blue blazing flashes. He saw trees split and crumple into ruin. He saw the monstrous dark cloud turn like a black disk overhead and hurl down a hundred other poles of electricity.

The man who had leaped up was now running, like someone in a great hall of pillars. He ran and dodged between pillars and then at last a dozen of the pillars slammed down and there was the sound a fly makes when landing upon the grill wires of an exterminator. The lieutenant remembered this from his childhood on a farm. And there was a smell of a man burned to a cinder.

The lieutenant lowered his head. "Don't look up," he told the others. He was afraid that he too might run at any moment.

The storm above them flashed down another series of bolts and then moved on away. Once again there was only the rain, which rapidly cleared the air of the charred smell, and in a moment the three remaining men were sitting and waiting for the beat of their hearts to subside into quiet once more.

They walked over to the body, thinking that perhaps they could still save the man's life. They couldn't believe that there wasn't some way to help the man. It was the natural act of men who have not accepted death until they have touched it and turned it over and made plans to bury it or leave it there for the jungle to bury in an hour of quick growth.

The body was twisted steel, wrapped in burned

leather. It looked like a wax dummy that had been thrown into an incinerator and pulled out after the wax had sunk to the charcoal skeleton. Only the teeth were white, and they shone like a strange white bracelet dropped half through a clenched black fist.

"He shouldn't have jumped up." They said it almost at the same time.

Even as they stood over the body it began to vanish, for the vegetation was edging in upon it, little vines and ivy and creepers, and even flowers for the dead.

At a distance the storm walked off on blue bolts of lightning and was gone.

They crossed a river and a creek and a stream and a dozen other rivers and creeks and streams. Before their eyes rivers appeared, rushing, new rivers, while old rivers changed their courses—rivers the color of mercury, rivers the color of silver and milk.

They came to the sea.

The Single Sea. There was only one continent on Venus. This land was three thousand miles long by a thousand miles wide, and about this island was the Single Sea, which covered the entire raining planet. The Single Sea, which lay upon the pallid shore with little motion . . .

"This way." The lieutenant nodded south. "I'm sure there are two Sun Domes down that way."

"While they were at it, why didn't they build a hundred more?"

"There're a hundred and twenty of them now, aren't there?"

"One hundred and twenty-six, as of last month. They tried to push a bill through Congress back on Earth a year ago to provide for a couple dozen more, but oh no, you know how *that* is. They'd rather a few men went crazy with the rain."

They started south.

The lieutenant and Simmons and the third man, Pickard, walked in the rain, in the rain that fell heavily and lightly, heavily and lightly, in the rain that poured and hammered and did not stop falling upon the land and the sea and the walking people.

Simmons saw it first. "There it is!"

"There's what?"

"The Sun Dome!"

The lieutenant blinked the water from his eyes and raised his hands to ward off the stinging blows of the rain.

At a distance there was a yellow glow on the edge of the jungle by the sea. It was, indeed, the Sun Dome.

The men smiled at each other.

"Looks like you were right, Lieutenant."

"Luck."

"Brother, that puts muscle in me, just seeing it. Come on!" Simmons began to trot. The others automatically fell in with this, gasping, tired, but keeping pace.

"A big pot of coffee for me," panted Simmons, smiling. "And a pan of cinnamon buns. Boy! And just lie there and let the old sun hit you. The guy that invented the Sun Domes, he should have got a medal!"

They ran faster. The yellow glow grew brighter.

"Guess a lot of men went crazy before they figured out the cure. Think it'd be obvious! Right off." Simmons panted the words in cadence to his running "Rain, rain! Years ago. Found a friend. Of mine. Out in the jungle. Wandering around. In the rain. Saying over and over, 'Don't know enough, to come in, outta the rain. Don't know enough, to come in, outta the rain. Don't know enough—' On and on. Like that. Poor crazy fool."

"Save your breath!"

They ran.

They all laughed. They reached the door of the Sun Dome, laughing.

Simmons yanked the door wide. "Hey!" he yelled. "Bring on the coffee!"

There was no reply.

They stepped through the door.

The Sun Dome was empty and dark. There was no synthetic yellow sun floating in a high gaseous whisper at the center of the blue ceiling. There was no food waiting. It was cold as a vault. And through a thousand holes which had been newly punctured in the ceiling water streamed, the rain fell down, soaking into the thick rugs and the heavy modern furniture and splashing on the glass tables. The jungle was growing up like a moss in the room, on top of the bookcases and the divans. The rain slashed through the holes and fell upon the three men's faces.

Pickard began to laugh quietly.

"Shut up, Pickard!"

"Ye gods, look what's here for us—no food, no sun, nothing. The Venusians—they did it! Of course!"

Simmons nodded, with the rain funneling down on his face. The water ran in his silvered hair and on his white eyebrows. "Every once in a while the Venusians come up out of the sea and attack a Sun Dome. They know if they ruin the Sun Domes they can ruin us."

"But aren't the Sun Domes protected with guns?"

"Sure." Simmons stepped aside to a place that was relatively dry. "But it's been five years since the Venusians tried anything. Defense relaxes. They caught this Dome unaware."

"Where are the bodies?"

"The Venusians took them all down into the sea. I hear they have a delightful way of drowning you. It takes eight hours to drown the way they work it. Really delightful."

"I bet there isn't any food here at all." Pickard laughed.

The lieutenant frowned at him, nodded at him so Simmons could see. Simmons shook his head and went back to a room at one side of the oval chamber. The kitchen was strewn with soggy loaves of bread, and meat that had grown a faint green fur. Rain came through a hundred holes in the kitchen roof.

"Brilliant." The lieutenant glanced up at the holes. "I don't suppose we can plug up all those holes and get snug here."

"Without food, sir?" Simmons snorted. "I notice the sun machine's dismantled. Our best bet is to make our way to the next Sun Dome. How far is that from here?"

"Not far. As I recall, they built two rather close together here. Perhaps if we waited, a rescue mission from the other might—"

"It's probably been here and gone already, some days ago. They'll send a crew to repair this place in about six months, when they get the money from Congress. I don't think we'd better wait."

"All right then, we'll eat what's left of our rations and get on to the next Dome."

Pickard said, "If only the rain wouldn't hit my head, just for a few minutes. If I could only remember what it's like not to be bothered." He put his hands on his skull and held it tight. "I remember when I was in school a bully used to sit in back of me and pinch me and pinch me and pinch me every five minutes, all day long. He did that for weeks and months. My arms were sore and black and blue all the time. And I thought I'd go crazy from being pinched. One day I must have gone a little mad from being hurt and hurt, and I turned around and took a metal trisquare I used in mechanical drawing and I almost cut his lousy head off. I almost scalped him before they dragged me out of the room, and I kept yelling, 'Why don't he leave me alone? Why don't he leave me alone?' Brother!" His hands clenched the bone of his head, shaking, tightening, his eyes shut. "But what do I do *now?* Who do I hit, who do I tell to lay off, stop bothering me, this damn rain, like the pinching, always *on* you, that's all you hear, that's all you feel!"

"We'll be at the other Sun Dome by four this afternoon."

"Sun Dome? Look at this one! What if all the Sun Domes on Venus are gone? What then? What if there are holes in all the ceilings, and the rain coming in!"

"We'll have to chance it."

"I'm tired of chancing it. All I want is a roof and some quiet. I want to be alone."

"That's only eight hours off, if you hold on."

"Don't worry, I'll hold on all right." And Pickard laughed, not looking at them.

"Let's eat," said Simmons, watching him.

They set off down the coast, southward again. After four hours they had to cut inland to go around a river that was a mile wide and so swift it was not navigable by boat. They had to walk inland six miles to a place where the river boiled out of the earth, suddenly, like a mortal wound. In the rain, they walked on solid ground and returned to the sea.

"I've got to sleep," said Pickard at last. He slumped.

"Haven't slept in four weeks. Tried, but couldn't. Sleep here."

The sky was getting darker. The night of Venus was setting in and it was so completely black that it was dangerous to move. Simmons and the lieutenant fell to their knees also, and the lieutenant said, "All right, we'll see what we can do. We've tried it before, but I don't know. Sleep doesn't seem one of the things you can get in this weather."

They lay out full, propping their heads so the water wouldn't come to their mouths, and they closed their eyes.

The lieutenant twitched.

He did not sleep.

There were things that crawled on his skin. Things grew upon him in layers. Drops fell and touched other drops and they became streams that trickled over his body, and while these moved down his flesh, the small growths of the forest took root in his clothing. He felt the ivy cling and make a second garment over him; he felt the small flowers bud and open and petal away, and still the rain pattered on his body and on his head. In the luminous night—for the vegetation glowed in the darkness—he could see the other two men outlined, like logs that had fallen and taken upon themselves velvet coverings of grass and flowers. The rain hit his face. He covered his face with his hands. The rain hit his neck. He turned over on his stomach in the mud, on the rubbery plants, and the rain hit his back and hit his legs.

Suddenly he leaped up and begun to brush the water from himself. A thousand hands were touching him and he no longer wanted to be touched. He no longer could stand being touched. He floundered and struck something else and knew that it was Simmons, standing up in the rain, sneezing moisture, coughing and choking. And then Pickard was up, shouting, running about.

"Wait a minute, Pickard!"

"Stop it, stop it!' Pickard screamed. He fired his gun six times at the night sky. In the flashes of powdery illumination they could see armies of raindrops, suspended as in a vast motionless amber, for an instant, hesitating as if shocked by the explosion, fifteen billion droplets, fifteen billion tears, fifteen billion ornaments, jewels standing out against a white velvet viewing board. And then, with the light gone, the drops which had waited to have their pictures taken, which had suspended their downward rush, fell upon them, stinging, in an insect cloud of coldness and pain.

"Stop it! Stop it!"

"Pickard!"

But Pickard was only standing now, alone. When the lieutenant switched on a small hand lamp and played it over Pickard's wet face, the eyes of the man were dilated, and his mouth was open, his face turned up, so the water hit and splashed on his tongue, and hit and drowned the wide eyes, and bubbled in a whispering froth on the nostrils.

"Pickard!"

The man would not reply. He simply stood there for a long while with the bubbles of rain breaking out in his whitened hair and manacles of rain jewels dripping from his wrists and his neck.

"Pickard! We're leaving. We're going on. Follow us."

The rain dripped from Pickard's ears.

"Do you hear me, Pickard!"

It was like shouting down a well.

"Pickard!"

"Leave him alone," said Simmons.

"We can't go on without him."

"What'll we do, carry him?" Simmons spat. "He's no good to us or to himself. You know what he'll do? He'll just stand here and drown."

"What?"

"You ought to know that by now. Don't you know the story? He'll just stand here with his head up and let the rain come in his nostrils and his mouth. He'll breathe the water."

"No."

"That's how they found General Mendt that time. Sitting on a rock with his head back, breathing the rain. His lungs were full of water."

The lieutenant turned the light back to the unblinking face. Pickard's nostrils gave off a tiny whispering wet sound.

"Pickard!" The lieutenant slapped the face.

"He can't even feel you," said Simmons. "A few days in this rain and you don't have any face or any legs or hands."

The lieutenant looked at his own hand in horror. He could no longer feel it.

"But we can't leave Pickard here."

"I'll show you what we can do." Simmons fired his gun.

Pickard fell into the raining earth.

Simmons said, "Don't move, Lieutenant. I've got my gun ready for you too. Think it over; he would only have stood or sat there and drowned. It's quicker this way."

The lieutenant blinked at the body. "But you killed him."

"Yes, because he'd have killed us by being a burden. You saw his face. Insane."

After a moment the lieutenant nodded.

They walked off into the rain.

It was dark and their hand lamps threw a beam that pierced the rain for only a few feet. After a half hour they had to stop and sit through the rest of the night, aching with hunger, waiting for the dawn to come; when it did come it was gray and continually raining as before, and they began to walk again.

"We've miscalculated," said Simmons.

"No. Another hour."

"Speak louder. I can't hear you." Simmons stopped and smiled. He touched his ears. "My ears. They've gone out on me. All the rain pouring finally numbed me right down to the bone."

"Can't you hear anything?" said the lieutenant.

"What?" Simmons' eyes were puzzled.

"Nothing. Come on."

"I think I'll wait here. You go on ahead."

"You can't do that."

"I can't hear you. You go on. I'm tired. I don't think the Sun Dome is down this way. And, if it is, it's probably got holes in the roof, like the last one. I think I'll just sit here."

"Get up from there!"

"So long, Lieutenant."

"You can't give up now."

"I've got a gun here that says I'm staying. I just don't care any more. I'm not crazy yet, but I'm the next thing to it. I don't want to go out that way. As soon as you get out of sight I'm going to use this gun on myself."

"Simmons!"

"You said my name. I can read that much off your lips."

"Simmons."

"Look, it's a matter of time. Either I die now or in a few hours. Wait'll you get to that next Dome, if you ever get there, and find rain coming in through the roof. Won't that be nice?"

The lieutenant waited and then splashed off in the rain. He turned and called back once, but Simmons was only sitting there with the gun in his hands, waiting for him to get out of sight. He shook his head and waved the lieutenant on.

The lieutenant didn't even hear the sound of the gun.

He began to eat the flowers as he walked. They stayed down for a time, and weren't poisonous; neither were they particularly sustaining, and he vomited them up, sickly, a minute or so later.

Once he took some leaves and tried to make himself a hat, but he had tried that before; the rain melted the leaves from his head. Once picked, the vegetation rotted quickly and fell away into gray masses in his fingers.

"Another five minutes," he told himself. "Another five minutes and then I'll walk into the sea and keep walking. We weren't made for this; no Earthman was or ever will be able to take it. Your nerves, your nerves."

He floundered his way through a sea of slush and foliage and came to a small hill.

At a distance there was a faint yellow smudge in the cold veils of water.

The next Sun Dome.

Through the trees, a long round yellow building, far away. For a moment he only stood, swaying, looking at it.

He began to run and then he slowed down, for he was afraid. He didn't call out. What if it's the same one?

What if it's the dead Sun Dome, with no sun in it? he thought.

He slipped and fell. Lie here, he thought; it's the wrong one. Lie here. It's no use. Drink all you want.

But he managed to climb to his feet again and crossed several creeks, and the yellow light grew very bright, and he began to run again, his feet crashing into mirrors and glass, his arms flailing at diamonds and precious stones.

He stood before the yellow door. The printed letters over it said THE SUN DOME. He put his numb hand up to feel it. Then he twisted the doorknob and stumbled in.

He stood for a moment looking about. Behind him the rain whirled at the door. Ahead of him, upon a low table, stood a silver pot of hot chocolate, steaming, and a cup, full, with a marshmallow in it. And beside that, on another tray, stood thick sandwiches of rich chicken meat and fresh-cut tomatoes and green onions. And on a rod just before his eyes was a great thick green Turkish towel, and a bin in which to throw wet clothes, and, to his right, a small cubicle in which heat rays might dry you instantly. And upon a chair, a fresh change of uniform, waiting for anyone—himself, or any lost one—to make use of it. And farther over, coffee in steaming copper urns, and a phonograph from which music would soon play quietly, and books bound in red and brown leather. And near the books a cot, a soft deep cot upon which one might lie, exposed and bare, to drink in the rays of the one great bright thing which dominated the long room.

He put his hands to his eyes. He saw other men moving toward him, but said nothing to them. He waited, and opened his eyes, and looked. The water from his uniform pooled at his feet, and he felt it drying from his hair and his face and his chest and his arms and his legs.

He was looking at the sun.

It hung in the center of the room, large and yellow and warm. It made not a sound, and there was no sound in the room. The door was shut and the rain only a memory to his tingling body. The sun hung high in the blue sky of the room, warm, hot, yellow, and very fine.

He walked forward, tearing off his clothes as he went.

Reviewing and Interpreting the Story

Record your answers to these comprehension questions in your personal literature notebook. Follow the directions for each part.

Reviewing Try to complete each of these sentences without looking back at the story.

Recalling Facts

1. The lieutenant and his men are lost on the planet
    a. Mars.
    b. Jupiter.
    c. Mercury.
    d. Venus.

Identifying Sequence

2. Just after the men circle back to the site of the rocket crash,
    a. they encounter an electrical storm.
    b. they enter the abandoned Sun Dome.
    c. they crash into the planet.
    d. one of the men shoots another.

Understanding Main Ideas

3. The Sun Domes are important to settlers on Venus because they
    a. offer protection from the Venusian creatures.
    b. provide relief from the constant rain.
    c. are pleasant vacation spots.
    d. are centers for research.

Identifying
Cause and Effect

4. Simmons shoots Pickard because

   a. Pickard is working with the Venusians.
   b. he doesn't like Pickard.
   c. Pickard is attacking Simmons.
   d. Pickard has become insane and a burden.

Recognizing
Story Elements
(Plot)

5. Which event happens during the falling action?

   a. The lieutenant takes off his wet clothes and walks into the Sun Dome.
   b. The four men find the ruined Sun Dome.
   c. The lieutenant finds that his hands are numb.
   d. Simmons stays behind with his gun.

Interpreting To answer these questions, you may look back at the story if you like.

Making Inferences

6. The Venusians must live

   a. under water.
   b. inside a waterproof dome, similar to the Sun Dome.
   c. in constant discomfort.
   d. in the forests.

Predicting
Outcomes

7. Based on the experiences of this mission, in the future the army will most likely

   a. stop flights to Venus.
   b. pack waterproof gear for the crew on every flight to Venus.
   c. send more men on every flight.
   d. try to change the weather patterns on Venus.

Making
Generalizations

8. The most important message you learn from this story is this:

a. You don't realize how important the simple pleasures in life are until they are gone.

b. Travel to other planets poses too great a risk for humans to attempt.

c. Creatures from other planets should never be trusted.

d. It is always better to live in a sunny climate than in a rainy one.

Analyzing

9. The lieutenant survived mainly because he

a. was lucky.

b. followed the rules.

c. never gave up.

d. knew more about the planet than the others.

Understanding
Story Elements
(Mood)

10. Which word best describes the mood of this story?

a. humorous

b. gloomy

c. hopeful

d. cheerful

Now check your answers with your teacher. Study the questions you answered incorrectly. What types of questions were they? Talk with your teacher about ways to work on those skills.

Descriptive Language

Did you ever see a movie made from a story or novel you had read? Sometimes the movie is perfect; it captures the characters and settings and feelings just as you saw them when you read the author's words. But at other times, the movie is somehow wrong. The characters, setting, and feelings are different from they way you had pictured them when you read the story. You find that you would rather go back to the book than watch the movie. You like your own interpretation of the author's words better than the moviemaker's interpretation.

This happens because good authors can make you share what they see, hear, feel, smell, and taste by painting vivid word pictures. You see through the writer's eyes so well that you create your own world, guided by the writer's words.

One way that writers communicate their ideas is by using exact words. Sometimes it takes a long time to find the best word, but the more precise a noun or specific a verb, the better the reader will understand what the writer means

Writers also use *figurative language,* or *figures of speech,* to help their readers see ordinary things in different ways. Figurative language uses words in imaginative ways to get across ideas or create mental images. *Similes* and *metaphors* are figures of speech that involve comparing unlike things in unexpected ways. *Exaggeration* and *personification* are other figures of speech that make writing lively. Exaggeration is used for emphasis. Personification gives human characteristics to nonhuman animals or things.

In this lesson, we will look at these ways in which Ray Bradbury uses language to paint mental pictures and to open up readers' minds to new images and ideas:

1. Bradbury chooses exact words—precise nouns and specific verbs to make the setting and action clear to readers.

2. He uses comparisons to create images in readers' minds.

3. He uses figures of speech such as exaggeration and personification to create special effects.

1 • Exact Words

When you were younger, you probably used the same words over and over again. If someone asked you how you felt when you were in a good mood, you would answer, "good." If you were in a bad mood, you might answer, "sad" or "mad." Words like *good, bad, happy*, and *sad* were your only ways to describe your feelings. Now that you are older, you might use words such as *excellent, disappointed, contented,* and *dejected* instead. These adjectives give your listener a better idea of what has created your feeling as well as your exact reaction.

Good writers not only use vivid, colorful, descriptive adjectives and adverbs; they also use precise nouns and specific verbs to express exact meanings. They are not satisfied with just coming close to the meaning they want to get across. They want to hit a bull's-eye with every word. That is why they work so hard at choosing the exact word.

Read this passage from "The Long Rain" to see how Ray Bradbury uses exact words to describe the deserted Sun Dome.

> The Sun Dome was empty and dark. There was no synthetic yellow sun floating in a high gaseous whisper at the center of the blue ceiling. There was no food waiting. It was cold as a vault. And through a thousand holes which had been newly punctured in the ceiling water streamed, the rain fell down, soaking into the thick rugs and the heavy modern furniture and splashing on the glass tables. The jungle was growing up like a moss in the room, on top of the bookcases and the divans. The rain slashed through the holes and fell upon the three men's faces.

The author gives us a chilling picture of the abandoned Sun Dome. The roof "punctured" with holes. The rain doesn't just *fall;* it *streams* through the ceiling holes. It *soaks,* and *splashes,* and *slashes*. And it doesn't simply fall on furniture in general; it falls on *thick rugs, heavy modern furniture, glass tables, bookcases,* and *divans*. The writer has painted the picture with words so exact that you can see and feel the scene along with the characters in the story.

Exact words can also help to create the mood of the story. In the following passage, notice how the author uses words associated with the sense of touch to build up to the lieutenant's violent reaction to the rain:

There were things that crawled on his skin. Things grew upon him in layers. Drops fell and touched other drops and they became streams that trickled over his body, and while these moved down his flesh, the small growths of the forest took root in his clothing. He felt the ivy cling and make a second garment over him; he felt the small flowers bud and open and petal away, and still the rain pattered on his body and on his head. In the luminous night—for the vegetation glowed in the darkness—he could see the other two men outlined, like logs that had fallen and taken upon themselves velvet coverings of grass and flowers. The rain hit his face. He covered his face with his hands. The rain hit his neck. He turned over on his stomach in the mud, on the rubbery plants, and the rain hit his back and hit his legs.

The author uses specific verbs to describe the rain, such as *crawled, trickled*, and *pattered*. He uses repetition to show how steady and unchanging the rain is. Reading this passage, you begin to feel uncomfortable yourself. You can hardly stand to feel the rain hitting over and over again. You share the mood of the unlucky lieutenant.

Exercise 1

Read this passage, which gives a vivid description of the Sun Dome. Use what you have learned in this lesson to answer the questions that follow.

They crossed the river, and in crossing they thought of the Sun Dome, somewhere ahead of them, shining in the jungle rain. A yellow house, round and bright as the sun. A house forty feet high by one hundred feet in diameter, in which was warmth and quiet and hot food and freedom from rain. And in the center of the Sun Dome, of course, was a sun. A small floating free globe of yellow fire, drifting in a space at the top of the building where you could look at it from where you sat, smoking or reading a book or drinking your hot chocolate crowned with marshmallow dollops or drinking something else. There it would be, the yellow sun, just the size of the Earth sun, and it was warm and continuous, and the rain world of Venus would be forgotten as long as you stayed in that house and idled your time.

1. Which words and phrases in this passage paint vivid word pictures? What mood is created with these words?

2. Compare the images in this passage with those in other passages in this lesson. How are the moods of the passages different?

Check your answers with your teacher. Review this part of the lesson if you don't understand why an answer was incorrect.

Writing on Your Own 1

In this exercise you will use what you have learned in the lesson to write a paragraph describing the place where the sport or game you chose takes place. Follow these steps:

- Review your list of details. Now picture yourself in the place where the activity happens. For example, what do you see as you step up to the plate or take your mark before the race? What and whom do you hear? Think of exact nouns, verbs, and adjectives to describe your situation. Record them in a chart like the one that follows.

My Favorite Game	
See	
Hear	
Smell	
Taste	
Touch	

- Write a paragraph describing the place from the first-person point of view. Use words from your chart to show the reader exactly what the place is like.

- Reread your paragraph. Replace any tired, overused words with words that describe sights, sounds, and feelings exactly.

2 • Similes and Metaphors

Similes and metaphors are two ways of comparing unlike things. Sometimes it is not good enough just to describe something in a normal, everyday way. You can use words imaginatively to compare two unlike things and help your readers see ordinary things in new ways. For example, a fast person might be described as "quick as a rabbit" or as "quick as greased lightning."

A simile is a comparison that uses the word *like* or *as*. Find the simile in the following passage from "The Long Rain":

> The two men sat together in the rain. Behind them sat two other men who were wet and tired and slumped like clay that was melting.

The author compares the slumping men to melting clay. Their heads are down, their shoulders are rounded, and their faces register no expression but exhaustion. They are wet and cold. This simile creates a vivid mental picture for the reader.

A metaphor compares one thing to another without using *like* or *as*. A metaphor states that one thing *is* another. The following passage contains an extended metaphor. What is the author comparing to a monster?

> And the monster came out of the rain.
> The monster was supported upon a thousand electric blue legs. It walked swiftly and terribly. It struck down a leg with a driving blow. Everywhere a leg struck a tree fell and burned. Great whiffs of ozone filled the rainy air, and smoke blew away and was broken up by the rain. The monster was

a half mile wide and a mile high and it felt of the ground like a great blind thing. Sometimes, for a moment, it had no legs at all. And then, in an instant, a thousand whips would fall out of its belly, white-blue whips, to sting the jungle.

This metaphor compares an electrical storm to a monster that is walking over the jungle. The streaks of lightning coming from the storm clouds are compared to the monster's legs or thousands of whips falling from its belly. This metaphor not only paints a frightening picture. It also creates a mood of dread and fear.

Exercise 2

Read this passage and answer the questions about it using what you have learned in this part of the lesson.

> The lieutenant turned and looked back at the three men using their oars and gritting their teeth. They were white as mushrooms, as white as he was. Venus bleached everything away in a few months. Even the jungle was an immense cartoon nightmare, for how could the jungle be green with no sun, with always rain falling and always dusk? The white, white jungle with the pale, cheese-colored leaves, and the earth carved of wet Camembert, and the tree boles like immense toadstools—everything black and white.

1. Find two similes in this passage. What two things are being compared in each simile?

2. To what is the jungle compared? How does the metaphor help to create a mood in the passage?

Check your answers with your teacher. Review this part of the lesson if you don't understand why an answer was incorrect.

Writing on Your Own 2

In this exercise you will continue to work on your description of the sport or game you wrote about in Writing on Your Own 1.

- Reread the paragraph you wrote to describe the place where your game is played. Add at least one simile and one metaphor to your paragraph. Make sure your comparisons give readers not only a sensory description but also a feeling about what you are describing. Help them share your feeling about the place. The similes and metaphors you choose should create a mood for your readers.

- Read your paragraph aloud. Listen for words or phrases that don't sound quite right or could be made more specific. If necessary, take a few moments to make your paragraph more descriptive.

3 • Other Figures of Speech

Exaggeration and personification are two other figures of speech that add life to your writing. Look at the pair of statements below. Which is more descriptive?

It was very hot.
It was so hot that we ate fried tomatoes right off the vine.

Exaggeration stops readers in their tracks. Because it is so intense, it makes readers think about what the speaker is really feeling. Exaggeration is like a stop sign that warns readers to watch out for strong emotions.

Read the following passage from "The Long Rain." See if you can find the exaggeration in it. Think about what strong feeling it indicates.

The rain continued. It was a hard rain, a perpetual rain, a sweating and steaming rain; it was a mizzle, a downpour, a fountain, a whipping at the eyes, an undertow at the ankles; it was a rain to drown all rains and the memory of rains. It came by the pound and the ton, it hacked at the jungle and cut the trees like scissors and shaved the grass and tunneled the soil and molted the bushes. It shrank men's hands into the hands of wrinkled apes; it rained a solid, glassy rain, and it never stopped.

How has the narrator exaggerated? Is it possible that rain could fall by the ton? Could rain cut trees like scissors? Could it shrink human hands into the hands of apes? These events are all impossible. However, the exaggerations let readers know that the narrator is overwhelmed by the rain. The rain is too overpowering to be described in a normal way. It can be understood only through exaggeration.

Personification is another way for a writer to describe something difficult to explain. Personification is a figure of speech in which an animal, an object, or an idea is described as though it were human. Like a metaphor, personification makes you see something in a new way. Read this example: "The rain danced on their skin. . . ." Rain can't dance. Only humans can dance. Authors use this technique to create a vivid picture in a reader's mind.

Exercise 3

Read these passages and answer the questions about them using what you have learned in this part of the lesson.

Passage A

The lieutenant and Simmons and the third man, Pickard, walked in the rain, in the rain that fell heavily and lightly, heavily and lightly; in the rain that poured and hammered and did not stop falling upon the land and the sea and the walking people.

Passage B

At a distance there was a yellow glow on the edge of the jungle by the sea. It was, indeed, the Sun Dome.

The men smiled at each other.

"Looks like you were right, Lieutenant."

"Luck."

"Brother, that puts muscle in me, just seeing it. Come on!" Simmons began to trot. The others automatically fell in with this, gasping, tired, but keeping pace.

1. Which passage uses exaggeration? What is the effect of this exaggeration? What does it tell you about the feelings of the speaker?

2. Which passage uses personification? What thing is being given human characteristics?

Check your answers with your teacher. Review this part of the lesson if you don't understand why an answer was incorrect.

Writing on Your Own 3

In this exercise you will use exaggeration and personification in a paragraph about one event that happens during your chosen game. Follow these steps:

- Make a list of exciting events that could happen in the course of a game. For example, you could write about the play that scores a touchdown, the final spurt of energy it takes to win a race, or the process of executing a double play in baseball. Choose the event you can see most clearly in your mind.

- Jot down notes about the sights, sounds, and feelings of the event. Then write a paragraph using those notes. Choose one or two details or emotions to exaggerate or personify. Make readers say, "That's impossible, but I know what you mean" when they read your paragraph. For example, you might write, "As I ran to catch the ball, my legs suddenly weighed a ton" or "The right field fence taunted me, sure that I could never hit a ball anywhere near it."

- Read your paragraph aloud to a partner. Read it with just the right amount of excitement or humor in your voice. After you hear your description read aloud, you may want to make changes.

Discussion Guides

1. Make a list of five of your favorite similes from "The Long Rain." Below each simile, translate it into more common, everyday language. Then get together with other students and compare the different ways of saying the same things. Decide which way you like better and explain why.

2. According to this story, the Venusian environment is wet and chilly. Yet the Earthmen still feel a need to settle there. If you were a Venusian, would you welcome the settlement of Earthlings on your planet? Together with another student, stage a debate. One of you should take the position that it is the right of Earth's inhabitants to travel and settle anywhere they choose in the universe. The other should argue that any planet with intelligent life should be left alone. Present your debate to the class.

3. Space travel seems to be filled with danger. Why would a person choose to put himself or herself in danger in this way? How could a person be persuaded to become a space traveler? Together with a friend, create a television commercial that advertises a school for space travelers and settlers. Include good reasons for trying this risky career. Practice your commercial and present it to the rest of the class.

4. This story is set on the planet Venus. In the years since the story was written, there have been space probes to Venus that have shown no evidence of life on the planet. How do these findings affect the believability of the story? Do you think that the story would be better if it were set on a planet in another solar system or galaxy? Why or why not? Discuss the issue in a small group and come to a decision. If necessary, you may agree to disagree. Report your group's decision to the rest of the class.

Write a Vivid Description

Throughout the unit you have been working on several descriptive paragraphs. Now you are going to write a one- or two-page description of an entire game, using all the skills you have learned in this unit.

If you have any questions about the writing process, refer to Using the Writing Process, beginning on page 306.

- Assemble the writing you did for all the exercises in this unit. You should have four pieces of writing: *a)* a list of details about a favorite sport or game, *b)* a paragraph that uses precise nouns, specific verbs, and vivid modifiers to describe the setting for your game, *c)* a paragraph that includes similes and metaphors, *d)* a paragraph that includes exaggeration and personification. Reread these pieces of writing now to get ideas for the description you are about to write.

- Now write a description of an entire game, including the setting and events that happen during the game. You may write your description from the first-person or the third-person point of view. Use phrases or sentences from your earlier paragraphs, as appropriate. Remember to use exact words, similes, metaphors, exaggeration, and personification to give your reader a realistic but fresh look at the game.

- Reread your description to make sure that you have brought the game to life for your readers and have used at least one simile, one metaphor, one exaggeration, and one personification. Then read it to a friend or family member for feedback. Ask your listener to tell you what mental images your writing creates for him or her. If something isn't clear to your listener, revise your writing to make it clear. Add any details that seem to be missing.

- Proofread to find spelling, grammar, and punctuation errors. Make a clean copy of your writing and share it with your classmates. If you wish, you may write a short story using your description. Save your work in a portfolio of your writing.

Unit 8 Discussing Literature

Lob's Girl
by Joan Aiken

About the Illustration

Describe the people in the scene and explain what you think they are doing. Talk about what might be happening here. Use details from the illustration as clues. Give reasons for your answers.

These questions will help you begin to think about the story:

- What is the setting of this story?

- Who do you suppose are the main characters? What makes you think as you do?

- What is the man carrying? How does he expect to use it? What problem might that cause for the girl?

Unit 8

Introduction

About the Story

When a young dog walking on a beach along the southern coast of England meets a little girl, it's love at first sight for both of them. The dog's owner, on vacation from a city in northwestern England, takes Lob back home a few days later. Lob, however, is unwilling to leave his girl, Sandy. He walks 400 miles to get back to her. His owner separates them once more, but when Lob runs away again to rejoin Sandy, his owner gives up, and Lob becomes part of Sandy's family. For the next nine years, Lob and Sandy are companions. Then, when Sandy is hurt in a traffic accident and is confined to a hospital bed, Lob overcomes even greater obstacles to get back to her side.

About the Author

Joan Aiken (1924–   ) is the daughter of the U.S. poet Conrad Aiken and sister of two other writers, and has referred to writing as "the family business." She was born in England in a haunted house where the ghost reportedly threw vases now and then. Aiken's parents divorced when she was four years old, and she stayed with her mother and grew up as a British citizen. By the time she was five, she knew she wanted to be a writer. After jobs with the BBC, a magazine, and an advertising agency, she became a full-time fiction writer in 1962. She has produced a large number of novels and short stories for children and for adults, as well as plays and poetry. She is married to an American landscape painter, has two children, and divides her time between England and the United States.

Many of Aiken's tales weave together fantasy, suspense, and a love of the absurd. Often, imaginative and weird situations lead to startling endings. Some of her best-known books are *The Wolves of Willoughby Chase* and its sequels. Her short story collections include *A Whisper in the Night: Tales of Terror and Suspense,* the source of "Lob's Girl."

About the Lessons

The lessons that follow "Lob's Girl" focus on skills that are helpful in analyzing and discussing literature. Almost everyone has an opinion about what he or she reads. Sometimes that opinion is based almost entirely on the piece of writing. At other times it is based on matters outside the writing, such as your mood when you begin to read. Most often, your opinion grows out of both what is in the story and how you approach it. When you discuss a short story, it is important to understand the reasons for your opinion. Even when you dislike a story, you will get more out of the literature when you can discuss it logically, focusing on important characteristics that everyone will recognize.

Writing: Writing About Literature

The lessons and exercises following each selection in this book guide you in recognizing the story's important passages. They provide starting points for talking about the story's elements. But when you read a story in your free time, or watch a story acted out, no one provides guiding questions. It's up to you to decide what you want out of a story and whether a particular story or type of story is worth your time. Sometimes you'll want to share your opinions about stories with your friends, especially if you have strong feelings for or against the writing. Then it's up to you to choose what you will tell others to help them decide whether or not they want to read a story.

After you read this story and complete the exercises, you will know more about how to examine a story, judge it, and explain your opinions to others. In addition, you will use your reactions to another writer's work as a guide to your own writing. At this time, prepare by trying these suggestions:

- Review stories you have read, whether in this book, as assignments in other classes, or in your free time. Pick your three favorites. List the titles and write a brief summary of each.

- For each story on your list, write several phrases to explain why you chose it.

- Think about what you like about these stories. What qualities do they have in common that make them appealing to you?

Before Reading

As you read this story, think about the answers to these questions:

1. What is your opinion of the story? How did your opinion change as you were reading it?

2. What do you notice about the characters, setting, plot, language, and other characteristics of this short story?

3. How does this story compare with others you have read?

Vocabulary Tips

This story includes a few words that may be unfamiliar to you but are useful for understanding the story. Below you will find some of these words, their definitions, and sentences that show how the words are used. Look over the words before you begin to read.

living spit an exact copy. One kitten is the <u>living spit</u> of its mother.

pilchards small fish in the herring family; a kind of sardine. The London grocery store carried canned and frozen <u>pilchards</u>.

midriff the part of the body just above the waist. Terry's shirt had a zigzag design across the <u>midriff</u>.

topaz yellow, as in the <u>topaz</u> gem. Marika received topaz earrings for her birthday.

erstwhile former; in the past. Leroy's <u>erstwhile</u> friend stopped calling after he moved to the suburbs.

shrouds ropes on a boat's mast. Early in the sailboat race, the crew of the *Liberty* pulled on the <u>shrouds</u> to raise more sails.

constitution a person's physical makeup. My grandmother has a strong <u>constitution</u> and will probably live many more years.

Lob's Girl

Joan Aiken

Some people choose their dogs, and some dogs choose their people. The Pengelly family had no say in the choosing of Lob; he came to them in the second way, and very decisively.

It began on the beach, the summer when Sandy was five, Don, her older brother, twelve, and the twins were three. Sandy was really Alexandra, because her grandmother had a beautiful picture of a queen in a diamond tiara and high collar of pearls. It hung by Granny Pearce's kitchen sink and was as familiar as the doormat. When Sandy was born everyone agreed that she was the living spit of the picture, and so she was called Alexandra and Sandy for short.

On this summer day she was lying peacefully reading a comic and not keeping an eye on the twins, who didn't need it because they were occupied in seeing which of them could wrap the most seaweed around the other one's legs. Father—Bert Pengelly—and Don were up on the Hard painting the bottom boards of the boat in which Father went fishing for pilchards. And Mother—Jean Pengelly—was getting ahead with making the Christmas puddings because she never felt easy in her mind if they weren't made and safely put away by the end of August. As usual, each member of the family was happily getting on with his or her own affairs. Little did they guess how soon this state of things would be changed by the large new member who was going to erupt into their midst.

Sandy rolled onto her back to make sure that the twins were not climbing on slippery rocks or getting cut off by the tide. At the same moment a large body struck her forcibly in the midriff and she was covered by flying sand. Instinctively she shut her eyes and felt the sand being wiped off her face by something that seemed like a warm, rough, damp flannel. She opened her eyes and looked. It was a tongue. Its owner was a large and bouncy young Alsatian, or German shepherd, with topaz eyes, black-tipped prick ears, a thick, soft coat, and a bushy black-tipped tail.

"*Lob!*" shouted a man farther up the beach. "Lob, come here!"

But Lob, as if trying to atone for the surprise he had given her, went on licking the sand off Sandy's face, wagging his tail so hard while he kept on knocking up more clouds of sand. His owner, a gray-haired man with a limp, walked over as quickly as he could and seized him by the collar.

"I hope he didn't give you a fright?" the man said to Sandy. "He meant it in play—he's only young."

"Oh, no, I think he's *beautiful*," said Sandy truly. She picked up a bit of driftwood and threw it. Lob, whisking easily out of his master's grip, was after it like a sand-colored bullet. He came back with the stick, beaming, and gave it to Sandy. At the same time he gave himself, though no one else was aware of this at the time. But with Sandy, too, it was love at first sight, and when, after a lot more stick-throwing, she and the twins joined Father and Don to go home for tea, they cast many a backward glance at Lob being led firmly away by his master.

"I wish we could play with him every day," Tess sighed.

"Why can't we?" said Tim.

Sandy explained. "Because Mr. Dodsworth, who owns

him, is from Liverpool, and he is only staying at the Fisherman's Arms till Saturday."

"Is Liverpool a long way off?"

"Right at the other end of England from Cornwall, I'm afraid."

It was a Cornish fishing village where the Pengelly family lived, with rocks and cliffs and a strip of beach and a little round harbor, and palm trees growing in the gardens of the little whitewashed stone houses. The village was approached by a narrow, steep, twisting hillroad, and guarded by a notice that said LOW GEAR FOR 1½ MILES, DANGEROUS TO CYCLISTS.

The Pengelly children went home to scones with Cornish cream and jam, thinking they had seen the last of Lob. But they were much mistaken. The whole family was playing cards by the fire in the front room after supper when there was a loud thump and a crash of china in the kitchen.

"My Christmas puddings!" exclaimed Jean, and ran out.

"Did you put TNT in them, then?" her husband said.

But it was Lob, who, finding the front door shut, had gone around to the back and bounced in through the open kitchen window, where the puddings were cooling on the sill. Luckily only the smallest was knocked down and broken.

Lob stood on his hind legs and plastered Sandy's face with licks. Then he did the same for the twins, who shrieked with joy.

"Where does this friend of yours come from?" inquired Mr. Pengelly.

"He's staying at the Fisherman's Arms—I mean his owner is."

"Then he must go back there. Find a bit of string, Sandy, to tie to his collar."

"I wonder how he found his way here," Mrs. Pengelly said, when the reluctant Lob had been led whining away and Sandy had explained about their afternoon's game on the beach. "Fisherman's Arms is right round the other side of the harbor."

Lob's owner scolded him and thanked Mr. Pengelly for bringing him back. Jean Pengelly warned the children that they had better not encourage Lob any more if they met him on the beach, or it would only lead to more trouble. So they dutifully took no notice of him the next day until he spoiled their good resolutions by dashing up to them with joyful barks, wagging his tail so hard that he winded Tess and knocked Tim's legs from under him.

They had a happy day, playing on the sand.

The next day was Saturday. Sandy had found out that Mr. Dodsworth was to catch the half-past-nine train. She went out secretly, down to the station, nodded to Mr. Hoskins, the stationmaster, who wouldn't dream of charging any local for a platform ticket, and climbed up on the footbridge that led over the tracks. She didn't want to be seen, but she did want to see. She saw Mr. Dodsworth get on the train, accompanied by an unhappy-looking Lob with drooping ears and tail. Then she saw the train slide away out of sight around the next headland, with a melancholy wail that sounded like Lob's last good-bye.

Sandy wished she hadn't had the idea of coming to the station. She walked home miserably, with her shoulders hunched and her hands in her pockets. For the rest of the day she was so cross and unlike herself that Tess and Tim were quite surprised, and her mother gave her a dose of senna.

A week passed. Then, one evening, Mrs. Pengelly and the younger children were in the front room playing snakes and ladders. Mr. Pengelly and Don had gone fishing on the evening tide. If your father is a fisherman, he will never be home at the same time from one week to the next.

Suddenly, history repeating itself, there was a crash from the kitchen. Jean Pengelly leaped up, crying, "My blackberry jelly!" She and the children had spent the morning picking and the afternoon boiling fruit.

But Sandy was ahead of her mother. With flushed cheeks and eyes like stars she had darted into the kitchen, where she and Lob were hugging one another in a frenzy of joy. About a yard of his tongue was out, and he was licking every part of her that he could reach.

"Good heavens!" exclaimed Jean. "How in the world did *he* get here?"

"He must have walked," said Sandy. "Look at his feet."

They were worn, dusty, and tarry. One had a cut on the pad.

"They ought to be bathed," said Jean Pengelly. "Sandy, run a bowl of warm water while I get the disinfectant."

"What'll we do about him, Mother?" said Sandy anxiously.

Mrs. Pengelly looked at her daughter's pleading eyes and sighed.

"He must go back to his owner, of course," she said, making her voice firm. "Your dad can get the address from the Fisherman's tomorrow, and phone him or send a telegram. In the meantime he'd better have a long drink and a good meal."

Lob was very grateful for the drink and the meal, and made no objection to having his feet washed. Then he flopped down on the hearthrug and slept in front of the fire they had lit because it was a cold, wet evening, with his head on Sandy's feet. He was a very tired dog. He had walked all the way from Liverpool to Cornwall, which is more than four hundred miles.

The next day Mr. Pengelly phoned Lob's owner, and the

following morning Mr. Dodsworth arrived off the night train, decidedly put out, to take his pet home. That parting was worse than the first. Lob whined, Don walked out of the house, the twins burst out crying, and Sandy crept up to her bedroom afterward and lay with her face pressed into the quilt, feeling as if she were bruised all over.

Jean Pengelly took them all into Plymouth to see the circus on the next day and the twins cheered up a little, but even the hour's ride in the train each way and the Liberty horses and performing seals could not cure Sandy's sore heart.

She need not have bothered, though. In ten days' time Lob was back—limping this time, with a torn ear and a patch missing out of his furry coat, as if he had met and tangled with an enemy or two in the course of his four-hundred-mile walk.

Bert Pengelly rang up Liverpool again. Mr. Dodsworth, when he answered, sounded weary. He said, "That dog has already cost me two days that I can't spare away from my work—plus endless time in police stations and drafting newspaper advertisements. I'm too old for these ups and downs. I think we'd better face the fact, Mr. Pengelly, that it's your family he wants to stay with—that is, if you want to have him."

Bert Pengelly gulped. He was not a rich man; and Lob was a pedigreed dog. He said cautiously, "How much would you be asking for him?"

"Good heavens, man, I'm not suggesting I'd *sell* him to you. You must have him as a gift. Think of the train fares I'll be saving. You'll be doing me a good turn."

"Is he a big eater?" Bert asked doubtfully.

By this time the children, breathless in the background listening to one side of this conversation, had realized what was in the wind and were dancing up and down with their hands clasped beseechingly.

"Oh, not for his size," Lob's owner assured Bert. "Two or three pounds of meat a day and some vegetables and gravy and biscuits—he does very well on that."

Alexandra's father looked over the telephone at his daughter's swimming eyes and trembling lips. He reached a decision. "Well, then, Mr. Dodsworth," he said briskly, "we'll accept your offer and thank you very much. The children will be overjoyed and you can be sure Lob has come to a good home. They'll look after him and see he gets enough exercise. But I can tell you," he ended firmly, "if he wants to settle in with us he'll have to learn to eat a lot of fish."

So that was how Lob came to live with the Pengelly family. Everybody loved him and he loved them all. But there was never any question who came first with him. He was Sandy's dog. He slept by her bed and followed her everywhere he was allowed.

Nine years went by, and each summer Mr. Dodsworth came back to stay at the Fisherman's Arms and call on his erstwhile dog. Lob always met him with recognition and dignified pleasure, accompanied him for a walk or two— but showed no signs of wishing to return to Liverpool. His place, he intimated, was definitely with the Pengellys.

In the course of nine years Lob changed less than Sandy. As she went into her teens he became a little slower, a little stiffer, there was a touch of gray on his nose, but he was still a handsome dog. He and Sandy still loved one another devotedly.

One evening in October all the summer visitors had left, and the little fishing town looked empty and secretive. It was a wet, windy dusk. When the children came home from school—even the twins were at high school now, and Don was a full-fledged fisherman—Jean Pengelly said, "Sandy, your Aunt Rebecca says she's lonesome because Uncle Will Hoskins has gone out trawling, and she wants one of you to go and spend the evening with her. You go, dear; you can take your homework with you."

Sandy looked far from enthusiastic.

"Can I take Lob with me?"

"You know Aunt Becky doesn't really like dogs—Oh, very well." Mrs. Pengelly sighed. "I suppose she'll have to put up with him as well as you."

Reluctantly Sandy tidied herself, took her schoolbag, put on the damp raincoat she had just taken off, fastened Lob's lead to his collar, and set off to walk through the dusk to Aunt Becky's cottage, which was five minutes' climb up the steep hill.

The wind was howling through the shrouds of boats drawn up on the Hard.

"Put some cheerful music on, do," said Jean Pengelly to the nearest twin. "Anything to drown that wretched sound while I make your dad's supper." So Don, who had just come in, put on some rock music, loud. Which was why the Pengellys did not hear the truck hurtle down the hill and crash against the post office wall a few minutes later.

Dr. Travers was driving through Cornwall with his wife, taking a late holiday before patients began coming down with winter colds and flu. He saw the sign that said STEEP HILL. LOW GEAR FOR 1½ MILES. Dutifully he changed into second gear.

"We must be nearly there," said his wife, looking out of her window. "I noticed a sign on the coast road that said the Fisherman's Arms was two miles. What a narrow, dangerous hill! But the cottages are very pretty—Oh, Frank, stop, *stop!* There's a child, I'm sure it's a child—by the wall over there!"

Dr. Travers jammed on his brakes and brought the car to a stop. A little stream ran down by the road in a shallow stone culvert, and half in the water lay something that looked, in the dusk, like a pile of clothes—or was it the body of a child? Mrs. Travers was out of the car in a flash, but her husband was quicker.

"Don't touch her, Emily!" he said sharply. "She's been hit. Can't be more than a few minutes. Remember that truck that overtook us half a mile back, speeding like the devil? Here, quick, go into that cottage and phone for an ambulance. The girl's in a bad way. I'll stay here and do what I can to stop the bleeding. Don't waste a minute."

Doctors are expert at stopping dangerous bleeding, for they know the right places to press. This Dr. Travers was able to do, but he didn't dare do more; the girl was lying in a queerly crumpled heap, and he guessed she had a number of bones broken and that it would be highly dangerous to move her. He watched her with great concentration, wondering where the truck had got to and what other damage it had done.

Mrs. Travers was very quick. She had seen plenty of accident cases and knew the importance of speed. The first cottage she tried had a phone; in four minutes she was back, and in six an ambulance was wailing down the hill.

Its attendants lifted the child onto a stretcher as carefully as if she were made of fine thistledown. The ambulance sped off to Plymouth—for the local cottage hospital did not take serious accident cases—and Dr. Travers went down to the police station to report what he had done.

He found that the police already knew about the speeding truck—which had suffered from loss of brakes and ended up with its radiator halfway through the post-office wall. The driver was concussed and shocked, but the police thought he was the only person injured—until Dr. Travers told his tale.

At half-past nine that night Aunt Rebecca Hoskins was sitting by her fire thinking aggrieved thoughts about the inconsiderateness of nieces who were asked to supper and never turned up, when she was startled by a neighbor, who burst in, exclaiming, "Have you heard about Sandy Pengelly, then, Mrs. Hoskins? Terrible thing, poor little soul, and they don't know if she's likely to live. Police have got the truck driver that hit her—ah, it didn't ought to be allowed, speeding through the place like that at umpty miles an hour, they ought to jail him for life—not that that'd be any comfort to poor Bert and Jean."

Horrified, Aunt Rebecca put on a coat and went down to her brother's house. She found the family with white shocked faces; Bert and Jean were about to drive off to the hospital where Sandy had been taken, and the twins were crying bitterly. Lob was nowhere to be seen. But Aunt Rebecca was not interested in dogs; she did not inquire about him.

"Thank the lord you've come, Beck," said her brother. "Will you stay the night with Don and the twins? Don's out looking for Lob and heaven knows when we'll be back; we may get a bed with Jean's mother in Plymouth."

"Oh, if only I'd never invited the poor child," wailed Mrs. Hoskins. But Bert and Jean hardly heard her.

That night seemed to last forever. The twins cried themselves to sleep. Don came home very late and grim-faced. Bert and Jean sat in a waiting room of the Western Counties Hospital, but Sandy was unconscious, they were told, and she remained so. All that could be done for her was done. She was given transfusions to replace all the blood she had lost. The broken bones were set and put in slings and cradles.

"Is she a healthy girl? Has she a good constitution?" the emergency doctor asked.

"Aye, doctor, she is that," Bert said hoarsely. The lump in Jean's throat prevented her from answering; she merely nodded.

"Then she ought to have a chance. But I won't conceal from you that her condition is very serious, unless she shows signs of coming out from this coma."

But as hour succeeded hour, Sandy showed no signs of recovering consciousness. Her parents sat in the waiting room with haggard faces; sometimes one of them would go to telephone the family at home, or to try to get a little sleep at the home of Granny Pearce, not far away.

At noon next day Dr. and Mrs. Travers went to the Pengelly cottage to inquire how Sandy was doing, but the report was gloomy: "Still in a very serious condition." The twins were miserably unhappy. They forgot that they had sometimes called their elder sister bossy and only remembered how often she had shared her pocket money with them, how she read to them and took them for picnics and helped with their homework. Now there was no Sandy, no Mother and Dad, Don went around with a gray, shuttered face, and worse still, there was no Lob.

The Western Counties Hospital is a large one, with dozens of different departments and five or six connected buildings, each with three or four entrances. By that afternoon it became noticeable that a dog seemed to have taken up position outside the hospital, with the fixed intention of getting in. Patiently he would try first one entrance and then another, all the way around, and then begin again. Sometimes he would get a little way inside, following a visitor, but animals were, of course, forbidden, and he was always kindly but firmly turned out again. Sometimes the guard at the main entrance gave him a pat or offered him a bit of sandwich—he looked so wet and beseeching and desperate. But he never ate the sandwich. No one seemed to own him or to know where he came from; Plymouth is a large city and he might have belonged to anybody.

At tea time Granny Pearce came through the pouring rain to bring a flask of hot tea with brandy in it to her daughter and son-in-law. Just as she reached the main entrance the guard was gently but forcibly shoving out a large, agitated, soaking-wet Alsatian dog.

"No, old fellow, you can *not* come in. Hospitals are for people, not for dogs."

"Why, bless me," exclaimed old Mrs. Pearce. "That's Lob! Here, Lob, Lobby boy!"

Lob ran to her, whining. Mrs. Pearce walked up to the desk.

"I'm sorry, madam, you can't bring that dog in here," the guard said.

Mrs. Pearce was a very determined old lady. She looked the porter in the eye.

"Now, see here, young man. That dog has walked twenty miles from St. Killan to get to my granddaughter. Heaven knows how he knew she was here, but it's plain he knows. And he ought to have his rights! He ought to get to see her! Do you know," she went on, bristling, "that dog has walked the length of England—*twice*—to be with that girl? And you think you can keep him out with your fiddling rules and regulations?"

"I'll have to ask the medical officer," the guard said weakly.

"You do that, young man." Granny Pearce sat down in a determined manner, shutting her umbrella, and Lob sat patiently dripping at her feet. Every now and then he shook his head, as if to dislodge something heavy that was tied around his neck.

Presently a tired, thin, intelligent-looking man in a white coat came downstairs, with an impressive, silver-haired man in a dark suit, and there was a low-voiced discussion. Granny Pearce eyed them, biding her time.

"Frankly . . . not much to lose," said the older man.

The man in the white coat approached Granny Pearce.

"It's strictly against every rule, but as it's such a serious case we are making an exception," he said to her quietly. "But only *outside* her bedroom door—and only for a moment or two."

Without a word, Granny Pearce rose and stumped upstairs. Lob followed close to her skirts, as if he knew his hope lay with her.

They waited in the green-floored corridor outside Sandy's room. The door was half shut. Bert and Jean were inside. Everything was terribly quiet. A nurse came out. The white-coated man asked her something and she shook her head. She had left the door ajar and through it could now be seen a high, narrow bed with a lot of gadgets around it. Sandy lay there, very flat under the covers, very still. Her head was turned away. All Lob's attention was riveted on the bed. He strained toward it, but Granny Pearce clasped his collar firmly.

"I've done a lot for you, my boy, now you behave yourself," she whispered grimly. Lob let out a faint whine, anxious and pleading.

At the sound of that whine Sandy stirred just a little. She sighed and moved her head the least fraction. Lob whined again. And then Sandy turned her head right over. Her eyes opened, looking at the door.

"Lob?" she murmured—no more than a breath of sound. "Lobby, boy?"

The doctor by Granny Pearce drew a quick, sharp breath. Sandy moved her left arm—the one that was not broken—from below the covers and let her hand dangle down, feeling, as she always did in the mornings, for Lob's furry head. The doctor nodded slowly.

"All right," he whispered. "Let him go to the bedside. But keep a hold of him."

Granny Pearce and Lob moved to the bedside. Now

she could see Bert and Jean, white-faced and shocked, on the far side of the bed. But she didn't look at them. She looked at the smile on her granddaughter's face as the groping fingers found Lob's wet ears and gently pulled them. "Good boy," whispered Sandy, and fell asleep again.

Granny Pearce led Lob out into the passage again. There she let go of him and he ran off swiftly down the stairs. She would have followed him, but Bert and Jean had come out into the passage, and she spoke to Bert fiercely.

"*I* don't know why you were so foolish as not to bring the dog before! Leaving him to find the way here himself—"

"But, Mother!" said Jean Pengelly. "That can't have been Lob. What a chance to take! Suppose Sandy hadn't —" She stopped, with her handkerchief pressed to her mouth.

"Not Lob? I've known that dog nine years! I suppose I ought to know my own granddaughter's dog?"

"Listen, Mother," said Bert. "Lob was killed by the same truck that hit Sandy. Don found him—when he went to look for Sandy's schoolbag. He was—he was dead. Ribs all smashed. No question of that. Don told me on the phone—he and Will Hoskins rowed a half mile out to sea and sank the dog with a lump of concrete tied to his collar. Poor old boy. Still—he was getting on. Couldn't have lasted forever."

"*Sank him at sea?* Then what—?"

Slowly old Mrs. Pearce, and then the other two, turned to look at the trail of dripping-wet footprints that led down the hospital stairs.

In the Pengellys' garden they have a stone, under the palm tree. It says: "Lob. Sandy's dog. Buried at sea."

Reviewing and Interpreting the Story

Record your answers to these comprehension questions in your personal literature notebook. Follow the directions for each part.

Reviewing Try to complete each of these sentences without looking back at the story.

Identifying
Cause and Effect

1. The real reason that Sandy's father decides to accept Lob as a gift from Mr. Dodsworth is that

   a. Lob is a pedigreed dog and would cost a great deal.

   b. Lob is not a big eater for his size.

   c. the Pengelly children want Lob.

   d. Mr. Pengelly wants to save Mr. Dodsworth the trouble of coming for Lob.

Understanding
Main Ideas

2. Mr. Dodsworth's reactions to Lob's efforts to stay with Sandy show that he

   a. is disgusted with Lob.

   b. believes that Sandy has intentionally turned Lob against him.

   c. really doesn't care about dogs.

   d. likes Lob and wants what's best for him.

Recalling Facts

3. Lob is brought into the hospital by Sandy's

   a. grandmother.

   b. aunt.

   c. mother.

   d. brother Don.

4. Lob dies

   a. when Don puts a weight on his neck
     and drowns him.

   b. after he leaves the hospital.

   c. before Sandy is taken to the hospital.

   d. while Sandy is in the hospital.

5. Which of these statements is not true
about the town Sandy lives in?

   a. It is too small to have a hospital with a
     critical care unit.

   b. It has wide roads to accommodate a
     great deal of traffic.

   c. It is built on hills and cliffs overlooking
     the shore.

   d. There are many more people living
     there during the tourist season than
     during the winter.

Interpreting   To answer these questions, you may look back at the
story if you like.

6. The first hint that something has happened to Lob is that

   a. Dr. Travers and his wife find Sandy, but
     Lob is not with her.

   b. when Granny Pearce brings Lob to
     Sandy's room, Sandy's parents look
     shocked.

   c. Don, after looking for Lob, comes home
     late and grim-faced.

   d. at the hospital, Lob often shakes his
     head as if to loosen something around
     his neck.

7. Don tells no one but his parents about Lob's death because he

   a. plans to get another dog that looks like Lob and let Sandy think it is Lob.

   b. hasn't had time yet to tell anyone else.

   c. doesn't want the twins to be even sadder.

   d. thinks it was an unimportant matter, not worth mentioning.

8. Now that Lob has brought Sandy out of the coma,

   a. Sandy's parents will never admit what they saw.

   b. Sandy will get well.

   c. Sandy will miss Lob so much that she will never get well.

   d. Lob will come back every time Sandy is in trouble.

9. The saying that best describes this story is

   a. "A dog is a person's best friend."

   b. "It's a dog's life."

   c. "Love is blind."

   d. "Love conquers all."

10. The turning point of this story comes when

    a. Sandy is struck by a runaway truck.
    b. Sandy sighs and turns her head at the sound of Lob's whine.
    c. Sandy's parents tell her grandmother that Lob is dead.
    d. Lob appears in front of the hospital.

Now check your answers with your teacher. Study the questions you answered incorrectly. What types of questions were they? Talk with your teacher about ways to work on those skills.

Discussing Literature

Literature can be analyzed and discussed orally or in writing. Suppose you and some friends all read the same book. The conversation you have about it may be productive without any of you spending much time in preparation. Your friends' questions often help you to focus on parts of the story you didn't pay attention to at first. Someone else's opinions or reasons may cause you to change your opinion or to understand something that wasn't clear to you. On the other hand, other people's comments may help you understand why you reacted as you did.

When writing a literary analysis, however, you must think through your judgments on your own. By planning ahead how you will examine the story, you are more likely to discover all the important points you should mention. You will answer your readers' questions before they are asked. You will be more accurate in separating factual statements about the work from your opinions of it. Your opinions will be expressed more clearly because you will better understand the reasons for them. You can focus on the issues that you find most interesting or most important, and lead your reader to look at the work through your eyes.

In this unit, you will explore how to analyze a short story in order to discuss it thoroughly. The approach has three steps:

1. You recognize your first response to the story and consider how it is shaped by the personal interests, attitudes, and experiences that you, the reader, bring to the story.

2. You examine how the author develops the elements of a short story in a distinctive way.

3. You compare this story with other stories, make judgments about the elements, and state your conclusions.

1 • Responding

Does this experience sound familiar to you? Three friends go to a movie, a murder mystery involving a stamp collector and his valuable stamps. Even as they leave the theater, the friends begin to wonder if they all saw the same movie. One person says, "That was great! I'll be sure to see it again." The second objects, "All that violence was disgusting! I couldn't wait for the end. That movie will probably give me nightmares." The third says, "I slept through most of the film. The only thing worth watching was the car chase through all that gorgeous scenery."

How could three such different responses come from the same experience? The movie didn't change for each viewer. However, how each viewer approached it was unique. The first person, who thought the movie was great, was pleased because she, too, was a stamp collector. Her background knowledge of and fondness for stamp collecting gave this viewer much pleasure in plot developments that involved rare stamps.

The second viewer was much less interested in the plot than in the characters. When her favorite characters were threatened and later reported killed, she became too upset to enjoy the movie.

The third person wasn't impressed by either plot or characters. Tired by her day's activities, she couldn't pay close attention to the plot developments. All she was looking for was exciting sights and sounds.

As you read the following paragraph from "Lob's Girl," be aware of your personal response to it:

> Sandy rolled onto her back to make sure that the twins were not climbing on slippery rocks or getting cut off by the tide. At the same moment a large body struck her forcibly in the midriff and she was covered by flying sand. Instinctively she shut her eyes and felt the sand being wiped off her face by something that seemed like a warm, rough, damp flannel. She opened her eyes and looked. It was a tongue. Its owner was a large and bouncy young Alsatian, or German shepherd, with topaz eyes, black-tipped prick ears, a thick, soft coat, and a bushy, black-tipped tail.

Did you enjoy the thought of a friendly dog jumping on you? If you personally like dogs, this passage probably gave you a warm feeling. You are likely to feel appreciative of a dog that shows its love so strongly. On the other hand, if you fear dogs or, worse, have been attacked by a dog, this passage may have upset you. You might be disturbed by the thought of being knocked down by an overeager animal, or disgusted by imagining it licking your face. How you reacted to this single paragraph may have strongly affected your feeling toward the story as a whole.

Exercise 1

Read this passage, which follows Mrs. Pengelly's statement that the dog in Sandy's hospital room could not have been Lob. Use what you have learned in this lesson to answer the questions that follow.

> "Not Lob? I've known that dog nine years! I suppose I ought to know my own granddaughter's dog?"
>
> "Listen, Mother," said Bert. "Lob was killed by the same truck that hit Sandy. Don found him—when he went to look for Sandy's schoolbag. He was—he was dead. Ribs all smashed. No question of that. Don told me on the phone—he and Will Hoskins rowed a half mile out to sea and sank the dog with a lump of concrete tied to his collar. Poor old boy. Still—he was getting on. Couldn't have lasted forever."
>
> "*Sank him at sea?* Then what—?"
>
> Slowly old Mrs. Pearce, and then the other two, turned to look at the trail of dripping-wet footprints that led down the hospital stairs.

1. In general, do you like tales about ghosts and the supernatural? Do you believe such things are possible? How did you feel about this ending? Did your attitude toward unexplained phenomena make it easier or harder for you to accept this development?

2. Did you react emotionally to news of Lob's death? Did you have a strong feeling of sympathy for Sandy because of her loss of Lob? How do you suppose your mood in response to this passage was affected by your own experiences with pets or with the loss of a good friend?

Check your answers with your teacher. Review this part of the lesson if you don't understand why an answer was incorrect.

Writing on Your Own 1

In this exercise you will use what you learned in this lesson to write about your opinion of "Lob's Girl." Follow these steps:

1. First, write a paragraph or two stating your overall opinion of the story. Tell whether you enjoyed reading the story and how you felt at the end.

2. Now examine at least two of the following elements in the story. Think about how the experiences you brought to the story affected the way you reacted to it. Write a paragraph or two about how the elements you chose affected your feelings. Here are examples:

   - *Setting* If you have never been in a small coastal town like Sandy's, you may find it difficult to imagine the town. That could make you believe that the author did not describe it adequately.
   - *Characters* You may see a similarity between Sandy's father and a character in another story that you have enjoyed. That could lead you to think highly of the author's ability to create characters.
   - *Plot* You may either dislike or be delighted by surprise endings.
   - *Language* The unfamiliar British terms may interfere with your enjoyment of the story or they may make it more interesting and intriguing.

You could also consider your feelings about pets, ghosts, and sad endings.

2 • Analyzing

Even though your background and experiences affect your personal response to any writing, you can still judge a story objectively by considering the elements discussed in the first seven units of this book.

You have a right to dislike a story, for any number of reasons. But if you find that the story has memorable characters, a vivid setting, a logical plot, a clear theme, and well-chosen language, you cannot say that it is bad or poorly written.

On the other hand, you may like a piece of writing because you agree with its major theme. But if you find it has an unclear setting and characters, an illogical and hard-to-follow plot, and language that doesn't fit either the topic or the audience, you cannot claim it is a good story.

When you discuss or write about a story, you must do your best to separate your personal opinions from your analysis of the work. Let others know which of your statements grow out of your own attitudes and which are supported by the text. Then even people who disagree with your opinion can tell from your discussion whether the story is worth their attention.

Read this excerpt, the second paragraph of "Lob's Girl." What information does it give you about the elements of the story, such as characters, setting, and language?

> It began on the beach, the summer when Sandy was five, Don, her older brother, twelve, and the twins were three. Sandy was really Alexandra, because her grandmother had a beautiful picture of a queen in a diamond tiara and high collar of pearls. It hung by Granny Pearce's kitchen sink and was as familiar as the doormat. When Sandy was born everyone agreed that she was the living spit of the picture, and so she was called Alexandra and Sandy for short.

A reader might complain that the paragraph uses some unfamiliar phrases and is vague about who the queen in the picture is. But even without understanding what "the living spit" means, or knowing a thing about Empress Alexandra of Russia, a reader learns that the main character in this story is a little girl in a family of four children. It is clear that the family lives close to the children's grandmother, and that they spend a good deal of time with the grandmother. With its description of the grandmother's kitchen, the paragraph establishes a comfortable, friendly tone.

Even a reader who dislikes the story would agree that the author quickly establishes the characters and tone, and begins to describe the setting. These are the characteristics on which the story should be judged.

Exercise 2

Read the following passage. Use what you have learned in this lesson to answer the questions that follow.

> It was a Cornish fishing village where the Pengelly family lived, with rocks and cliffs and a strip of beach and a little round harbor, and palm trees growing in the gardens of the little whitewashed stone houses. The village was approached by a narrow, steep, twisting hillroad, and guarded by a notice that said LOW GEAR FOR 1½ MILES, DANGEROUS TO CYCLISTS.
>
> The Pengelly children went home to scones with Cornish cream and jam, thinking they had seen the last of Lob. But they were much mistaken. The whole family was playing cards by the fire in the front room after supper when there was a loud thump and a crash of china in the kitchen.
>
> "My Christmas puddings!" exclaimed Jean, and ran out.
>
> "Did you put TNT in them, then?" her husband said.

1. What details about the setting does this passage provide? Why do you suppose the author mentions the road sign? Why is the description of the sign mixed in with details about trees and houses?

2. How do the details about food—scones with Cornish cream and jam, and Christmas puddings—emphasize the English setting?

3. What do you infer about the characters from their actions in this excerpt? What do you discover, in particular, about Mr. Pengelly's sense of humor?

Check your answers with your teacher. Review this part of the lesson if you don't understand why an answer was incorrect.

Writing on Your Own 2

In this exercise you will analyze a specific story element in several stories. Review your list of three favorite stories that you made at the beginning of this unit. Then follow these steps:

- Choose one of these story elements to examine carefully in "Lob's Girl": character, plot, conflict, theme, narrator. Write a paragraph or two describing how the author develops that element. Point out examples throughout the story that support your analysis.

- With the same element in mind, skim each of the three stories that you selected. How well or poorly was that element developed in each story? Give each of your chosen stories a grade for the use of that element.

3 • Evaluating

Suppose a friend wants to know if a movie you have seen is one that he or she would enjoy. It would be natural for the friend to ask you to compare this movie with *Star Wars, The Wizard of Oz, Jurassic Park,* or any other movie that you are both familiar with. To help your friend make a decision, you don't need to say that one movie is better or worse than the other. You just need to point out how the two movies are alike or different.

When you discuss a short story, it's helpful to do the same thing: compare this story with others that you have read. Usually, you'll want to focus on such major elements as characters, plot, and speaker. In some cases, you might look at other characteristics that are important in the specific stories being compared, such as humor, the author's purpose, and the audience for whom the story was written.

Consider, for example, what you might do if you were asked to compare the characters in "Lob's Girl" with characters in other stories in this book. First, since discussing ten stories at once would be rather difficult, you would want to reduce the number of stories you'll consider. "Lob's Girl" involves both parents and children. So you might compare the story with one or more of the others that involve parents and children: "Tuesday of the Other June," "Almost a Whole Trickster," "President Cleveland, Where Are You?" "Catch the Moon," and "Many Moons." Then you could focus on a manageable issue or two.

For example, you might compare parent-child relationships in "Lob's Girl" and the other five stories, or only the father-daughter relationships in "Lob's Girl" and "Many Moons." Which families are more realistic? Can you prove your point with excerpts from the stories?

You might focus on just the young girl characters in "Lob's Girl," "Tuesday of the Other June," and "Many Moons." Which girl is portrayed in greatest depth? Which is easiest to picture outside the story?

Or you might compare Sandy's extended family with its children, parents, grandparent, and aunt and uncle, to June's small family of herself and her mother. How do the different family relationships influence the plots? Could the two families trade stories without changing the plots and themes of the stories? Read the following comparison. Notice how this reader backs up the opening statement on this issue with details from the story:

> In both "Tuesday of the Other June" and "Lob's Girl," the size of the main character's family is important to the plot. June's mother has no one else to worry about besides June, and June dreads the thought of disappointing her mother. Because she knows her mother expects so much of her, she is slow to fight back when the Other June bothers her.
>
> In "Lob's Girl," the crisis begins when Sandy's mother learns that Aunt Rebecca is lonesome while her husband is off on his boat, and asks Sandy to keep her company. After Sandy is hurt, it is her brother who finds Lob dead and buries him at sea, and her grandmother who insists on bringing what she thinks is Lob into the hospital to comfort Sandy. If Sandy didn't have such a big family, no one would know how mysterious Lob's visit to the hospital is.

You might bring your own experience into the discussion of a story by explaining how similarities between the fictional characters and your own family made it easier for you to understand or appreciate the characters.

Exercise 3

Read these three statements and review the story "Lob's Girl." Use what you have learned in this lesson to answer the questions below. If necessary, look back at the stories being compared.

- Of all the stories in this book, only "Lob's Girl" has an important character that is an animal.

- The setting of "Lob's Girl" is more realistic than the setting of "Many Moons."

- Sensory detail is not as important in "Lob's Girl" as it is in "The Long Rain," but it is more important than in "The Richer, the Poorer."

1. Which of the statements is most easily proved by examining the stories? Explain your answer.

2. Which of the statements is least easily proved by examining the stories? Explain your answer.

Check your answers with your teacher. Review this part of the lesson if you don't understand why an answer was incorrect.

Writing on Your Own 3

Review your answers for Exercise 3, above. Then do the following:

- Write a page or two supporting the second statement in Exercise 3. If you have not read "Many Moons," substitute one of these stories that you have read: "The Professor of Smells" or "The Long Rain."

- Reread your writing. Have you backed up the statement with specific details and excerpts from both of the stories?

Discussion Guides

1. Imagine that Lob could talk. What might he say to Mr. Dodsworth to explain why he keeps running away to be with Sandy? Develop a speech that Lob might make, and present it to your class.

2. In this story, Mr. Dodsworth comes to the Cornish fishing village every summer for vacation. The author also notes that the town is full of visitors throughout the summer months, emptying out in the fall. What makes the village so attractive to vacationers? With a small group, discuss the author's details about the setting and develop a travel brochure to advertise Sandy's town. Make up a name for the village. If possible, include a map showing the beach, the twisting road to town, the hotel where Mr. Dodsworth stayed, the railroad station, and other places mentioned in the story. Add businesses that you think vacationers would need to know about.

3. How do you suppose Sandy eventually learned about Lob's death? Who told her—her father, mother, grandmother, brother, or several family members together? With one or more partners, work out a scene in which Sandy is given the bad news. Present your scene to others.

4. How do the people in your class feel about the ending of this story? Have any of them ever heard of such a thing happening? Do they believe such a thing could happen? Discuss the possibilities. Then conduct a poll to record the opinions of the participants in the discussion.

Write a Story Analysis

Think about what you have learned about analyzing stories. Now examine one of the other stories in this book in detail. Follow these steps:

If you have questions about the writing process, refer to Using the Writing Process on page 306.

- Review the writing assignments you completed for this unit. You should have the following: *a)* a paragraph or two telling whether you liked the story and how you felt at the end, *b)* an explanation of how two of the story elements contributed to your feeling, *c)* an analysis of how the author developed one important story element, and *d)* support for a statement comparing the setting of two stories.

- Reread the story you chose to analyze. Take notes about how the author develops the various story elements and how your experiences affect your reaction to those elements and the story.

- Now write a page or two stating your opinion of the story. Decide which story elements affected your opinion and how. Point out parts you especially liked or disliked. Tell whether you would recommend the story to other readers.

- Read your analysis to be sure it makes sense and that you include details to support your opinions. Will your readers understand, for example, why the way the author developed the characters, or used dialogue, or described the setting was important for understanding the story. Revise your writing.

- Read your revised paper to one or more classmates for feedback. Make any final revisions they suggest.

- Proofread for errors in spelling, grammar, and punctuation. Make a clean copy. You may wish to share your analysis with a small group or your class.

Using the Writing Process

This reference section will help you complete the writing exercises in this book. It explains the major steps in the writing process. Read the information carefully so that you understand the process thoroughly. Whenever you need a quick review of important things to think about when you write, refer to the handy checklist on page 312.

Most tasks worth doing have several steps. For example, houses can be built only after the builder follows a number of complicated, logical steps. Moviemakers must go through a series of steps before releasing a film. Even a task as simple as making a peanut butter and jelly sandwich requires that the sandwich maker perform specific steps in order. So it should be no surprise that anyone who wants to write a good story, poem, report, or article must follow certain steps. Taken together, the steps a writer takes are called the writing process.

The writing process is divided into three main stages: prewriting, writing, and revising. Each stage is important for good writing.

Stage 1: Prewriting

Prewriting consists of all the preparation you do before you put a single word down on paper. There are many decisions that must be made in order for your writing to be interesting, logical, and easy to read. These are the steps you should take before you begin to write:

1. **Decide on your audience.** Who will read your writing? Are you writing for your teacher? Are you writing for readers of the school newspaper? Are you writing for yourself or your friends? Your writing will change, depending on who you think your audience will be.

2. **Decide on your purpose.** Why are you writing? Do you want to teach your audience something? Do you want to entertain? Do you want to change someone's mind about an issue? Think about your purpose before you begin to write.

3. **Choose a topic.** What are some topics that interest you? Make a list of topics that you are familiar with and could write about. Make another list of topics that interest you and you want to learn about.

   One technique that works for some writers at this stage is to brainstorm. When you brainstorm, you let your mind wander freely. Without criticizing yourself, you scribble down ideas as they come to you—even if the ideas seem silly or farfetched. Good ideas often develop from crazy thoughts. You may want to talk your ideas over with a partner or a group of classmates. Toss out ideas as you think of them. Brainstorming either alone or with others should give you a long list of possible topics.

4. **Limit your topic.** It is impossible to cover every aspect of a given topic in one piece of writing. Say, for example, you are interested in the possibility of life on other planets. In a single story or a single report, you could not include everything that is known about extraterrestrial life. You must choose one or two aspects to focus on. Otherwise, you might overload your story or report with too many ideas. Concentrate on telling about a few things thoroughly and well.

5. **Research your topic.** In working on factual reports, you have probably had to look up topics in the encyclopedia, at the library, or on the Internet. Even to write a story, you often need to do some research. In a story set during the Civil War, for example, you wouldn't talk about pocket cameras or knights in armor.

   You may use books, magazines, newspapers, encyclopedias, or other sources of information for your research. Some topics may require you to interview knowledgeable people. For realistic stories set in the present time, you may find that the best research is simple observation of everyday life. Thorough research will help insure that your facts and details are accurate.

6. **Organize your ideas.** Now you have the facts, ideas, and details you need to write. How will you arrange them? Which order will you choose? No matter what you are writing, it is

always helpful to begin with a written plan. If you are writing a story, you will probably tell it in time order. Make a list of the story events, from first to last.

Arranging details in time order is not the only way to organize information. Some writers make *lists* (informal outlines) of the facts and ideas they have gathered and rearrange the items in their lists until they have the information in the correct order that will work well in their writing.

Other writers make formal *outlines,* designating the most important ideas I, II, III, IV, etc., and related details as A, B, C, 1, 2, 3, and so on. An outline is a more formal version of a list, and like a list, the items in an outline can be rearranged until you decide on a logical order. Both outlines and lists help you organize and group your ideas.

Mapping or *clustering* is another helpful technique used by many writers. With this method you write down your main idea and then show how other facts and ideas are connected to that main idea. Here is an example of a cluster map one student created before writing a science fiction story:

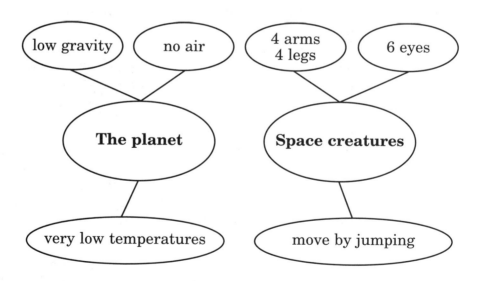

Stage 2: Writing

1. **Get started.** Begin with an introductory sentence or paragraph. A good introduction can become a guide for the rest of your story or essay. For ideas on good opening sentences, take a look at all the stories in this book. Your introduction should give the reader a hint about what is coming next. It sets the tone and mood for the story. It tells the reader the narrator's point of view. It may introduce the reader to the writer's purpose, the main characters, and the setting. Do the best you can with your introduction, but remember that, if you wish to, you can change it later.

2. **Keep writing.** Get your thoughts down as quickly as possible, referring to your prewriting notes to keep you on track. Later, when you are done with this *rough draft,* you will have a chance to revise and polish your work to make it correct and attractive. But for right now, don't stop for spelling, grammar, or exact wording problems. Come as close as you can to what you want to say, but don't let yourself get bogged down in details at this stage.

Stage 3: Revising

Now you're ready to revise your work. Careful revision includes editing and reorganizing that can make a big difference in the final product. You may wish to get feedback from your classmates or your teacher to help you decide how to revise your work.

1. **Revise and edit your work.** When you are revising, ask yourself these questions:

   - *Did I follow my prewriting plan?* Reread your entire first draft. Compare it to your original plan. Did you skip anything important? If you added an idea, did it work logically with the rest of your plan? Even if you decide that your prewriting plan is no longer what you want, it may include ideas you don't want to lose.

   - *Is my writing clear and logical?* Does one idea follow the other in a sensible order? Do you want to change the order or add ideas to make the organization clearer?

- *Is my language interesting?* Have you chosen strong verbs, nouns, and adjectives? For example, have you used forms of the verb *to be (is, are, being, become)* more than you should? If so, replace them, or change your sentence to make them unnecessary. Include precise action words such as *jumped, slouched, grinned,* and *sobbed* in place of overused verbs. Instead of using vague nouns, choose exact nouns, such as *lagoon, emerald,* and *cascade.* Replace common adjectives like *beautiful* and *nice* with precise ones such as *elegant, luscious,* and *exquisite.*

- *Is my writing exact and to the point?* Take out words that repeat the same ideas. For example, don't use both *bright* and *intelligent*. The words are synonyms. Choose one word or the other.

2. **Proofread for errors in spelling, grammar, capitalization, and punctuation.** Anyone reading your writing will notice errors in spelling, grammar, and other mechanics of writing immediately. These errors can confuse your readers or make them feel that you just don't care enough to bother to do things right. Readers may start to doubt your accuracy in every detail just because of these small errors.

   If you are in doubt about the spelling of a word, look it up. If you are not sure whether your grammar is correct, read your writing aloud and listen carefully. Does anything sound wrong? Check with a friend or classmate if you need a second opinion or refer to a grammar handbook. Make sure every group of words is a complete sentence. Is any of your sentences a run-on?

   Do proper nouns begin with capital letters? Is the first word of every sentence capitalized?

   Do all your sentences have the correct end marks? Should you add any commas or apostrophes to your writing? Is dialogue (quotations) punctuated correctly?

3. **Make a clean final draft to share.** After you are satisfied with your writing, it is time to share it with your audience. If you are lucky enough to be writing on a computer, you can print out a final copy easily, after running a spell check. If you

are writing your final draft by hand, make sure your handwriting is clear and easy to read. Leave margins on either side of the page. If you are writing on lined notebook paper, you may want to skip every other line. Make your writing look inviting to your readers. After all, you put a lot of work into this piece. It's important that someone read and enjoy it.

A Writing Checklist

Ask yourself these questions before beginning a writing assignment.

- Have I chosen a topic that is both interesting and manageable? Should I narrow it so that I can cover it in the space I have?

- Do I have a clear prewriting plan?

- What should I do to gather my facts and ideas? Read? Interview? Observe?

- How will I organize my ideas? A list? An outline? A cluster map?

- Do I have an intriguing opening sentence or paragraph?

- Do I need to add more information? Switch the order of paragraphs? Take out unnecessary information?

Ask yourself these questions after completing a writing assignment.

- Did I use my prewriting plan?

- Is the organization of my writing clear? Should I move, add, or delete any paragraphs or sentences to make the ideas flow more logically?

- Do all the sentences in one paragraph relate to one idea?

- Have I used active, precise words? Is my language interesting? Do the words say what I mean to say?

- Is the spelling correct?

- Have I used correct grammar, capitalization, and punctuation?

- Is my final draft legible, clean, and attractive?